DIS

The Recreation Handbook

THE RECREATION HANDBOOK

*342 Games and Other
Activities for Teams
and Individuals*

by

Robert L. Loeffelbein

McFarland & Company, Inc., Publishers
Jefferson, North Carolina, and London

British Library Cataloguing-in-Publication data are available

Library of Congress Cataloguing-in-Publication Data

Loeffelbein, Robert L.
   The recreation handbook : 342 games and other activities for
teams and individuals / by Robert L. Loeffelbein.
     p. cm.
   Includes index.
   ISBN 0-89950-744-1 (sewn softcover : 50# alk. paper) ∞
   1. Games — Juvenile literature. 2. Sports for children — Juvenile
literature. I. Title.
GV1203.L58 1992
793′.01922 — dc20   92-50310
                                               CIP
                                             AC

Manufactured in the United States of America

McFarland & Company, Inc., Publishers
* Box 611, Jefferson, North Carolina 28640*

To look at our children now
you'd never think
these are our doctors,
lawyers, scientists, astronauts...
& parents of tomorrow.
But, then neither did our parents
think thus of us as children.
And so this book is dedicated
to all mothers and fathers—
to whom we have been, we hope,
the biggest surprise endings
they could have imagined.

Contents

Introduction   xiii
Special Notes on a Few of the Games   xvii

The Games

Aquatic Games

Sliding Statues	1
Mermaid Angling	2
Clown Diving Competition	2
Surf Jai Alai	3
Surf Hockey	3
Aquaball	4
Socko	5
Surfmat Polo	6
Underwater Blind Man's Bluff	7

Basketball Type Games

Bucketball	8
Guard Ball	8
Crab Basketball	10
Soccer-Basketball	11
Borden Ball	12
Court Ball	13
Cage Ball	14
American Ball	15
Boxers' Basketball	16
Sideline Basketball	16
Funnel Basketball	17
4-Corner Basketball	18
Korfbal	19
Hoop Shoot Tournament	20

Bat and Ball Games

Sock-It	22

Zippie	22
German Bat Ball	23
Beginner Baseball	24
Scoop Softball	24
Hockey-Baseball	25
Fly-Up	25
Ping Pong Baseball	26
Katie Ball	26
Three-Player Baseball	27
Straight-Line Baseball	27
In-Line Softball	28
Tag Ball	29
Can Cricket	29
Two-Pin Cricket	30
Cricketball	31
American Cricket	32
Toppleball	33
Half Ball	34
Indian Ball	35
Corkball	36
Sack-it	37
Bellevue Whiffleball	37

Bowling Type Games

Coin Lag	38
Setting Your Cap	39
Button Bowling	39
Spaceman's Shooting Gallery	40
Migs Bowling	41
Bridge Bowling	41

Hole Bowling	42
Kick Bowling	42
Bag-It Bowling	43
Holes in the Head	43
Ping-Pong™ Pockets	44
Goalie	44
Six-Hole Bowling	45
Bowling Bounce	46
Anty-In	46
Puck Pitch	47
Box Score	48
Washer Pitch	48
Backyard Bocce	49
Bocce Pole	49
Target Bowling	50
Potty	51
Skid Pins	52
Summer Curling	52
Skittles	53
Putt Pins	53
Box Carom Bowling	54
Control Bowling	55
Carom Bowling	55

Football, Soccer and Other
Kicking Type Games

Kick Golf	56
Hole-in-One Kickball	57
Hop-Kick Golf	57
Codeball-on-the-Green	57
Crab Soccer	58
Soccer-Tennis	58
Volley-Soccer	59
Kicker's Ball	60
Kick Carom Volleyball	61
Field Pool	61
Kick Baseball	62
Cannonade	63
Line Soccer	64
Melee	65
Dog Fight	65
Fieldball	66
Soccer Shoot	68
Circle Soccer	68

Scrambleball	69
Scramble Soccer	70
Football Skills Tournament	71
Speed-a-Way	72
Speed Football	74
Touch Rugby	74
Hocker	75
Flicker Ball	76
5-Man Football	77

Combative Sports
and Games

Dueling	78
Playground Sumo	79
Push Duel	79
Indian Dueling	80
Swat the Dancing Bear	80
Horse Hassle	81
Push-o-War	81
Pushball	82
Team Bar Wrestling	82
Hot Spot	83
Tethered Dodgeball	84
Arm Wrestling	84
Greek Tug-of-War	85
Pony Jumping	85
Gang Rush	86
Battleball	87
Battleball II	87
Blindfold Smoker	89

Hand Striking and
Throwing Games

Bird-on-a-Rock	90
Two-Up	90
Ring-a-Balloon	91
Ring-Tac-Toe	91
Ring-a-King-Tac-Toe	93
Super Ring-a-Tac-Toe	93
Ring Scrabble	94
Poker Toss	94
Dart Baseball	95
Ring Tennis	97

Table of Contents

Flying Rings	97
Flying Horseshoes	98
Flying Saucers	99
Pie-Pan Horseshoes	100
Frisbee Baseball	100
Ring Tag	101
Frisbee Volleyball	101
Flying Saucers Skill Tournament	102
Crosscatch	103
Star Ball	104
Wind Up	105
Squares	106
Stoop Ball	107
Tchouk Ball	108
Crazy Bounce	109
Giant Wallball	110
Rumble Ball	111
Anty-Over	112
Balloon Volleyball	113
Volleyball Serving Skill Test	113
Volleying Football	114
Three-Way Volleyball	114
Long Volley	115
Cage Ball	115
Blind Volleyball	116
Peteka Rio	116
Gaucho Tennis	117
Hoover Ball	118
Gorodke	118
Team Handball	119
Foxball	120

Mallet-Club-Stick Games

Placement Pool	122
Cross the Line	122
Three-Ball Pool	123
Billiard Baseball	124
Hammer Pool	124
Marble Golf	125
Mini-Golf	125
Handicap Golf Driving	126
Putter Pool	126

Wall Golf	127
Team One-Ball Golf	128
Speed Golf	128
Croquet Bowling	128
Target Bowling	129
Hole-in-One Croquet	130
Croquet Field Pool	131
Super Croquet	132
Snoo-Quet	133
Whopolo	134
Slalom Hockey	135
Broom Hockey	136

Paddle, Racquet and Cesta Games

Roof Ball	136
Cup Jai Alai	137
99	137
Twist Table Tennis	138
Floor Tennis	138
Cornerball	139
Volley-Pong	140
Paddle Volleyball	140
Cesta Cornerball	141
Jug Ball	141
Cesta Wallball	142
Lob Hockey	143
Jai Alai–Volleyball	144
Jug Tennis	144
Pin Hit	145
Rolling Scoop Throw	146
Scoop Jai Alai	147
Badminiature	148
Pingminton	148
Winter Badminton	149
Bird Dunk	149
Pickle Ball	150
Serving Games	151
Three-Man Tennis	152
Pole Tennis	152

Table Games

Solo Survivor Puzzle	153
Rubberband Writing	154

Sea War   154
Nisei Go   155
Auto Race   156
Elimination   157
"Free Hand" Pinochle   157
Bermuda Bridge   158
Board Golf   159
Blow Ball   159
Poker Dice   160
"Wind" Hockey   160
Clock Golf   161
Wink Golf   162
Wink Tennis   162
Wink Basketball   163
Tiddley Baseball   164
Box Basketball   165
Muhle   166
Overthrow Checkers   167
Double-Decker Checkers   167
Scramble-Amble Checkers   168
Bocce Dice   169
Golfer's Dice   170
Dice Baseball   170
Mini Shufflboard   171
Pencil Pool   172
Go-Mo-Ko   172
Clip-a-Tac-Toe   172
Junk Jackstraws   173
Peg Ball   173
Flick Football   174

Track & Field, Tag
    Relay Games
A Cup of Blow   175
Frog Hunt   176
Happy Hooligan Race   177
Kleenex Sprint   177
Lame Dog Race   178
Mother Nature's Relay   178
Handicap Race   178
Trio Racing   179
Commando Obstacle
    Course   180
Blackout   180

The Hexathlon   181
Jelly Roll Relay   181
Tunnel Race   182
Ball Dogging   183
Land Grab   183
Gauntlet   184
Fox and Geese   186
Hare and Hounds   186
Criss-Cross Tag   187
Bronco Roundup   188
Invasion   188
Moving Maze Race   189

Word-Play and Story-
    Telling Games
Your Name's the Game   190
Deft-nitions   191
Dictionary Doodling   193
Math Matching   193
Trademark Recall   193
Ad Tic-Tac-Toe   194
Baby Says   194
Imagineering   195
Who Am I?   195
Ego Trip   196
Stage Coach   196
Story Board   197

Special Equipment Games
Belli-Ball   197
Balance Beam   198
Button Capture   198
Jackstones   199
Snake Stomp   200
Woggle Sticks   201
Tilt Tennis   201
Jungle Climb   202
Snow Snake Slinging   203
Bike Drag Races   203
Bike Polo   205
Tot Train   205
Four-Season Sliding   206
Push-Bug Derby   207
Bronco Buster   208

Jousting 208
Playground Zoo 210

Recreation for Rainy
Days, Play Days,
Carnivals and Parties
Penny Crawl 210
American Hopscotch 211
British Hopscotch 211
Hop-Scotch Rope Jumping 212
Hopscotch Obstacle Course 213
Dutch Rope Jumping 213
Hurricane 213
Mummy Wrapper Race 214
Ego Game 214
Flag Pin 214
Name Bingo 215
Tree Bingo 215
Olympic Seed Spit 216
Statues 217
Beastie Dancing 217
Seat Scramble 218
Belly-Laugh 218
Sardines 218
Balloons-to-the-Moon 219
Balloon Bounce 219
Chopstick Balloon Relay 220
Balloon Steeplechase 220
The Candy Tree 220
Grab Bag 221
Swap Carnival 221
Cukoo 222

Picnic Scramble 222
Mud Scrabble 223
Mud Sliding 223
Mud Disco 223

Crafts Play and Game
Constructions
Homemade Play Dough,
  Paints and Bubble
  Blowing Compound 224
Bubbling-Up 224
Box Play 225
Electricity Play 226
Snake Swirl 227
Feet Painting 227
Worm Painting 228
Leaf Ink Prints 228
Leaf Spatter Prints 229
Ink Blot Flowering Plant 229
Creature Crafting 230
Bottle Cap Bugs 230
Martian Art 231
Snip Shopping 231
Peephole Binoculars 232
Bottle Cap Boat Racing 232
Hop Ring 233
Stompers 234
Chigger 234
Japanese Wish Tree 235
A Bird Feeder 236
Dirty Harry 236

Introduction

Amusing ourselves is almost a lost art. A number of factors have contributed to the changes in play over the past two generations. Kids perhaps get too much, too soon and too easy, and become blasé. Perhaps they get too much television. Perhaps there is too much highly organized sport, where too many adults are organizing leagues, controlling the games, and furnishing top grade uniforms, equipment and fields of play. Perhaps too many toys do all the play by themselves. Perhaps too little free space is available now for pickup play.

This book hopes to help reverse this trend and head back toward "pickup" games — where, basically, a group of kids pick up whatever is handy and make a game. It presents more than 300 such made-up sports, games and other recreational activities for children's and teenagers' play during informal and loosely structured leisure time.

If players or leaders find ways to change any of them to make them more fun for themselves, go to it. I don't know who it was that said, "Ideas are very much like children. Your own are very wonderful," but that is especially true when kids make up their own games. And it isn't as hard to do as you might think.

All you have to remember is a few simple suggestions. First, the rules of the game must be kept as few and as simple as possible so every player can remember them easily. Secondly, playing equipment should be simple, cheap and easy to get. Thirdly, a game is best that can be played by different numbers of players, and different ages of players together. And last, you should be able to play the game in whatever size playing space you have.

The easiest way to make up a game is to take parts of one game you may like and put them together with parts of another game you may like.

A BALL AND A WALL

Nearly everyone at some time has played a game by himself, throwing a ball against a wall and catching it as it bounces back. This actually is one of the simplest make-up games discovered by every junior athlete.

Add an opponent, and three simple rules to this, though, and you have invented one of your first real games, according to the dictionary definition: "A physical competition played according to rules, with players in opposition."

The three simple rules needed to make this a game would be: (1) The ball is served against the wall by one player, using open or clenched hand; (2) Players take turns hitting the ball against the wall after the serve; and (3) Player who misses the ball or knocks the ball out of the agreed playing area loses the point. Any number of points may be agreed upon as a game.

Everything else about the game can be sort of "catch-as-catch-can," meaning you, the players, agree on things as they come up. Any type ball, from a volleyball or playground ball to an old tennis ball or a Ping-Pong™ ball, can be used. Just changing the type ball you use sometimes makes a different game. For example, a volleyball will bounce further and make a game with much more running in it than using a Ping-Pong™ ball. So each of the two games will need different skills.

ADD A BAT OR PADDLE

Add bats or paddles to the game and you have made up still another game.

Bats and paddles don't have to be bought, either, to have fun. Some of the things I've seen used to hit tennis balls and playground balls are rolled-up magazines, old tin pans (the kind with handles), and old books. Smaller balls, like Ping-Pong™ balls, can be hit with folded newspapers, paperback books or LP record album covers.

If you want to play a game more like badminton than tennis, where the "ball" is hit back and forth in the air without touching the ground, these same items may be used as paddles or racquets. Instead of a ball, though, you can use a paper cup, a balloon, a small ball of yarn, or even a tightly balled piece of paper. You can use a net or not.

If there are a group of players, this game, which I call "Badminiature," can be played two ways. The first way is to form a ring. Players bat the object back and forth around the ring, with the one missing it dropping out, until only a winner is left. Or one person can be put inside the ring and the rest play keep-away by batting the item around and over him, until he gets it and replaces the person who made the bad hit to him.

The second way to play is form sides and play over a net or a designated "no-man's land" between the sides, or to play "keep-away" by teams.

ADD A NET

The games above usually involve only two items of equipment, a paddle and a ball-like object. If you want a more organized game, you can add a net and mark off boundaries with chain, string, tape, twigs, or whatever is handy. The net can also be made from whatever is handy, like a string tied between two sticks in the ground or just a box set on its side.

Such a game is "Sidewalk Tennis." This is played with a small ball, like a tennis ball or a Ping-Pong™ ball, which is hit with the hand back and forth over the net until one player misses or knocks it out of bounds. Of course, a sidewalk doesn't have to be used. Any hard surface will do, like a driveway, patio, or floor.

MOVE A GAME

Sometimes just moving a game from where it is usually played to a new surface can make a new game.

A few years ago, for example, table tennis was moved to the gym floor, where the playing area was made bigger and the net was raised higher, and the game called "Smash" was invented. This is a simple change to make, so anyone could play it almost anywhere.

Shuffleboard can become a new game, too, by adding empty cardboard quart milk cartons at the end of the pushway as bowling tenpins. Then, instead of throwing a ball at them, you push shuffleboard discs at them. Scoring can be done as in bowling, or by having each pin count one point, without bonuses for strikes and spares.

OLD COURT, NEW USE

There are times when city, school or playground tennis courts are not in use. It's then they make great courts for playing new types of tennis games, like volley-tennis and soccer-tennis. Volley-tennis was invented when two people started batting a volleyball back and forth over a tennis net with hand, fist and both fists clenched together. Soccer-tennis was invented the same way, with two people kicking a soccer ball back and forth over a tennis net. Others modified this idea by using a lighter playground ball. Others modified this into a game they called volley-soccer, kicking a soccer ball back and forth over a volleyball net, allowing one bounce between each kick, two or four persons to a side.

There are scores of variations possible like those. Most of them will never turn up on the *Wide World of Sports,* but in the diversified world of the playground, gym and playing field they can become joyful additions.

You can alter the court — from a wall to a corner area, making a novel table tennis–wallball combination, for example. You can change the number of players — which is how pro beach volleyball got started, two players to a side. You can change the size of the ball used — which is how playground wallball, hitting a rubber playground ball with the fist, evolved from standard handball. You can change the shape of the ball used — like Australian football, which uses a blunter, more rounded ball, because it is dribbled as well as passed and kicked. You can use equipment in different ways — like using a tennis racquet and ball to play softball. You can change a rule — like allowing one bounce between each hit in volleyball. Or you can alter the size of the playing area — like miniaturizing equipment so pool can be played on a card table, or using croquet equipment to play pool on a park lawn.

Anyhow, these are some of the type things done to innovate the sports, games and other activities introduced in this book. I hope perhaps, to have shown that it really isn't whether you win or lose, but how you play the game that is important in playtime.

Special Notes on a Few of the Games

Ping-Pong™ (Introduction, p. xiv) is a copyrighted name for the game now known more universally as Table Tennis. The company originating the game would not allow other manufacturers to use the name Ping-Pong™, thus the change.

Mermaid Angling (#2, p. 2), as a stunt, was originated at the Royal Aquarium in London, England, in the summer of 1895.

U.S. Navy Special Services (#4, p. 3) was formerly named the Recreation & Welfare Department of the Navy. The author set up the original Special Services Training School and directed it for five years. One training assignment there was to "invent" a new game so recreation administrators would recognize how difficult this is and thus would have a greater appreciation for the games they supervised.

Zippie (#25, p. 22–23) is a variation of Spindle Baseball from an old-time street game, called Nipsie or Ards-Off in different areas of the U.S.

Cesta (#28, p. 24, and #35, p. 28) is a large, rattan scoop attached by thongs to the forearm of a jai alai player in Spain and Mexico. It is used to catch-and-throw a ball against a wall at terrific speed. Toy makers have adapted these in plastic for playground use in various games. They may also be handcrafted from gallon plastic jugs (*see* Jug Tennis).

Cricket (#37, p. 29; #38, p. 30; #39, p. 31) is a British game often believed to have been the forerunner of American baseball since it utilizes ball, bats and base running. But it uses 11 players to a side, runs mount into the hundreds, and batters stand in front of "wickets" to protect them from balls thrown by the "pitcher."

Sacket (#39, p. 31) is a commercial game (U.S. Games Co.) modified from British Cricket for playground use.

H'Penny (#47, p. 39) refers to the British half-penny coin often used in this popular pub game.

Curling (#66, p. 49; #67, p. 50; #70, p. 52) is a Canadian sport where round, handled "stones" are shoved down an ice course to a marker.

Sumo (#104, p. 79) is a form of Japanese wrestling where opponents try to force each other out of a small ring.

Whiz-Ring (#130, p. 97) is basically a light Frisbee with a hole in its middle, merchandized originally by North Pacific Products, Inc. of Bend, OR.

Foxball (#161, p. 120) is a game modified from International Handball, marketed about 1978 by James B. McCarthy of Verona, PA.

Nisei (#211, p. 155) is a term from the World War II era denoting American citizens of Japanese ancestry. Thus the name here denotes an Americanized version of a Japanese game.

Dictionary Doodling Game (#264, p. 193) is adapted from the author's hobby. It became a panel-column in the *Long Beach Southland* paper in the early 1960s and later became a book, titled *The Doodler's Dictionary,* 1971, after the author had gone through the entire dictionary "doodling" words so they became self-explanatory.

Imagineering (#269, p. 195) is a term invented by the author combining "*imagin*ation" with "engin*eering*" to show the way games are innovated.

The Games

AQUATIC GAMES

1. Sliding Statues

*An innovative variation of the game of Statues
using an aquatic format*

Age level: 6 and up
Organizational level: Medium
Number of players: Open
Supervision: Play leader
Playing time: Open-ended
Space needed: Beach or lawn area that can be
reached by a water hose, about $10' \times 30'$

Equipment: Slip-n-Slide (commercial, available from Wham-O) or equivalent sheet of heavy plastic, hose and stand sprinkler (if on grass area), old barrel and bucket (if at beach), plus a hammer and large nail

Directions: Lay Slip-n-Slide, or plastic sheet, on ground that preferably slants somewhat. If on grass, place sprinkler so it keeps the plastic wet. If at the beach, set the barrel at the side of the uphill end of the plastic sheet. With the hammer and nail, make several holes across the barrel about 6″ up from the bottom facing the plastic. Fill the barrel with buckets of lake or seawater. The holes should keep the plastic wet enough to slide easily on.

One at a time, players take a run and slide on the plastic. When this begins to lessen in interest, institute contests, judging the funniest pose while sliding, the hardest trick while sliding (as on knees, back, one foot, spinning around, bellywhopper), or try tandem sliding (holding hands, seated like on a sled, several at once, each holding waist of person in front, etc.). You can also have a hurdle contest, jumping over an obstacle or person laying down, while in mid-slide. If you have plenty of plastic you can have distance sliding contests.

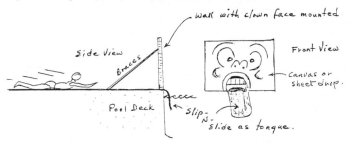

1

Variation: A Slip-n-Slide can be utilized in an aquacade also. Put up a large wood frame, covered with chicken wire, then tack butcher paper over the front. Paint a huge clown face on the front, with a large mouth (see illustration, p. 1). Cut the chicken wire and the paper mouth out, leaving the paper mouth hanging from the top. Put the Slip-n-Slide to the mouth, with the mouth exiting right into the pool of water. Then the performers can slide right through the mouth into the water for a novel entrance.

2. Mermaid Angling

Fisherman stunt for aquacade

Age level: 14 and up
Organizational level: Medium
Number of players: Several strong anglers, swimmers
Supervision: Referee
Playing time: 3–5 minutes per swimmer
Space needed: Water area deep enough so swimmers can't touch bottom by standing, with deck or platform adjacent for the angler
Equipment: Deep sea fishing gear, belt or harness (for swimmers to wear) and stopwatch

Directions: Contest may be waged by individuals, between boy and girl swimmers on a team, or as an elimination tournament, with swimmers who can last the time limit, without being reeled in or stopping swimming, going on to the next brackets.

Each swimmer wears the belt or harness that has fishing line attached to it at the back and is on a reel and pole the angler holds on deck. The swimmer starts with a prespecified length of line out. On the "go" signal by a referee, angler tries to reel in swimmer, who starts swimming away from him.

Variation: *Sucker Fishing*—Teams are selected (can include both male and female swimmers, so long as each team has an equal number of each). One team becomes the fishermen, the other, the fish. Then they switch places, when a whole team has been fished.

Girls fish for girls, boys for boys. Team captains can select the pairings.
The team with the most members staying the time limit is the winner.

3. Clown Diving Competition

*An adjunct to springboard diving competition
for those divers who specialize in comedy*

Age level: 10–13, 14–17, 18 and up
Organizational level: High
Number of players: Open
Supervision: 3 judges, lifeguards, recorder-scorekeeper
Playing time: 5 dives per contestant. May count "pair dives" points for both divers.
Space needed: Diving pool, or area of pool or lake, with 2 3-meter diving boards
Equipment: 3 diving flash card sets (for judges), whistle (to signal judges to show flash cards and next diver to go ahead), hand calculator (for score-keeper)

Directions: Divers register, listing the names of the dives they will do, in the order they will do them. They draw numbers from hat to determine their turn diving.

Each performs 5 dives, one at a time in rotation with other divers. As each one is diving, the next one gets ready on the other board.

Judges will base awards of 1–10 points on (1) difficulty, (2) novelty and (3) excellence of performance. Difficulty and novelty can earn 3 points; excellence 4 points, including board takeoff and water entrance. Three judges' scores are totalled and divided by 3 to get average score for each dive, which is listed by the scorekeeper. At the end of competition, scores are totalled and the winner is high point earner.

4. Surf Jai Alai

A variation of the usual water games

Age level: 10 and up
Organizational level: Medium
Number of players: 2 teams, 1, 2, or 4 each
Supervision: None
Playing time: 21-point game
Space needed: 20′ × 20′ area in surf or shallow end of swim pool

Equipment: Ball (tennis ball sized that floats), plastic hand cesta (scoops – available from Cosom Co.) for each player, 1 rebound net (commercial), 2 boundary floats and anchors

Directions: Anchor boundary floats. Rebound net is placed on edge of pool or beach. Players are in the water facing it. Each has a hand cesta to catch and throw the ball from and to the rebound net.

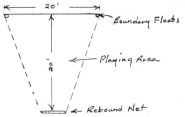

Determine first server. He serves 5 times, then opponent serves 5, and so on until game is decided. Serve by throwing the ball against the rebound net, with opponents alternating catches-and-return throws. (If playing teams, any player of a team may play the ball when it is his team's turn.)

Any missed ball landing inside the playing area is a point against the team missing it. Any thrown ball that doesn't rebound from the net is a point against the throwing team.

Variations: *Mini-Jai Alai* – Same game may be played on the beach or on a lawn area. *Cut Throat Jai Alai* – Played by 3 players, the server playing against the other two. Server remains serving as long as he makes points. When he misses, another server takes over and the two others play against him as a team, though still playing the ball in rotation sequence.

Game source: Modified from game idea by Bruce R. Fox, U.S. Navy Special Services, 1967.

5. Surf Hockey

New aquatic challenge

Age level: 8 and up
Organizational level: Medium
Number of players: 2 teams, 3 per team
Supervision: Referee and scorekeeper
Playing time: 6 5-minute periods
Space needed: Beach surf (water covering ankles of players)

Equipment: Waterball (big enough so it can't be grasped in one hand), 30′ canvas net, 1 paddleboard, water polo goals (modified to float in surf on a floating platform)

Directions: Start the game, and after each goal, at the offensive line, with an offensive player throwing the ball into the playing area to a teammate. All players must remain with ankles covered by water during play periods.

Ball may be thrown, kicked or hit to move it or put it into goal. A goal is 3 points. All players may rove the playing area. One defense player may serve as goalie, but only one offensive series there, then must switch off with another teammate. The goalie may use the paddleboard to help guard the goal, but only while he is in the goalie slot. No carrying ball.

Scoring may only be done by the offensive team. If the defense intercepts the ball, it takes it out at the offensive line and becomes the offensive team.

Any ball going up onto the beach is thrown into play by the referee. He throws it at least 10' overhead and so it lands near the center of the playing area on a line with the spot where it went onto the beach. A ball going out of bounds in any of the other 3 directions is given to the team not touching it last at the offense line.

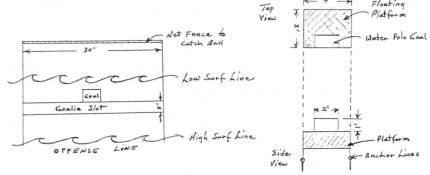

Variation: *Out of the Surf*—Same game, except the net is placed on the beach, at the surf's edge. Players play from the water.

Game source: Modified from an idea proposed at a U.S. Navy Special Services Training School class in 1972 by Bob McLeay of Kamiseya Naval Base, Japan.

6. Aquaball

A form of baseball played in the water

Age level: 14 and up
Organizational level: High
Number of players: 2 teams, 8 each (swimmers)
Supervision: 2 umpires, lifeguards, scorekeeper
Playing time: 5 innings, 5-minute rest after 3 innings
Space needed: Beach or pool area deep enough so players have to tread water

Equipment: 3 floating base pads (kickboards or inflated pillows), life jackets or innertubes for all officials and players (catcher, pitcher, first base, second base, third base and 3 outfielders for each team), surfmat or surfboard (for umpire), ball (inflated, size of softball), bat (canoe paddle, kickboard, plastic bat), 4 concrete or pumicestone blocks (to anchor bases, via detachable plastic lines)

Directions: Bases anchored 30' apart. Pitcher is 15' from home plate. Basic slowpitch softball rules.

Ball is pitched overhand, but in an arc as in slowpitch softball. No walks for batter hit by pitched ball. Base runners must touch bases above water, and must swim last 10 yards to any base on top of water. Base-swimmers may steal bases, and may advance one base on an overthrow or wild pitch.

Batted ball is foul if it strikes home plate.

Game source: Baseball while swimming was introduced in the summer of 1953 at Split Rock Lodge on Lake Harmony in Pennsylvania's Poconos. Editor Nelson Bryant of *Resort Management* magazine, June 1953, printed a revised version he called Aquaball. This is a much modified version of that game.

7. Socko (or Guard Ball)
Innovative aquatic game for either informal or intramural/league play

Age level: 8 and up
Organizational level: High
Number of players: 2 teams, any number up to 10
Supervision: 2 scoring monitors
Playing time: 4 10-minute periods
Space needed: Any pre-determined area of a swimming pool. This may include deep or shallow water, or half and half. The area needed is best determined by the number of players playing the game and the skills of the swimmers (whether non-swimmers or advanced swimmers).

Teams' home ends decided by coin flip and changed at half.
Equipment: Six waterproof balls of the same size — three one color and the other three any contrasting color. Two out of each three-set shall have been painted into quarters with a white ½" to 1" stripe, so as to be easily distinguishable from the plain colored ones. The plain balls shall be called "throw balls" and the striped ones "goal balls." Swimming caps of 2 contrasting colors (to differentiate team members).

Directions: One team must throw its "throw ball" and hit one or both of the opponent's "goal balls," either on the fly or the bounce. At the same time, they shall try to block attempts by the opposing players to hit their "goal balls" with the opposing "throw ball."

Play at the start of each quarter starts with all goal balls tossed into the center of the playing area by the monitors. Each monitor shall toss one ball of each color. Team captains will hold the throw balls at their respective ends of the pool until the starting whistle by the senior monitor, senior being decided before the start of the game.

Fouls: Fouls shall be called for (1) body contact, (2) unsportsmanlike conduct, which includes intentionally throwing at a player's face, (3) catching the opponent's throw ball, (4) touching any goal ball, or allowing one to touch you. Numbers 1 and 2 receive two throws, taken consecutively by the same person, the second being thrown from the spot it ends up from the first throw. Numbers 3 and 4 receive one free throw. No free foul throws may be blocked, under penalty of an added free throw from the point of the block. All free throws are taken from the spot where the infraction occurred, and must be taken within 10 seconds after the handoff from the monitor.

On completion of a foul throw, or throws, play commences immediately with all balls remaining in position they end up (on the whistle of the monitor designating that the ball has completed its flight). Even though a score is made, the play goes on without interruption.

Variations: *Double Socko* — Includes using five balls (three goal balls and two throw balls) for each team. Other rules remain the same. Three monitors used. *Elimination Socko* — Three or more teams playing in the same area, each team designated by colored caps (as in water polo) to match their balls, which their team uses.

Each team is eliminated as it has 15 points scored against it by the other teams. Last one to remain in the game, or the one with the lowest number of points scored against it, is the winner at the end of the playing period.

No less than four monitors shall be used, one designated as senior monitor. Each of those, other than the senior monitor, will keep the points scored against one of the playing teams. He shall be designated by either a cap or a tie-on vest of the color of the ball of the team he is scoring.

8. Surfmat Waterpolo

A less strenuous and skilled version of water polo

Age level: 10–12, 13–16, 17 and up
Organizational level: Medium
Number of players: 2 teams, 7 each
Supervision: Referee, scorekeeper & lifeguard
Playing time: 30 minutes
Space needed: Pool area 25 yards × 25 yards minimum

Equipment: Auto innertube for each player (14), 2 goals (boxes, chairs set on sides of pool), waterpolo ball (or rubber volleyball, playground ball), 2 differently colored sets of swim caps, marking pen (to put player's numbers on caps) and a watch

Directions: Basic water polo rules. Players play while seated in innertubes, passing the ball or trying to block or intercept it, or scoring from that position. Each team has a goalie.

Game starts with referee tossing the ball into the center of the pool and both teams racing from their goal lines to play it.

Players may tip and dunk anyone holding the ball, until they turn loose of it. Any other time this is a foul, with a penalty throw awarded to the fouled player from the point of the foul. No opponent may be closer than 3′ on a penalty throw.

If any player gets out of the seated position in his tube during play, it is also a foul. Penalty: the ball goes to the opposite team. If that team already has possession, it then gets a penalty throw at the goal from the point where the foul was made. However, if a shot on goal is being taken and an opposition player climbs out of his tube, the shooter has his choice of the goal shot or the penalty shot.

A ball thrown into the goal counts 1 point.

Two scoring monitors (or referees) are preferred. One located on each side of the playing area. Each shall be armed with: (1) whistle, (2) sticks with colored flags on each end, one denoting the color of the caps being used by one team and the other denoting the color of the caps being used by the opposite team ... to signify fouls and scores, (3) golf stroke marker to keep track of points (goals) scored. Each monitor keeps score for one team, though there shall be a composite scorer to keep the running score for both teams. Scoring shall be compared at each quarter rest period to make sure there are no discrepancies.

Substitutions may be made only between quarters, or in case of injury, in which case the clock would be stopped.

If a game ends in a tie score, each team receives one-half a win. Overtime play is done away with to aid scheduling of pools' activities.

Scoring: One point (goal) is awarded each time a throw ball contacts an opposition goal ball, providing it touches a person before it contacts the same goal ball a second time. (This avoids the problem of balls clinging together, making it impossible for monitors to judge the scoring.)

Throw balls must be thrown and never carried while swimming. They may be bounced off another person or dribbled as in water polo. If a throw ball hits both opposing goal balls on the same throw, a "billiard" is scored, counting 5 points. Should the throw ball hit the first opposing goal ball, then the second, then the first one again, it shall be scored 10 points as a "double billiard."

Goal balls must remain free-floating at all times, though they may be moved by splashing water at them. No one is allowed to touch them except a monitor, or unless a monitor directly calls for someone to touch them. An example would be to recover a ball which has been knocked or thrown out of bounds. In such case, the ball is put back into play by the monitor at the point where it went out and no more than 3' inside the boundary line. Players must hold positions at whistle.

Scores may be stopped by blocking thrown balls with the body, but the ball may never be caught or trapped, scooped or held in any way for any length of time. Nor may it be dribbled away by the opposition. The opponent's throw ball may, however, be hit and knocked away at any time.

Variations: *Kickboard water polo* — Basic water polo, but with each player allowed to hold onto a kickboard as an aid, instead of sitting in an innertube. *Pong Polo* — Basic water polo for small area. Can use a Ping-Pong™ (table tennis) ball, and tubes to sit in.

Game Source: The University of California at Davis innovated Surfmat Water Polo in its intramural program in 1967-68. In 1971, it made its debut at the Ravenswood Parks and Recreation District, E. Palo Alto, CA.

9. Underwater Blind Man's Bluff

A real challenge for breath control, to build up lung capacity.
Training for lifeguards and skin divers in use of equipment.

Age level: 12 and up
Organizational level: Medium
Number of players: 4–8 swimmers
Supervision: 2 referees and lifeguards
Playing time: Open ended
Space needed: 20' × 20' area in deep end (8–12' swim pool

Equipment: 1 blindfold, skin diving face masks and snorkels for all players, one float, 40' of netting, 2 anchors to hold netting to pool sides, 2 whistles for referees and swim fins for all, if wished

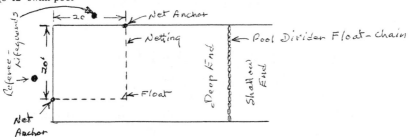

Directions: Basic Blind Man's Bluff, where person who is "it" is blindfolded. He tries to tag one of the other players, who must touch him every 10 seconds while, at the same time, avoiding his return touch. A tagged player becomes "it" until he, in turn, tags another. Or, a player not touching "it" every 10 seconds may be called by a referee and he becomes "it."

Variation: *Double Bluff*— If more people want to play (up to 20), enlarge playing area to entire end of pool and blindfold two players. Post 4 lifeguards — referees.

BASKETBALL TYPE GAMES

10. Bucketball

Teaches basic basketball skills without necessity of expensive courts and equipment. Also can be played by handicapped.

Age level: 6–8 and 9–12 play together
Organizational level: Low
Number of players: Two teams of equal numbers, from 1 on 1 to 5 on 5
Supervision: None (except, possibly, for some handicapped)
Playing time: Open

Space needed: 40–60′ length, 15–40′ width, depending on availability and ages and skills of players. Indoors or outdoors.
Equipment: 1 playground ball, 2 metal buckets, waste baskets, bushel baskets or boxes as goals

Directions: 1 on 1 game: Ball can only be dribbled to advance toward basket. With more players, ball can be passed and dribbled among players to advance it. No physical contact by defense or offense. Foul allows fouled player to shoot, unguarded, at his basket from point of infraction. Successful free shots score one point.

Field goals may be scored by shooting or bouncing the ball into the shooting team's basket. They count 2 points, if successful. Ball must stay in basket to count. (This keeps hard throwing out of the game.)

At start of game, at quarters, and after each goal scored, play starts by one player holding the ball at mid-court. Coin flip can decide which team gets ball to start game. After that, it is the team scored on. (Or, this rule can be changed to "alternating possession of ball after each score," regardless of which team scores.)

11. Guard Ball (Also called Waste-ket Ball)

Active game for limited space,
as in a hallway. (Can be played by handicapped.)

Age level: 8 and up
Organizational level: Low

Number of players: 2 2-person teams
Supervision: None

Playing time: 7 innings
Space needed: Unused end of hallway, narrow areaway between two buildings, or in shipboard passageway. Need about 12′ length.

Equipment: 2 waste baskets, 10 small rubber balls (or even 10 tightly-wadded paper balls with tape around them). Chalk for marking off court.

Directions: Object is for one team to shoot or throw as many of the 10 balls as possible into the waste baskets, while the other team tries to block the balls. Time limit, if wished, of 3–4 minutes. Then teams switch places.

Play 6 or 7 innings. An inning is when both teams have been on offense once. Winner is the team scoring the most total baskets. Each basket is one point.

Offense (throwing team) can throw only from behind the throw line. Stepping over is penalized by taking away one point. Balls may be thrown, bounced or caromed off floor, ceiling or walls.

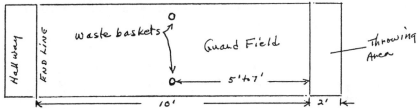

Variations: *(1)* Same game, but with throwing areas at each end of court, one offensive player in each, and waste baskets set one foot out from the walls in the middle of the guard field. Balls that go through the guard field into the opposite throwing area may be replayed by throwing team. Any ball ending up in guard field, however, is dead, whether it has been thrown or blocked or caught by defensive team.

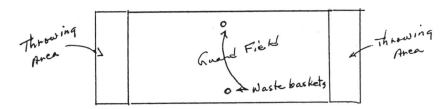

(2) Same rules and court as variation #1, except the waste baskets are set about two feet apart in the middle of the guard area.

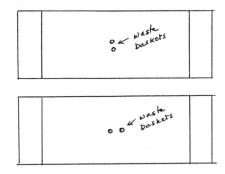

12. Crab Basketball

Uses a lot of muscles that no other games seem to use much,
especially in wrists and arms, ankles and legs

Age level: 10 and up
Organizational level: Medium
Number of players: 2 teams, 10–12 persons per team
Supervision: None for informal play. Referee-scorekeeper for tourneys.
Playing time: 4 8-minute quarters, 3-minute rest periods between each or game can be played to a pre-set number of points, with no quarters

Space needed: Court size can be varied according to age and skills of participants. A circle 22 yards in radius makes a good court for elementary and junior high ages.
Equipment: Ball (volleyball, basketball or rubber playground ball), cardboard box (large enough for the ball to go into easily) weighted with a sandbag in the bottom.

Directions: Basic "sideline" basketball rules, where only one goal is used for both teams. This goal is located in the center of a circle, rather than at one end of the squared playing court, however.

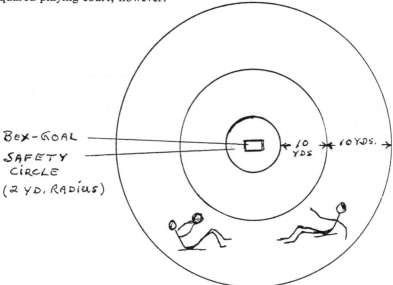

Players play from the crab position, backside to floor, moving about on hands and feet, sitting to catch, pass and shoot the ball. Both arms and feet may be used in blocking, passing and shooting also, however.

Goal is placed in the center of the circles. Goal is scored by throwing or bouncing the ball into the box-goal. Field goal is 2 points. Players cannot go inside the small safety circle around the box-goal. Loss of ball and cancellation of goal, if one is made, is the penalty.

Free throws are taken for fouls, being shot from anywhere outside the safety circle. They count 1 point.

Fouls: Fouls are called for a player standing up to play the ball in any way, and the basic basketball rules concerning contact, sportsmanship, et al.

After any basket, the ball goes to the team not making the basket, outside the outer circle. A shot that does not go into the goal, whether it touches the box-goal or not, may be played by either side, though no player may reach inside the safety circle to retrieve the ball. If the ball stays inside the safety circle, the referee gives it to the team last on defense, out of bounds.

Variations: *Crab Funnelball*—Instead of a box-goal on the ground, an overhead hoop, without a backboard, is mounted in the center of the circles about 5' high. (An old washtub without the bottom in it makes a good hoop, mounted by nailing the side handles to posts in the ground.) *Crab Fieldball*—Same game as above, except a smaller ball is used, a playground ball of rubber or plastic that can be held and thrown one-handed. The goal can be made smaller, too, like a plastic bucket with the bottom cut out of it.

13. Soccer-Basketball

Soccer action game for variety and training in passing,
touch control and accuracy of kicking

Age level: Any age good soccer players

Organizational level: High

Number of players: 2 teams, 4–6 players each

Supervision: 2 referees, one of which can keep score

Playing time: Set to fit age, fitness and skill of players, with suggested length of 4 10-minute quarters, short rest periods between them

Space needed: Basketball court, indoors or out

Equipment: Soccer ball. Basketball standards with backboards

Directions: Basic basketball rules, except players use feet to play the ball as in soccer.

One-point score is made by kicking or "heading" ball so it hits opponent's backboard. If ball goes through hoop, from top, it counts 4 points.

Variations: *4-Corner Soccer-Basketball* — Four teams of 4 players each play on same court at same time by utilizing 4 (moveable) basketball standards, located in each of the four corners of the court (which must then be squared off so all sides are equidistant).

Each team is assigned a different goal to protect. *Soccer-Funnelball* — Using Funnel Ball standard (see Funnel Basketball) placed in center of court, 2 or 4 teams of 4 players each can compete. Use basic Funnel Basketball rules, except players use feet instead of hands on ball.

14. Borden Ball

Modification of Olympic handball adapted to the Canadian
familiarity with football and basketball handling

Age level: 10 and up
Organizational level: High
Number of players: 2 teams, 6 each
Supervision: Referee — scorekeeper
Playing time: 2 15-minute halves, 5-minute rest period. Overtime — 5 minutes playing time each way.
Space needed: Field 65' × 165'
Equipment: Rugby ball (or football), 2 hockey type goals

Directions: To start play, referee throws ball to center-forward of team winning coin toss. Other team then gets ball to start second half.

Ball is advanced by throwing it from one player to another until a try on goal can be attempted. A player may take only three steps with the ball. (Penalty is loss of ball at point of foul.) A player holding the ball may only remain at a standstill 3 seconds. (Penalty: loss of ball.)

If a pass is missed, the ball goes to the other team at point where missed. All players must remain at least 3' away from player with the ball. (Penalty: free shot from a point 7 yards in front of goal.)

Fouls: Unsportsmanlike conduct, holding or otherwise restricting personal movement of an opponent. Penalty: penalty kick. Four personal fouls results in ejection from game.

Only the goal keeper can play in the "crease" (semi-circle in front of each goal). Penalty for offensive player in it is loss of ball. If offensive player follows a shot in, any score made is disallowed and fouled team is awarded a penalty shot.

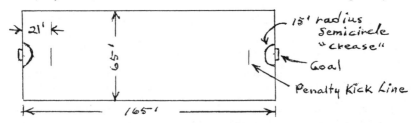

Variation: Played with another type ball, as a basketball or playground ball, the goal could be changed to anything that can reasonably be guarded by one goal keeper: hitting a box, knocking over bowling pins or Indian clubs, shooting through a hoop or wooden frame, or passing over an end line.

Game source: Modified from game instituted by the service secretary at Camp Borden in 1940.

15. Court Ball

Game of keep-away to teach basic basketball skills.
For use where basketball courts aren't available.

Age level: 8–11
Organizational level: Medium
Number of players: 2 teams, 6 players each
Supervision: Referee
Playing time: About 30 minutes
Space needed: Court area approximately
30′ wide by 60′ long, indoors or out

Equipment: Soccerball, playground ball or basketball. (Beanbag may be used for smaller or more inept players, or for handicapped players.) Lime or chalk to mark playing field.

Directions: Six players to team, composed of 3 guards, 2 forwards and a goalie. Goalies limited to area within free throw circle. Other players limited to the half court where they are assigned. Free substitution any time ball is dead.

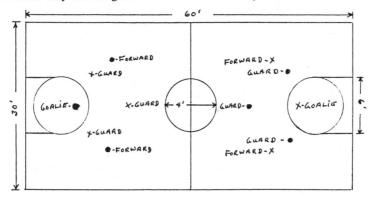

Play starts with referee throwing ball to a guard in the center circle, alternating sides at the start of each quarter (first throw decided by coin toss). Game consists of four 5-minute quarters, two minutes intermission at quarters and five minutes at half.

Each ball caught by a goalie, inside the goal area circle, counts one point for his side. Ball thrown into goal and not caught counts point for throwing team.

If a game ends tied, any number of one-minute overtimes shall be played until the tie is broken and remains broken at the end of that overtime.

After a score, the team scored on takes the ball in the center circle to start play again. He must pass the ball before leaving the circle.

Fouls: Fouls will be called for body contact, such as pushing, charging, tripping, hacking or face-guarding, as well as for stepping on or over out-of-bounds lines, center division line or goal area lines, and touching the ball while in the possession of an opponent. Penalty for these infractions is awarding of the ball to the fouled team at the point of infraction. *Exception:* if a guard invades the goal area circle, an automatic point will be awarded his opposing team.

Variations: *Massed Court Ball*—If you have more players than can be handled in the regular game, divide up sides evenly, then play, without timing, until one team reaches 15 points. *Scramble-Amble Court Ball*—Four teams of six players on court at same time, each team trying to score in an opponent's

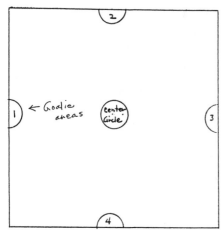

goal and protect its own. Other than that, basic Court Ball rules are used, except (1) any ball landing in a goal area untouched by the goalie earns the throwing team one point, and any ball caught by a goalie earns the goalie's team two points, (2) after each foul or each goal, the ball is given to the team with the lowest score, in the center circle (or, in case of a tie, to the last team scoring the tie).

Court may be any size, to fit age, skills and fitness of players, but should always be square so all teams have equal chance.

16. Cage Ball

Active field game combining soccer and field handball

Age level: 12 and up
Organizational level: High
Number of players: 2 teams, 6 each
Supervision: Referee, umpire (to assist), linesman and timekeeper
Playing time: 4 periods, 6 minutes each, with 2-minute intermissions and 10 minutes at half. Overtime, 5 minutes.
Space needed: 50′ × 180′ (see drawing)
Equipment: 8′ × 10′ × 36″ net, ball (rubber or leather with bladder, 12–14 oz. weight, 26–27″ circumference)

Directions: Start game, and half (and after each goal), with jump ball in the center circle. Player positions include center, left and right defense, left and right attack and goaltender. Sides exchanged at halftime.

Players advance ball by throwing, passing, hitting, rolling or dribbling ball, while trying to put it into the opponent's goal cage and at the same time, protecting their own. Players cannot run with the ball or kick it. One air-pass to oneself during a dribble is allowed by batting the ball into the air with one hand off the other. A dribble is completed when touched with 2 hands.

Held balls, between two opponents, requires a jump ball in the nearest special circle. Jump ball is also called if a player runs with or kicks the ball while in the attack or defense zones (adjacent goals), and after any penalty throw that fails to score.

Fouls: Player stepping into attack zone before the ball reaches the zone, unless he is advancing it. Defense plays ball through the neutral zone and beyond the opponent's goal line. Player holding ball over 5 seconds without playing it. (Penalty: jump ball.)

Penalty throw is awarded for personal fouls, including holding, hand checking, pushing, charging and tripping. Penalty throws are taken from behind zone lines. No scoring allowed from a rebound. Penalty throw awards 1 point if successful. Goal throw awards 2 points.

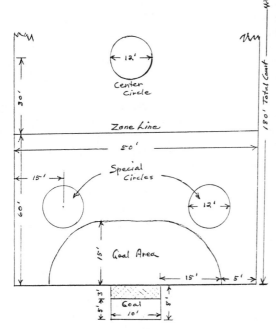

Goalkeeper may go out of goal area to stop shots when play is underway, but then becomes just another field player. Inside goal area he can use any part of body to bat, block, catch or trap the ball. When the ball leaves a team's defense zone, all but three of that team's defense men must leave that area immediately. (Penalty: jump ball.)

Ball going out of bounds is thrown back in by team not last touching it from the point it went out.

17. American Ball

Body contact game more accident-free than touch football.
The name was selected because elements of three big American
sports (baseball, basketball and football) are present in it.

Age level: 10 and up
Organizational level: High
Number of players: 2 teams, 9 each, though 20–30 can play if field is enlarged accordingly
Supervision: Referees, scorekeeper and timekeeper
Playing time: 2 20-minute halves, with 10-minute rest period between. Overtime: 5-minute period.
Space needed: Area 60′ × 108′, indoors or out
Equipment: 14″ diameter inflated round ball (or equivalent, like soccer, volleyball or playground ball)

Directions: Start game with center jump in center circle. Ball then may be carried or passed, but not kicked, in the area between the "scoring lines." If a player is tagged (two hands above waist) while in possession of the ball, ball goes to tagging player at that point. (Original rules allowed tackling, but that has been eliminated.)

Ball going out of bounds is thrown in by team opposite last team to touch it.

Scoring: Goal, 2 points; free throw, 1 point, made by throwing ball, on the fly, to your team's catcher, standing in the catcher's circle in your team's goal area. Goal throw may be made from anywhere in the field. A free throw is taken from the free throw circle.

Free throws are awarded for body contact or unsportsmanlike conduct or arguing with the referee. Opponents may mass between the free thrower and his catcher to try to stop the score. Center jump after each score.

If attempt for goal fails, and ball goes out of bounds over the end line, the catcher throws it back into play from where it crossed the end line. This is the only time a catcher may leave the goal area. (Penalty: free throw for opposing team, and same penalty against any player stepping into either goal area during play.)

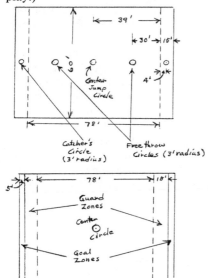

Catcher's Circle (3' radius)   Free throw Circles (3' radius)

Variation #2

Variations: *(1)* Change the scoring lines to semi-circles connecting to the two corners of the end lines. This allows more playing space around the catchers and more tries on goal. *(2)* Eliminate the catchers' circles. Each team's catcher is, thus, allowed to roam free in the "goal zone." However, the field is extended 5' at each end. That area will be the goal zone. The 15' wide strip that previously held the catcher's circles becomes a "guard zone" in which an opposing player is stationed and he may rove anywhere within it to try to stop players passing to their catchers.

Game source: George Haniford, an assistant professor at Purdue University, IN, innovated it in 1948–52. The original rules (modified here), which allowed tackling, were prepared by Larry A. Bidlake in 1934 for use by the Department of Physical Education and Health, School of Education, N.Y. University.

18. Boxer's Basketball

Short stunt sport for spectator fun

Age level: Junior high and above, adult
Organizational level: Low
Number of players: 2 teams, 5 each
Supervision: 2 referees
Playing time: 10–20 minutes

Space needed: Basketball court
Equipment: 1 basketball, 10 pairs boxing gloves (though heavy leather mittens may be substituted if boxing gloves are not available)

Directions: Basic basketball rules, except players will be wearing gloves.

Game source: Modified from Ensign Guerlick, USNR (MCB 40) innovation at U.S. Navy Special Services Training Facility, 1971.

19. Sideline Basketball

Uses easily procured items to teach basics of basketball in small space.
Can be played by the handicapped, too.

Age level: 6–10, or older handicapped
Organizational level: low
Number of players: Teams of 1 to 5
Supervision: None
Playing time: Set as wished, to fit interest and fitness of participants
Space needed: Any small area, at least 20′ × 20′, with a wall at one end that a "basket" can be attached to, like an auto garage apron. Also can be played in park or playground areas, with post erected for attaching "basket."
Equipment: 1 wire coat hanger, any ball that will fit easily through it when bent to form "basket" rim, post, if needed, 2″ × 4″, about 7′ long

Directions: Bend wire coat hanger into diamond, square or round shape, then attach it to wall or post by curved hanger part at height appropriate for age, size and abilities of players.

Basic basketball rules, except no jump balls. Team that scores gets to take ball out of bounds at midcourt to start each new play. Fouls are automatic points (one point each) for the team fouled, offensive or defensive, and fouled team gets the ball out of bounds at point of infraction.

Variations: *(1)* Same game can be played in shallow pool, with boxes set on chairs on sides of pool as hoops. Ball, instead of being dribbled, can be pushed in the water, but not grasped in the hand while push-dribbling. *(2)*Same game may be played using a beanbag instead of a ball, except there is no dribbling.

Game source: Modified from suggestion by Rich Nyquist, Ensign of USS *Caliente*, at Navy Special Services School.

20. Funnel Basketball

Agility, timing and hand-eye coordination training as basic basketball skills. (Also good game for wheelchair athletes.)

Age level: 8 and up
Organizational level: Medium
Number of players: 2 4-person teams
Supervision: Referee
Playing time: 4 quarters, 10 minutes each (or set to suit age, skill and fitness level of participants)
Equipment: 1 basketball, moveable funnel hoop which has return slots, no backboard (available from J. E. Burke Co.)

Directions: Basic basketball rules, with following exceptions. No centers, all 4 players are both forwards and guards. Both teams shoot at same basket, located in middle of round court. (Outer boundaries can be square.)

No jump balls. Held balls taken out of bounds at nearest point by alternating teams throughout contest. (Flip coin to see which team gets first one.)

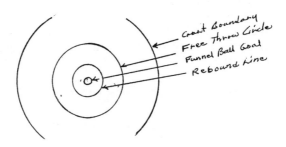

(This rule may be changed to "Held balls are played at point on court of held ball, alternating team possessions.")

Ball is put into play to start game and each quarter by referee tossing ball into Funnel Hoop from rebound line. Ball must go beyond rebound line before any player can touch it on missed shots. One free throw awarded team opposite player called for this foul, with fouling player's guard taking the free throw.

Free throws taken from anywhere outside the free throw circle.

After each basket, ball goes to team scored on outside the boundary line, but referee does not have to touch the ball.

Players cannot touch the Funnel hoop standard. One shot foul awarded.

21. 4-Corner Basketball

Adds variety to regular basketball play. Puts more people on each court when there are too many people for available courts. Teaches rapid ball movement (since ball handlers may have three guards).

Age level: Any age
Organizational level: Medium
Number of players: 4 teams of 4–6 players
Supervision: Referee, scorekeeper
Playing time: 4 quarters, 10 minutes each
Space needed: Square court, field or park area 40′ × 40′ or larger. The more skilled and larger the players, the larger the field should be.

Equipment: 1 basketball, 4 moveable basketball standards (Commercial available, or may be fashioned by cementing posts inside discarded auto tires and mounting boxes atop the posts as goal hoops. Bore a hole in the bottom of each box and have broom handles or other sticks at each goal to poke the ball out of the boxes, if they stay in.)

Directions: Basic basketball rules, except have four goal standards, one at each corner.

Start game with four centers standing at edges of center circle. Referee bounces ball on floor so it bounces high enough that centers have to jump to bat it to teammates.

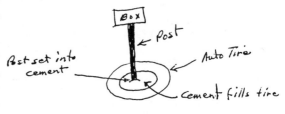

Each of four teams pass or dribble ball and attempt to shoot at their basket. No body contact allowed, guards must remain one foot from person with ball. Fouls are automatic points for team fouled, one point each, without any free throws taken.

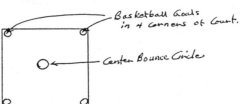

Variations: *4-Corner Beanbag Basketball*— Small children or handicapped persons may use beanbag instead of ball, with box-goals set on chairs or even on ground in four corners of field. Field may be smaller, too. (Then, as skills develop, the beanbag may be substituted with a ball.) *Any-goal Basketball*—Special basketball standard, with four hoops attached (see picture), is set at the connecting junction

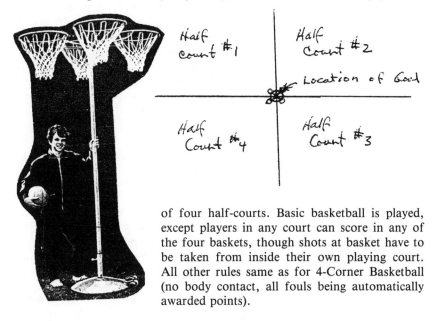

Half Count #1

Half Count #2

Location of Goal

Half Count #4

Half Count #3

of four half-courts. Basic basketball is played, except players in any court can score in any of the four baskets, though shots at basket have to be taken from inside their own playing court. All other rules same as for 4-Corner Basketball (no body contact, all fouls being automatically awarded points).

22. Korfbal

An outside basketball game that eliminates all contact.
Game stresses passing skills and teamwork.
All players get a chance to play all positions.

Age level: 8 and up
Organizational level: High
Number of players: 2 teams, 12 each team
Supervision: Referee-scorekeeper
Playing time: 2 45-minute halves, with 10 minute rest period between

Space needed: Basketball-size court (131' × 295') inside or outside
Equipment: 2 goal posts (wooden 4-by-4s) 10' tall (2' longer if they are to be driven into the ground), 2 hoops (without backboards), basketball

Directions: Court is divided into three sections. Four players from each team play in each section. Players change areas of play after every two goals. Goals are located inside the court, so shots can be taken from all around.

Center jump starts play to start the game, at the halftime, and after every goal.

Fouls include touching the ball with leg or foot, hitting the ball with the fist, holding the ball while in a fallen position, walking with the ball (pivoting is approved), dribbling the ball in any way or passing the ball to self, freezing the ball or delay of game, taking the ball from someone's hands, hindering an opponent in running, passing or shooting (though a player may maintain position if he or she doesn't move when the opponent approaches). Players may block the ball, but not the person.

Other fouls include playing outside the assigned section of the court, hindering someone already being guarded (two-on-one), and throwing the ball over the middle-section of the court. The ball must always touch either a player or the court before going from one end to another.

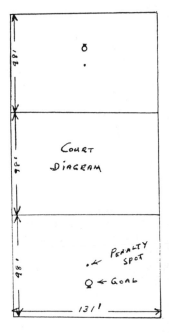

No shot at goal may be attempted unless an opponent is within an arm's length of the shooter and facing him or her, and either between the shooter and the goal or on the far side of the goalpost. The goal or post cannot be touched.

Free throws are taken for fouls, from the penalty spot fronting each goal. No player can do anything to distract a free throw shooter, and all must stand 11½ feet away.

Variations: *Micro-Korfbal*— Played inside a hall, the dimensions can be reduced to 132′ × 66′ or any larger size where the length to width ratio is 2 to 1. The center section is eliminated, leaving only two equal halves. Goalposts are positioned 1/6 court length in from each end. Teams will consist of 8 players. Match length is shortened to 2 30-minute halves, with 10 minutes between.

Other rules remain the same, except that a ball hitting the roof or other built-in obstruction is the same as a ball going out of bounds.

Game source: Invented in Holland in 1902 as a children's schoolyard game.

23. Hoop Shoot Tournament

A basketball skills field day test

Age level: By groups, aged 8–9, 10–11, 12–13, 14–15, 16–17, 18 and over. Events can be modified as wished for handicapped.
Organizational level: High
Number of players: Any number, taken in sequence
Supervision: Judge, recorder-timer, scorekeeper for each group, each event

Playing time: Varies for each event
Space needed: Basketball court or courts, with enough officials to run several groups simultaneously at different baskets
Equipment: Basketball for each court, whistle and stopwatch for judge and timer, clipboards, pencil and paper for recorder, tape to mark floor for various competitions

Directions: See individual events. (A subsequent hoop shoot tournament can be held to find out the improvement of skills for contestants. Subtract first score from second over-all score and put results on a curve to establish improvement.)

Event #1: Bounce & Shoot— Each contestant shoots as many baskets as he can within a one minute time limit. He may shoot from anywhere, but the ball must bounce once on the floor between each shot. The winner is the one scoring the most baskets. Enter the total on the score sheet.

Event #2: Speed Shooting— A half-circle is drawn on the court under the basket, using a 3-foot radius, from a spot directly under the basket.

Each contestant shoots as many baskets as he is able within a one minute time limit, with all shots being taken from outside the half-circle. The ball need not touch the floor during this contest. The winner is the one scoring the most baskets. Enter the total on the score sheet.

Event #3: Free Throw — Each contestant takes 20 consecutive free throws from the free-throw line, with someone else retrieving the ball and counting for him. Each basket counts one point. The winner is the one scoring the most points. Enter the total on the score sheet.

Event #4: Weaver Dribble — This is a dribbling proficiency contest to test use of each hand. Four chairs, or other obstacles, are placed equal distances apart on a line from basket to basket down the middle of the court. The contestant, dribbling against a stopwatch for time, starts at one end, on command. He dribbles around each obstacle, changing hands as he skirts each obstacle, using the left hand as he turns left and right hand as he turns right. As he reaches the end of the court, he will shoot left-handed (if he is right-handed) or right-handed (if he is left-handed) until he makes a basket. Then he makes a return run, weaving right and left around the obstacles again, switching hands, back to the starting point, where he shoots, with the opposite hand from the one he used previously, until he makes a basket there. His timed run stops as the ball goes through the hoop there.

The winner is the one with the least elapsed time for the run. The seconds are listed as points on the score sheet. This makes it easier in adding point totals, having all sub-totals in like terms.

Event #5: "Cripple" Stuffing — This is a dribbling lay-up contest. A "retriever" is needed under the basket. Each participant dribbles toward the basket from 20 feet out and makes a lay-up attempt. If he makes the basket on that try, he stays in line in the competition, but, if he misses, he drops out.

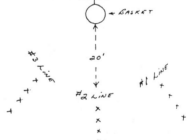

This is repeated from three positions: the right side of the basket, the center, and the left side. As a person misses, in each of the three section tests, he is given the number of points equal to the number of contestants still in line. Last person in the line to miss, thus, is the winner. Points are listed on the score sheet as minus points, and are subtracted from the total when finding the overall champion.

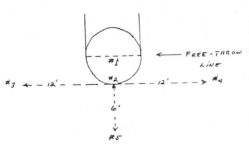

Event #6: Dead-eye Dick — This is a shooting contest for medium and long shots. Three shots are taken from each of five positions (see diagram). Scoring is as follows: each basket made at point #1 counts 2 points; each basket made at point #2 counts 3 points; each basket made at point #3 counts 4 points; each basket made at point #4 counts 4 points; each basket made at #5 counts 5 points. A perfect score would be 54 points.

Event #7: Hoop Golf—This is a shooting contest similar to miniature golf. The contestant shoots from each of nine spots laid out on the court (see diagram), shooting from each spot until he makes the basket. Note that spots 1, 2, 5, 8 and 9 each have two markings. The shortest distance in each case is for the use of elementary school ages, while the longer distances are used for all others.

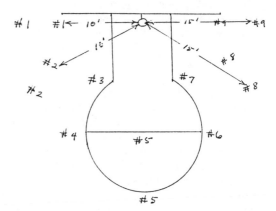

The total number of shots taken to complete a revolution of all nine positions is the competitor's score. Low score wins, as in golf. Points are listed on the score sheet as minus points and subtracted from the other totals in figuring up the overall winner.

BAT AND BALL GAMES

24. Sock-It (or Sack Practice)

Age level: Any age
Organizational level: Low
Number of players: One
Supervision: None
Playing time: Free play
Space needed: Small open area under a tree limb

Equipment: Rope (6–10 feet), bat (plastic, wood or metal baseball or softball bat, or even a cut-off broomstick), ball (baseball, softball, tennis ball or almost any other type ball), sack (burlap or plastic garbage sack)

Directions: Put ball inside bag. Tie bag's open end shut with one end of rope. Tie other end of rope to tree limb so bag hangs about chest high. Practice batting stance and swing without having to chase the ball. Good exercise for older players. For best exercise, switch batting from left- to right-handed periodically.

Variation: A plastic Whiffleball may be used without a bag, by tying the rope through two of the holes in the ball.

25. Zippie

Free play, exercise, practice batting skills and strengthening wrists

Age level: Any age
Organizational level: Low

Number of players: 1 or 2
Supervision: None

Playing time: Free play

Space needed: Open field or gym, at least 40' × 40'

Equipment: Spindle (section of round broomstick 3″ long and 1″ in diameter, with both ends whittled to points); bat (the rest of the broomstick, with the broom cut off)

Directions: Lay spindle on ground. Hit down on one of the pointed ends with bat so spindle flies into air. Try to keep it in air by successively hitting it.

If two people play, take turns at bat. Winner is batter who can keep spindle in air the longest (with the most successive hits).

Variations: *(1)* Lay spindle on ground, serve it up, then see how far batter can hit it. Winner is the one who hits it farthest in five turns at bat. Only the one longest hit out of the five is counted for each player. *(2)* A modified version of baseball may be played by laying out lines at distances of 5, 10, 15 and 20 yards from batter's "box" area. Each player takes five at-bats. A hit over the 5-yard mark is a single, over the 10-yard mark is a double, over the 15-yarder is a triple, and over the 20-yarder is a home run. Person with most runs driven in after five at-bats is winner. Ties are played off with another round of five at-bats, until a winner is determined. *(3)* Spindle Baseball — Even number of players on each of two teams. Each side bats, with each player batting in turn, as in basic baseball. Play 7 innings, extra innings to break ties. Use the field diagram below.

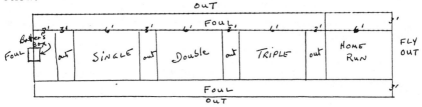

Each player bats until he or she either strikes out (misses the spindle three times) or hits a fair ball.

26. German Bat Ball

Age level: 9–12, 13–17

Number of players: 9 to a team, 2 teams; any number could play

Space needed: Outdoors, medium–large open space

Equipment: Volleyball or similar type playground ball, home plate and one base

Directions: Game is a combination of baseball, volleyball and dodgeball. Batter throws ball up and hits it into the field with hand or fist. It must go over a scratch line 10 feet from the batter in the air to be a fair hit. There are no strikeouts.

After a fair hit, the batter runs to the base, which should be 15–30 feet from the home plate (depending upon the age of the players) and back, pausing no more than 10 seconds on the base (which is "free," meaning he can't be tagged out while on it).

The fielders try to field the ball, then throw it to hit the batter before he can get back to home plate. The Batter-runner may duck, dodge and zig-zag to avoid being hit so long as he stays inside the playing field. Fielders are allowed to take only one step after retrieving the ball, and can only hold the ball five seconds before they must pass it or throw it at the batter-runner. They cannot dribble it, and two players cannot pass the ball back and forth between them more than twice.

Outs are scored by a caught fly ball or by hitting the runner before he gets home. There are three outs per team per inning, seven or nine innings to a game.

One point is scored per run. Batters bat in rotation.

Variation: The game may be played with one rule change, where the batter can remain on the base, if he chooses, rather than try to get back home. Then the next batter can try to knock both the runner and himself home. However, the opponents can then score two outs by putting both players out on the same play.

Game source: Modified from similar game at H. B. Ellison Junior High in Wenatchee, WA, in mid-1930s.

27. Beginner Baseball

Prepares younger or inexperienced children for softball and baseball. This is a good game for handicapped who might be discouraged using regular softball equipment.

Age level: 6–12, older handicapped
Organizational level: Medium
Number of players: 8–10 players per team. (Eliminate the shortstop if you use 8, add a short centerfielder if you use 10.)
Supervision: Plate and base umpires, scorekeeper

Playing time: 7 innings, more to play off ties
Space needed: Softball field, distances varied with age and skill groups involved
Equipment: Tennis racquet and tennis ball

Directions: Pitch to batter is underhand on one bounce. Four strikes are allowed before an out is called, no balls or walks.

Otherwise use basic softball rules.

Variations: Table tennis paddle and ball may be used in smaller inside area.

Game source: Modified from ideas presented in U.S. Navy Special Services games seminar by Tyrone Adams and John Trimarche.

28. Scoop Softball

A work-up softball variation using hand-crafted equipment

Age level: 8 and up
Organizational level: Medium
Number of players: 2 teams, 9 per team (10 if you use short-centerfielder)
Supervision: None informally, umpire-scorekeeper otherwise
Playing time: 5, 7 or 9 innings

Space needed: Softball field or equivalent area
Equipment: Cut off broom handle as bat, tennis ball (or Whiffleball), jug cestas (scoops) for all fielders (made from cutting off bottoms or side of plastic gallon milk or juice jugs)

Directions: Basic softball rules, except catching, fielding ground balls and throwing is all done with the cesta (scoop). (If pitchers have too hard a time pitching with the cesta, they can be exempted from this rule, but they would still have to use the cesta for fielding hit balls.)

No leading off base or base stealing allowed.

Fielders may remove the ball from the cesta to tag a runner between bases (to prevent injury to runner).

Variation: *Work-up Scoop Softball*—When not enough players are available to make up two teams, the game may be played with 9–10 fielders and 3 batters.

If a batter is put out, he goes to right field and all other fielders move up one position, from right field to center field to left field to third base, shortstop, second base, first base, pitcher, catcher, batter. A short-centerfielder and/or a second shortstop, between first and second bases, may also be added if there are enough players.

If a fly ball is caught, the player catching it and the batter exchange places, no one else moves up.

29. Hockey-Baseball

Introductory game for novices to field hockey

Age level: 8 and up
Organizational level: Medium
Number of players: 2 teams, 7 per team
Supervision: Referee-scorekeeper
Playing time: 4 quarters of 10–20 minutes

each, depending upon age, fitness and skill of players
Equipment: 4 base mats, field hockey sticks for batter and all fielders, field hockey ball (or rubber baseball, small Whiffleball or tennis ball)

Directions: Basic softball rules, except game is played all on the ground, like field hockey. Instruction should be given in safe use of hockey sticks.

Pitcher hits ball to batter on ground. Batter hits it and fielders play it with their sticks. If a ball touches a base before the runner gets to it, he is out.

Sticks cannot be used to tag, hit, trip, push or otherwise touch runners. A base is awarded all on-base runners at the time of such infraction.

Fielders cannot touch ball with hands. Penalty is awarding a base to the batter and any on-base runners.

Base runners cannot lead off or steal.

Game source: Modified from Lisa Beardsley, who innovated it at U.S. Navy Special Services Training School.

30. Fly-Up

*Uses baseball skills on an informal basis,
with varying numbers of players available*

Age level: 10 and up
Organizational level: Low
Number of players: Variable, according to size of playing area
Supervision: None

Playing time: Free play
Space needed: Playing field or gymnasium
Equipment: Bat (cut-off broomstick), ball (tennis or handball-racquetball type)

Directions: Batter hits ball into the air, then must drop bat to ground with its length facing the field. Batter plays against the field.

Fielders station themselves wherever they wish in the field, changing positions at will to play different batters. They try to catch the fly ball. The person catching it changes places with the batter.

Any non-fly ball hit can also earn an at-bat for a fielder by rolling the ball back so it hits the bat laid on the ground and bounces into the air off the bat. If the batter fails to catch the ball as it bounces up off the bat, the fielder and batter change places.

Variations: *(1)* Instead of changing batsmen every at-bat, the field can play to 500 points, with a caught fly counting 100, a one or two-bouncer 50, and a rolling grounder 25 points. First fielder to reach 500 points changes places with the batter. *(2)* Same game as above, except that fielders play 500-or-break. They must get exactly 500 points or they "break" and must start over. *(3)* All these games may be played with alternate equipment, such as standard softball or baseball equipment, plastic bat and ball, tennis racquet and ball, etc.

Game source: Old game called Stickball, Catch-a-fly-you're-up and other names in different parts of the country.

31. Ping-Pong™ Baseball

Active game for relatively large group
in a small area with inexpensive equipment.

Age level: 6 and up
Organizational level: Medium
Number of players: 2 teams, 9 per team
Supervision: None informally, umpire-scorekeeper otherwise
Playing time: 5, 7 or 9 innings

Space needed: About 30' × 30', indoors or outdoors (if no wind blowing)
Equipment: Table tennis paddle, table tennis ball (get extras, since they break) or a small Whiffleball or yarn ball, 4 base mats

Directions: Basic softball rules.

Variation: *Ping-Pong*™ Baseball Work-up—If not enough players are available for two teams, the game can be played with 9 fielders (plus a second shortstop between first and second bases and or a short-centerfielder) and 3 batters.

When a batter is put out, he goes to right field position and all other fielders move up one position: right field to center field to left field to short-centerfield to third base to shortstop, second base, first base, pitcher, catcher and batter.

If any fielder catches a fly ball, fair or foul, he exchanges places with the batter, and no one moves up.

32. Katie Ball (or Crosse Baseball)

Teaches novices the use of lacrosse sticks.
Interesting diversion for lacrosse practices for better players.

Age level: 8 and up
Organizational level: Medium
Number of players: 2 teams, 9-11 per team
Supervision: Umpire-scorekeeper
Playing time: 5, 7 or 9 innings

Space needed: Softball field
Equipment: Lacrosse, rubber baseball or tennis ball, racketball bat or tennis racket, lacrosse sticks for all fielders except pitcher and catcher

Directions: Basic softball rules, except lacrosse sticks must be used to catch, field and throw ball. Pitcher and catcher do not field hit balls. If they do, it is an automatic base hit. Pitcher must pitch underhand, slow-pitch style.

No tagging of runners with sticks in any way, including blocking, tripping or pushing. Runners may not lead off bases or steal bases.

Game source: Modified from Katie O'Neill, who innovated it at U.S. Navy Special Services Training School.

33. Three-Player Baseball

Change of pace from regular baseball, useful in smaller
areas and with fewer players. May also be played by handicapped
or others who might not be able to use regular bats.

Age level: All ages
Organizational level: Medium
Number of players: 2 teams, 3 per team
Supervision: Umpire-scorekeeper
Playing time: 7 innings, more to break ties

Space needed: Playground or gymnasium; base distances may be varied to fit needs
Equipment: Plastic ball, plastic bat, plastic scoop (available from Cosom Company) for each player in field (3)

Directions: Defensive team consists of 3rd baseman-left fielder, 2nd baseman-center fielder, and 1st baseman-right fielder. They catch and throw ball with scoops. An error is given any hand touch of ball, with a base advancement awarded each player on base. The only exception is taking ball out of scoop to tag a player.

The ball is placed on tip of the bat by the batter, pushed into the air and hit as it comes down. Batter is out on three swinging strikes or three fouled balls. There are no balls or walks.

No bunting, leading off from base, or base stealing allowed.

Variations: Scoops may be made from plastic gallon jugs, with tennis ball and a cut-off broomstick replacing plastic bat and ball.

34. Straight-Line Baseball

Baseball for smaller area, for beginners or recreational mixed group

Age level: 6–13
Organizational level: Medium
Number of players: 2 teams, 1–10 per team
Supervision: None, though players from each team, when batting, keep score
Playing time: 7 innings
Space needed: Rectangular field 60′ × 30′, indoors or outdoors
Equipment: Whiffleball and bat; lime (outside), chalk (inside) to mark field

Directions: Ball is thrown into air by batter, standing at home plate, and he tries to hit it before it falls to the ground. If he swings and misses, it is a strike. A foul hit is a strike. Three strikes is an out.

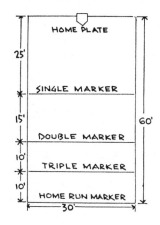

If hit ball lands beyond singles marker, it's a one-base hit; between the double and triple markers, a double; between the triple and home run markers, a triple; and past the home run marker, a home run. A caught fly ball is an out.

A single moves all base runners one base, a double, two bases, etc.

Game source: Modified from U.S. Navy recreation activities booklet (out of print).

35. In-Line Softball

Adds variety to the game. Teaches new skill
of using hand scoops, similar to jai alai cestas

Age level: 8–adult
Organizational level: Medium
Number of players: 2 teams, 7–10 per team
Supervision: Referee-scorekeeper
Playing time: Any number of pre-agreed innings or time limit with winner being team with most scores
Space needed: Any level area 100′ or more long, 40′ or more wide

Equipment: 4 base mats, plastic hand scoops (these can be made from gallon plastic milk jugs by cutting off bottoms or part of one side) for all fielders, Whiffleball bat and ball, field marker (commercial Saf-T-Bat, Fun Ball by Cosom Co.)

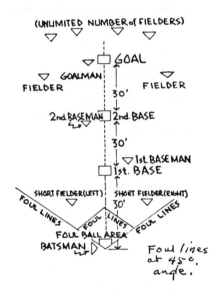

Directions: Player positions are first base, second base, third base (or goalie), short and long fielders. Each holds hand scoop to field, catch and throw ball with.

Batter throws ball into air and tries to hit it with bat before it falls to ground. He doesn't have to swing at the ball until he throws up one he likes, to a limit of three. Bunting is not allowed.

Outs are called: (1) when batter swings and misses ball, (2) when he fails to swing at three consecutive throws in the air, (3) when he hits two foul balls (whith are not counted as strikes) in same at-bat, (4) when fly ball is caught by fielding team, (5) when base runner is forced out before reaching base or tagged out while between bases. Two outs is side-out.

If a base runner overruns a base, he must continue on to the next one. Once past a base, the runner cannot return to it. No leading off or stealing bases. When a runner has stopped at a base, he can't advance until the next batter hits the ball. The only time a fielder can touch the ball with a hand is in tagging a runner (since tagging with the scoop could cause injury).

A run, or goal, is scored when a batter reaches third base (goal) safely. After scoring, the player returns, outside the playing area, to the batting team's area.

36. Tag Ball

Teaches teamwork passing. Good for "letting off steam" too,
since it allows players to hit runners with ball.

Age level: 8 and up
Organizational level: Low
Number of players: 2 teams, 10–15 per side
Supervision: None in informal play, with referee-scorekeeper otherwise

Playing time: 5, 7 or 9 innings
Space needed: Level area, indoors or out, 40–50' × 100'
Equipment: Volleyball, 2 base mats

Directions: Team consists of pitcher, catcher and fielders.

Pitcher tosses ball to batter, who hits it with fist or both hands clenched together.

Three foul hits (going behind the end line) is an out. Caught fly-ball is an out. Hitting a player between bases with the ball is an out. But, before the ball may be thrown at the runner, it must be passed 5 times among the fielding team (without two consecutive passes between the same two players). Fielding players cannot walk or run with the ball in their possession.

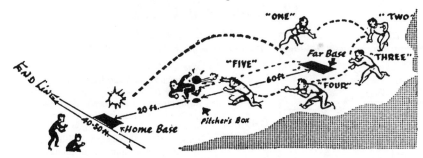

Batter, upon hitting ball fair, must run around the far base and return to home base (not running outside the field boundaries) to score a run.

Three outs is side-out.

Game source: Modified from Swat Ball in U.S. Navy recreational games booklet (out of print).

37. Can Cricket

Combines the simplicity of cricket with skills of baseball.
Teaches basics so the game of cricket can be understood.

Age level: All ages
Organizational level: Medium
Number of players: Two batters, pitcher, any number of basemen-fielders
Supervision: None

Playing time: Until all players have one turn batting
Space needed: 80' × 40', field or gym
Equipment: 2 tin cans (same size), tennis ball, bat, sawed off broom handle or table tennis paddle

Directions: Place two cans about 60 feet apart. Pitcher and batters stand by opposite cans. Catcher stands behind batter about 10 feet to return pitched balls or to catch fly balls in that area. Fielders are scattered beyond the pitcher.

Pitcher bowls ball underhanded toward batter, trying to knock over the can beside him. Batter tries to hit the ball to keep it from knocking the can over.

If the can is knocked over by the pitcher, the batter is out. If the batter hits the ball, he runs to the other can or tries for a home run, going to the other can and returning to the home can on the same hit. Batters continue until one is put out. Outs are made by catcher, pitcher or a fielder catching a fly ball, or by a thrown ball that knocks over a can before a runner reaches it.

All hits are fair and must be run out. When a batter or runner is put out, fielders move up — catcher becomes a batter, pitcher becomes catcher, player with longest time in field becomes pitcher.

Variations: *(1)* Same game may be played, but with batters staying up until they make three outs. Then everyone moves up two places and the put-out batters go into the field.

(2) Same game, except batters stay up until a player in the field scores 500 points. Points are scored: 100 for catching a fly ball, 50 for making a base put-out. Fielder making 500 points replaces the batter that gives him his last-needed points.

38. Two-Pin Cricket

Teaches basics of English game of Cricket,
using modified "pick-up" equipment for informal play

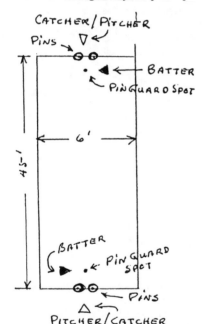

Age level: 8 and up
Organizational level: Medium
Number of players: 2 teams, 2 per team
Supervision: None (once players learn rules), referee-scorekeeper otherwise, who sit at midcourt, outside play area
Playing time: Pre-determined number of points (in even number of innings), or time limit (60 minutes minimum)
Space needed: Level rectangular area 6′×45′
Equipment: 4 bowling pins (Bow-lite Pins, Saf-T-Bat, Fun Ball commercially available by Cosom Co. or plastic, rubber, half-gallon milk cartons, or foot-long sections of 4′×4′ board can be used), Whiffle-ball and bat, 2 plastic hand scoops (or make scoops by cutting bottoms or one side off gallon plastic milk jugs

Directions: Players include 2 pitcher/catchers.

Flip coin to decide which team starts batting.

Pitcher throws ball, using hand scoop, toward opposite end of playing court, trying to knock over the two pins there. Catcher fields the pitch. Batter stands just in front, and to side of pins, and tries to hit ball and keep it from knocking over pins.

If ball knocks over one pin, it is one out; two pins, two outs, whether batter swings or not. If batter swings and misses pitch *and* ball knocks over both pins, it is 3 outs.

If pitcher or catcher catches fly ball, it is an out. If either runner is tagged with ball while running between bases, it is an out.

Three outs is side-out.

If batter hits ball, he runs to opposite batter's box. His teammate-batter there, at the same time, runs to the batter's box opposite him. If a hit is long enough, they may exchange again and again, scoring one run each time both of them successfully reach their opposite bases.

Same batter remains at bat so long as his team keeps scoring. If he ends his run at the opposite end of the court from where he first batted, the catcher there becomes the pitcher.

After an out, the second batter will be pitched to, at the base he ended up at, by the pitcher/catcher at the end opposite him.

Runners cannot run outside the court boundaries.

39. Cricketball

For variety in recreation program.
Also teaches rudiments of English game of Cricket.

Age level: 8 and up
Organizational level: Medium
Number of players: 2 teams, 5–12 per team
Supervision: None in informal play (once players have learned rules), but umpire-scorekeeper otherwise
Playing time: 3–5 innings, or pre-determined time limit (with equal number of innings for both sides since innings, especially as players get better, are apt to last longer than in baseball)
Space needed: Level area 90' × 40–50'
Equipment: Sacket or semi-flattened softball bat and softball (12–16"). Smaller field, with Whiffleball and bat or racketball paddle and tennis ball, may be used for smaller or handicapped players.

Directions: Player positions are catcher, pitcher, far baseman, fielders.

Pitcher's box and far base are 3' × 6' mats or marked areas.

Batter remains at bat until he hits the ball. Every hit is fair ball, even foul tips. Batter then runs to the far base, and chooses either to remain there or try to run back to home base to score a run.

Several runners may be on the far base at the same time, provided one player remains to bat. Any or all of them may run for home base on any hit. But, once a runner leaves the far base, he cannot return to it, except when a fly ball is caught. Runners cannot advance on caught fly balls.

A batter is out when (1) a fly ball is caught, (2) the ball is thrown to the far baseman before the runner reaches the base, (3) he is tagged or hit by underhand-thrown ball while he is off base, running for home base.

Side-out is three outs.

Game source: Modified from Long Ball in U.S. Navy recreational games booklet (out of print).

40. American Cricket

Teaches basics of the English game of Cricket

Age level: 8 and up
Organizational level: Medium
Number of players: 12–20, divided into
  2-person teams
Supervision: None in informal play, referee-scorekeeper otherwise
Playing time: 2–5 innings (since innings are apt to last much longer than in base-ball), or to time limit available (after an even number of innings)
Space needed: 30' × 60'
Equipment: 2 cricket bats with wrist strings, 5" circumference ball, 2 30" tall T-Ball type posts to hold tethered Whiffleball (commercial set — U.S. Games Company), scorecards, pencil

Directions: The game has two batter's plates, set opposite each other. Batter teammates stand to one side and in front of each, with bats in hand.

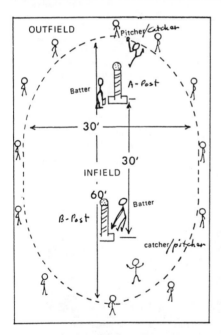

To start game, one pitcher (opponents are both pitchers and catchers alternately) throws the ball at the batter's post at the opposite end of the field, trying to knock the small ball off the stand. He can take a run to make his delivery, so long as he doesn't go past the batter's line beside the batter's stand at his end of the field. He may throw underhand, sidearm or overhand, and the ball can be thrown in the air or bounced off the ground.

If the batter hits the ball, he runs to the other batter's line, and the second batter there, runs to his batter's line. If they do this safely, it is a run. If the ball is hit far enough, they may run again and again, scoring another run each successful transfer of the both of them. A hit into the out-of-bounds area (marked out before the game) is an automatic two runs. Batters may also run on a bad pitch that is not struck at, if they think they can make a run. They may continue scoring runs if a fielder makes a bad throw.

If the batter does not swing at the ball, and it misses the post, it is caught, or recovered, by the catcher, who then becomes the pitcher and pitches the ball at the opposite side batter's post.

If a batter accidentally knocks the ball off a stand at any time, it is an out. If the wind blows the ball off, it is not an out. It is merely replaced before the next pitch.

If a fielder catches a fly ball, it is an out. If a runner is tagged while running, out of either batter's box, it is an out. If a pitched ball knocks the tethered ball off the stand (at the current batter's end of the field), either while he is batting or while running after a hit, and before he returns, it is an out.

After two outs, the team joins the other fielders in the circle, and the #2 team of two players become the pitcher-catchers, while the former pitcher-catchers become the batters. This rotation continues until all the two-person teams have batted. Winning team is the one with the most runs. Ties can be batted off be-tween tied teams.

Game source: Modified from British cricket.

41. Toppleball

*Active game, teaching teamwork for large number of players in
small area, almost anywhere from playground to park to gym to shallow pool*

Age level: 8 and up
Organizational level: Low
Number of players: 15–25
Supervision: None informally, referee-score-keeper otherwise
Playing time: One or two rounds of batting, roughly 30–60 minutes
Space needed: 60′ × 60′, indoors or outside; smaller area required for small players or handicapped

Equipment: Commercial Toppleball set (available from U.S. Games Company): flat-sided cricket-type bat, 30″ high ball stand with tethered Toppleball, playground ball (8½″ circumference); or make-do equipment: shop-crafted paddle-bat, T-Ball stand with line attached to small Whiffleball, playground ball

Directions: Mark 15′ radius ring, with out-of-bounds area beyond it. Players draw numbers from cap to determine batting order. Number 1 goes to batter's circle.

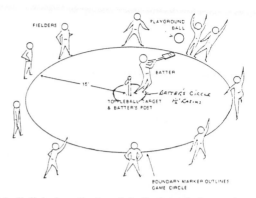

Number 2 pitches ball to batter, who tries to protect the toppleball by hitting the pitched ball. If it is a bad pitch, however, he doesn't have to strike. If a passed or struck-at ball dislodges the toppleball, though, batter is out.

If batter hits ball, he runs to any point of the circle, touches it with his bat, and runs back to the batter's circle. This scores a run. If hit far enough, he can make the run two or three times, scoring another run each time. He bats as long as he keeps scoring safely.

Fielders try to catch or field the hit ball, and may pass it around, so one of them may try to throw it—from outside the circle—and knock the toppleball off its stand before the runner gets back to the batter's circle, putting him out. Batter-runner may use his body and bat to block thrown balls during his run. But, if he knocks the toppleball off with his bat (even while batting) or with a throw he has blocked while running, he is out. (If he knocks the toppleball off with his body while batting, however, it is not an out. It is merely replaced before the next pitch.)

Batter with most runs after everyone has batted is the winner. Ties can be batted-off, until an ultimate winner is decided.

Variations: *Half-circle Toppleball*—Same game, except a semi-circle is formed around batter, who stands with his back against a wall. Batter, thus, must protect toppleball from rebounds from the wall also.

Special bats and playball is made for handicapped by U.S. Games Company.

Game source: Modified from British cricket.

42. Half Ball

Baseball type game for variety. Teaches eye contact.

Age level: 8 and up
Organizational level: Medium
Number of players: 2 teams, 7 per team

Supervision: None informally, umpire-score-keeper otherwise
Playing time: 5, 7 or 9 innings

Space needed: Half a softball diamond, or equivalent area

Equipment: Stickball bat (broomstick cut off), tennis or other rubber ball cut in half, three base mats

Directions: Basic softball rules, except have two instead of three bases and an odd shaped ball, which adds to the hilarity of the game because it does such erratic things when thrown.

Ball is controlled best by "skidding it," sort of like an inverted Frisbee, sidearm.

Pitcher can throw underhand, sidearm or overhand, depending upon age, skill of players.

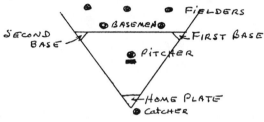

Variation: *Half-Ball Work-up*—Game can be played with 3 batters and from 5 to 8 fielders, work-up style, where a batter, when put out, goes to right field and all other players move up one position, from right field to center field, left field, third base, shortstop, first base, pitcher, catcher to batter.

Any fielder catching fly ball, fair or foul, trades places with batter, and no one moves up.

Game source: Modified from Charlestown, MA Recreation Department.

43. Indian Ball

Modified baseball for smaller area of play, and when fewer, or extra, players are on hand. Or for variety or "change-of-pace," when only nine players available, so play "work-up."

Age level: All

Organizational level: Medium

Number of players: 6–15 per team

Supervision: None

Playing time: 7 innings

Space needed: Playing area 55′ long, with outfield extending indefinitely. Field marked off at 45 degree angle at plate. All sides of triangle as near equal length as possible.

Equipment; Softball (12–16″ size) and bat (or can be played with tennis ball and wooden racketball paddle)

Directions: Each team composed of catcher, 2 infielders, 3 or more outfielders. Pitcher is member of batting team.

Pitcher stands anywhere in "neutral zone." No bases, so no base running. Scores are "force-ins," with every hit being regarded as a single, except a home run. Thus, it takes four singles to force in a run; a home run will score one run plus as many more as players were on bases at time.

Hits are made when (1) the ball hits the ground in the outfield, (2) the ball is dropped, or comes to rest, in the infield, (3) a fly is dropped in the neutral zone, (4) a home run is made by a fly ball being hit over the head of the last out-fielder.

Three outs retire the side.

Variations: *Indian Kickball*—Use soccer or playground ball and kick it instead of batting it. *Indian Whiffleball*—With smaller field available, use Whiffleball and bat. *Indian T-Ball*—For very young players, use smaller field and T-Ball equipment.

Game source: Modified from U.S. Navy recreation activities booklet (out of print).

44. Corkball

Baseball type game for four people, in relatively small area

Age level: 6 and up
Organizational level: Low
Number of players: 2 teams, 2 each
Supervision: None, though referee-score-keeper used for tournaments
Space needed: 100′×100′ (see drawings), though it can be played informally in any rectangular area as well, like a closed off street area
Equipment: Corkball (quart vacuum cork covered with single layer of tape), bat (broomstick cut to 36″ length), blackboard and chalk, or paper, pencil

Directions: Batter must remain inside batter's box while hitting. No bunting. Batters don't actually run the bases; scores are made by keeping track of hitters on bases and scores on blackboard or paper pad.

Pitcher must have both feet on rubber while pitching. Cork must be pitched with legal underhand softball motion (though overhand motion may be used when better players are competing).

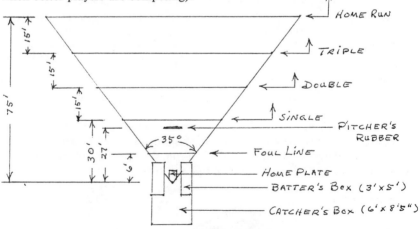

Batter is out if he: (1) swings and misses pitch that is caught be catcher, (2) hits fair or foul fly ball caught by catcher or pitcher, (3) hits ball while outside batter's box, (4) hits foul ball that doesn't go past foul line, (5) takes two swinging strikes without catcher catching cork. Side-out is three outs.

Batter gets base on 5 pitched balls.

Base hits are made by hitting cork in fair territory past the baseline marks. All runners advance one base if walk or single is hit (between single and double marks, two bases for double, and so on.

Tie score is played off until one team has scored more runs than the other in an equal number of innings.

Variations: Field can be enlarged by widening the angle between the sideline markers. Then more players can be used, adding short and long fielders, with fly outs being tallied. This has the advantage of the pitcher not having to chase the cork continually into the outfield. Recommended: no more than three fielders.

Game source: Modified from Chuck Rogers innovation at Jacksonville, FL Recreation Department, July 1937.

45. Sack-it

An indoors, small area baseball type game,
not requiring gloves, catcher's equipment, et al.

Age level: 8 and up
Organizational level: Medium
Number of players: Two teams: 5–9 players per team
Supervision: None in informal play; referee-scorekeeper otherwise
Playing time: 5, 7, or 9 innings
Space needed: Softball-sized field, indoors or out, though can be played on smaller area, like gym or multipurpose room, in paved parking lot, in park or closed off street

Equipment: Commercial Sacket (semi-flat) bat and Sacket ball, Sacket framed net, three bases (commercial available from U.S. Games Co.) or make-do equipment may be used: Whiffleball bat and ball, old softball bat shaved down semi-flat, with mushball (soft softball), or tennis raquet and tennis ball. Net can be made by tacking any type netting behind a wooden frame of approximately the same size as the Sacket net. Bases can be mats.

Directions: Basic softball rules, except Sacket net eliminates need for umpire at plate, since any pitch into the net is an automatic strike.

Two strikes is an out; three balls is a walk.

Any ball hit into the field is played. There is no foul ball.

Runner attempting to score at home can be put out by a thrown ball into the Sacket net before he reaches home. He can't return to third base once he has run past it.

Game source: Modification of game of British cricket by adding baseball elements.

46. Bellevue Whiffleball

Active softball type game in smaller area, using cheaper equipment. Good
for younger or handicapped players who can't handle regular softball equipment.

Age level: 6 up
Organizational level: Medium
Number of players: 2 teams: 7 players each
Supervision: Umpire-scorekeeper
Playing time: Any number innings fitting time available, and age, fitness and skill of players. Seven is best, because of special rule

Space needed: Gym or multi-purpose room, or level outside area layed out like softball field, but shortened up to fit equipment and age/skills of players
Equipment: Whiffleball and bat, four base mats 2′ × 3′ in size, field marker (lime, chalk, etc.)

Directions: Basic slow-pitch softball rules, except players are required to rotate field positions every inning, so everyone plays every position during the game. Positions are catcher, pitcher, first base, second base, shortstop, third base, rover. No gloves allowed.

Balls hit or thrown by fielders against walls or off ceiling are considered in play.

No sliding into bases. No blocking baseline unless ball is already in hand.

Pitched ball, thrown higher than the batter's head and landing on the home base mat will be called an automatic strike. Any ball swung at and missed will be called a strike. Ball missing mat and not swung at is a ball. Two strikes is an out; three balls is a walk. Three foul hits in same at-bat is an out.

Pitching distance is 30′ from home plate. (But can be lessened if needed for young, inept or handicapped players.)

Game source: Modified from Bellevue, NE Recreation Department, 1979.

BOWLING TYPE GAMES

47. Coin Lag (or Shove Ha'Penny)

Simple tabletop game for informal play almost anywhere by anyone

Age level: 8 and up
Organizational level: Low
Number of players: 1–10
Supervision: None informally, referee-score-keeper otherwise

Playing time: Short game, so many can be played in half-hour
Space needed: Hard table top
Equipment: Table, chalk to draw lag line, 4 large buttons per player (all same, or use quarter coins)

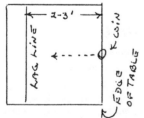

Directions: Lag for player sequence, closest to line, first, and so on.

Place button/coin half on edge of table, half off table. Push it with open palm of hand so it stops on or as near the lag line as possible.

All players push one button/coin around, then second, and so on. Any player may push his button/coin into another to knock it away or closer to the line.

When all buttons/coins have been lagged, winner is person on or closest to the lag line. Ties may be lagged off by those tied.

Variations: *Carom Shove*—Same game as previously mentioned, except button/coin must be caromed off a sideboard, or off a backboard.

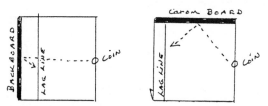

Game source: Modified from old Irish pub gambling game, Shove H'Penny.

48. Setting Your Cap (or Bottlecap Lagging)

Good inner-city game played with bottle caps

Age level: 6 and up
Organizational level: Low
Number of players: 2–5 per playing area
Supervision: None
Playing time: 5 minutes per game

Space needed: Three sections of sidewalk, or equivalent cement or wood surface area, about 9' length
Equipment: Supply of bottle caps for each player. Ruler for measuring.

Directions: Each player gathers own bottle caps. These can be polished and waxed, to make them slide smoother. Then they are filled with candle wax level to the opening.

Using three sections of sidewalk, make one line between sections the foul line, which players must remain behind when they shoot their caps, and shoot toward the second or third section line beyond that, as the scoring line, about 9' away.

Caps may be tossed, skidded with a sidearm motion, or shot like a marble.

Two ways of scoring: (1) Toss nearest the score line, on either side of it, wins or (2) any toss that goes beyond the score line is a foul (and it is considered beyond if more than half of it is beyond the line).

Winners win opponent's shooters. If a player is down to his last prepared shooter, he may wager 6 unfilled bottlecaps (in good shape) in its place.

Game source: Adapted from an old Brooklyn, NY street game.

49. Button Bowling

Informal game in which novice bowlers
can be taught how to score that game

Age level: 8 and up
Organizational level: Low
Number of players: 6 to a court is ideal
(2–6, playing individually or as teams)
Supervision: None; players re-set pins for
each other

Playing time: 10 frames per game, three games
Space needed: 2' × 3' space on table, floor or
cement area
Equipment: 9 cardboard center rolls from
toilet tissue rolls, 2–4 large flat buttons,
or coins (nickles or quarters)

Directions: Make design of spots for placement of tenpins on a paper sheet, so it may be taped to the playing court. It will make sure the pins are always reset the same way.

Buttons are placed half on, half off the end of the table, sidewalk edge, or on a strip of cardboard placed on the floor (to raise the buttons high enough to push). Player may also snap buttons with the fingernail, if preferred, especially if playing on floor where there is no raised area to push buttons from.

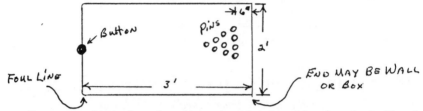

Buttons are hit or shoved or snapped, with palm of hand, or heel of hand, or finger, toward the pins. If all 10 are knocked over on first button, it is a strike; all with 2 buttons, it is a spare. Scoring is like bowling. (Booklets showing how to score are available at any local bowling lane.)

Two buttons per frame, for each bowler; 10 frames to a game; 3 games to a match. Winner is high total score.

Variation: *Tiddley-Bowling* — Bowling idea, but using tiddley-winks (or buttons that can be snapped like winks) to knock over pins. Player gets two "snaps" per frame, snapping the first time from the foul line, the second time from wherever it lands the first tme, even if it has knocked over pins. If the first snap knocks all the pins over, the second snap is taken from the foul line again.

50. Spaceman's Shooting Gallery

Craft project which can then be used in game situation

Age level: 8 and up
Organizational level: Low
Number of players: Any number space is available for
Supervision: Scrap-art instructor for making "monsters"
Playing time: Informal individual or group project and game. Craft work can be scheduled over several periods. Game at end keeps interest high.
Space needed: Tables for craft work. Any $3' \times 10'$ ground or rug covered area for game. If played on floor or cement, put blanket down as base to control marbles.
Equipment: Supply of small plastic bottles (washed clean), small art paint brushes, glue, several blunt scissors, bottles of colored paints, and box of colored cloth scraps, cardboard, colored poster paper, feathers, buttons, etc., for use in making "monsters"

Directions: Paste-and-paint plastic bottles as imaginative monsters from space. When completed, line them up as in a carnival shooting gallery. Group may also make a paste-and-paint background setting inside a large box set on its side, to set the monsters up in, or hang them from.

Competitors get as many marbles (or rubber bands) to shoot at monsters as there are monsters. They take turns shooting all their marbles (or rubber bands). Person who hits (or knocks over, for older players) the most monsters is winner. Shootoffs can be held for ties.

Variation: *Shootout*—Same game idea, except all shooters (limited to 6 at a time) shoot at the monsters at the same time. Each monster *knocked over* counts a point for the hitter. Those knocked over cannot be hit again. Game is over either when players are out of ammunition or all monsters have been knocked over. Winner is player with most scores.

51. Migs Bowling

Different marble games

Age level: 8 and up
Organizational level: Medium
Number of players: 2–8 in rotation, or by teams
Supervision: None

Playing time: 30–45 minutes
Space needed: 10′×10′ area with smooth floor
Equipment: 10 old penlight (AA) batteries, 2 marbles, bowling scoresheets and pencil

Directions: Make out a tenpin bowling formation design on a sheet of paper to tape to the floor, so batteries will be set in the same spots for each player.

Basic bowling rules and scoring. Players reset pins and keep scores for each other. Marbles may be shot, as in playing marbles, or rolled.

Variations: *Migs Croquet*—Set batteries up where croquet arches and stakes usually go, in a 20′×20′ hard-surfaced area. Play croquet rules, except

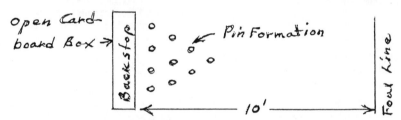

players shoot marbles instead of using mallets. *Sniper*—Set batteries up at various spots within a selected area, size depending on age and skills of players. Some may be placed behind rocks or other items. Players become "snipers," shooting their marbles through the course, one at a time, until they have hit all the batteries. Players can shoot any battery in any order. Person with least number of shots is winner.

52. Bridge Bowling

Age level: Any age, but more fun for elementary ages
Number of players: As many as have equipment for, but 6 at a time is best

Space needed: Indoors, large floor area
Equipment: Hula hoop, cardboard (for bridge), tape and 6 table tennis balls for each participant

Directions: Prepare the playing area (see diagram on the next page).

On signal, each player starts rolling his 6 balls, trying to get them all into the hoop over the bridge. Any that miss must be retrieved, taken back to the foul line and rolled again from there. Winner is first person to get them all inside the hoop. Ties can be played off.

Variation: *Blow Bowling*—Balls, instead of being rolled by hand, must be

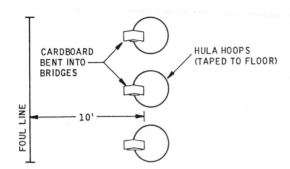

blown by mouth into the rings over the bridge. Players may follow the balls over the foul lines, on hands and knees, in guiding and blowing the balls, but cannot touch the balls.

Each person has to return back across the foul line to start each new ball.

Game source: Modified from George Hertzog, who innovated it at U.S. Navy Special Services Training School, 1972.

53. Hole Bowling

Simple game almost any child can play nearly anywhere outdoors

Age level: 6 and up
Organizational level: Low
Number of players: Any number, in rotation
Supervision: None
Playing time: Depends on number playing, about 5 minutes per person
Space needed: 5' × 23' area outside. Either

dig holes in ground or sink cans in ground so open ends are level with surface, in pattern of 18" circle around one central can (7 holes or cans altogether).
Equipment: 2 croquet balls (or rubber baseballs, Whiffleballs, tennis balls), 7 tin cans (30 oz. size or larger), old spoon to dig with

Directions: Bowlers roll two successive balls into can "holes." Middle can scores 3 points, others 1 point each. Each bowler gets three turns, in rotation. Winner is one with highest total score after three turns. (Or bowlers may keep going until one reaches 15 points. This may be varied by playing "15 points-or-break," where a bowler must score exactly 15 points to win. If he goes over that number, he has to start over.)

   Variation: Same game, except bowlers kick the balls into holes instead of rolling by hand. *Shuffle Hole-Bowling*—Shuffleboard sticks (or old pool cues) can be used to push (or shoot) "pucks" into holes. Pucks can be made from crushing used Dixie cups, or by using screw-on jar lids.

54. Kick Bowling (or Soccer-Bowling)

Simple game that can be played about anywhere by almost anyone

Age level: 8 and up
Organizational level: Low
Number of players: 1 on 1, or teams
Supervision: Scorekeeper who knows bowling scoring
Playing time: 10 frames for each bowler, opponents setting pins for each other
Space needed: 35' × 3-4' area, or shuffleboard court

Equipment: 10 bowling pins (plastic, quart milk cartons, or Pringle's potato chip canisters), 2 balls (softballs, large Whiffleballs, small playground balls), (commercial bowling sets of Bowlite plastic pins and rubberized ball available from Cosom Company), bowling scoresheets (sample, plus scoring instruction booklets available at any bowling lane) and pencil

Directions: Mark spots on poster or wrapping paper for tenpins formation, so it can be taped to bowling lane. This way the pins will be set the same each time. The larger the ball used, the farther apart the pins should be spaced.

Each bowler gets two balls per frame, for ten frames, for a game. Three games are a match. Bowlers set pins for each other. Smaller children or handicapped may be given three balls per frame.

Balls are kicked with feet instead of being thrown by hand.

55. Bag-It Bowling

Good inside game for rainy days with equipment easy to find

Age level: 8 and up
Organizational level: Low
Number of players: Any number, individuals or teams of 2–5 players
Supervision: Chasers (one team chases balls and realigns bags for other)

Playing time: 10 "lines" per game, as in bowling
Space needed: Clear area against a wall, 12′ × 6′ minimum
Equipment: 1 paper grocery bag and 2 tennis balls (or other small balls) for each team member, paper and pencil

Directions: Sacks placed with open ends facing wall, folded back 2–3 inches, 2–3 feet apart, and 2 feet from wall.

While one team serves as chasers, the other team bowls. Each player, in turn, rolls his two balls, trying to rebound them from the wall into his sack.

The first ball in a sack scores a spare (worth 5 points). A second ball in a

NAMES	1	2	3	4	5	6	7	8	9	10

SCORECARD

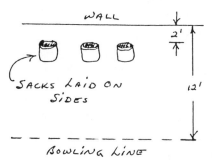

sack scores a strike (worth 10 more points). All team members' scores are summed each round for the score on that "line" on the scorecard. Winner is the team with the highest score after 10 lines.

If a rolled ball moves a sack, that sack must remain as moved until the end of the team's turn. Sacks are realigned only at the start of each team's turn or line.

56. Holes-in-the-Head

Good target game for picnics or campouts,
especially since it uses materials at hand

Age level: 6 and up
Organizational level: Low
Number of players: 1–6

Supervision: None
Playing time: About 30 minutes construction and play

Space needed: Tabletop, or floor/ground area 4′ × 6′

Equipment: Paper plate (stiff ones are best),

.3 small paper cups, 5 small pebbles per player, scissors, marking pen

FIG. 1

ROCK→

Directions: Cut part of the plate off (or fold it back) and 3 cup sized holes in the bottom (see fig. 1). Insert 3 cups into holes from front of the plate. Then prop the plate target up against a wall, table or rock, or hang it up. Mark amounts different holes are worth; top one, 3 points; bottom ones, 1 point each.

Players stand about 6 feet away and take turns tossing their pebbles at the plate, trying to hit the holes. Winner is highest scorer, or play may continue to a pre-set number of points, 15 or 25.

Variations: *3-Throw* — 3 players. Each claims one of the holes in the plate as his. Then, as players throw their pebbles, they try to hit only their own hole, since any thrown into the other holes count for the owners of those holes. (Each hole is worth 1 point per pebble.) *Bowlroll* — Prop the plate so the bent portion is flat on the table and the rest raised slightly. Players roll 5 marbles, in turns, up the inclined plate and into the holes.

57. Ping-Pong™ Pockets

Rainy day indoors game for especially "small fry"

Age level: 6 and up
Organizational level: Low
Number of players: 1–4
Supervision: None, after target constructed
Playing time: Open ended

Space needed: 5′ × 10′ area indoors, or outdoors away from wind
Equipment: 5 table tennis balls, 5′ square piece of cardboard, scissors, several colored marker pens

Directions: Cut our various sized holes, at different spots, in the cardboard. Paint 2 or 3 clown faces around the larger ones, using the holes for mouths, or smaller holes for ears or eyes.

Hang, or brace, the cardboard up so balls can be tossed through the holes. Each player, in rotation, stands 5–10 feet away (depending on age and skill of players) and tosses all five balls, trying to get as many points as possible. Each hole, depending on size, is marked with the number of points it is worth — 5 for smallest, 3 for medium-sized and 1 for largest.

58. Goalie (or Goal Bowling)

Good indoors rainy day game using materials easily gathered.
Teaches basic goalie skills used in many games.

Age level: 6 and up
Organizational level: Low
Number of players: 2 at a time

Supervision: None
Playing time: Free play
Space needed: 10′ × 15′ minimum, in or out

Equipment: Goal (made from large cardboard box), house broom, 6 tennis or Whiffle or Nerf balls

Directions: Decide order of play. Bowler moves to goalie position when finished bowling, then moves to end of the line of bowlers.

Bowler tries to roll ball into goal, while goalie tries to keep it out by using a broom from his position behind the box-goal. Next bowler in line serves as ball retriever.

Game may be played to 10 goals or be played to a time limit of 5 minutes.

Balls must be rolled underhand at the goal, from behind the bowling line. If the bowler goes over this line while bowling, a goal will be subtracted from his total.

GOAL BOX
(CUT CORNERWISE)

15'

Variations: *Subtraction goalie —* Same game except that goalie figures in the scoring more actively. The number of goalie "saves" is subtracted from the number of bowler "goals" for the bowler's total score.

59. Six-Hole Bowling (or Bowline)

Simple game requiring little equipment that can be played almost anywhere by nearly anyone, including handicapped persons. Teaches lag-bowling skill.

Age level: 8 and up
Organizational level: Low
Number of players: Any number, in rotation.
Supervision: None
Playing time: 10 minutes per game

Space needed: Any dirt area 6' × 20' or larger, where holes may be dug
Equipment: Ball (same type) for each player (Whiffle, playground, golf or croquet balls). Can use one ball for all if have a retriever.

Directions: Decide player rotation. First player throws ball, trying to put it into the nearest circle (#1). Whether he succeeds or not, he goes to end of line, while other players throw in turn.

On second time around, those who succeeded at hole #1, try for hole #2; those who didn't succeed, keep trying for hole #1.

Continue in this manner until a player puts his ball into hole #6. If players tie, in the same round, they each get three throws and the one with the most in the #6 hole wins.

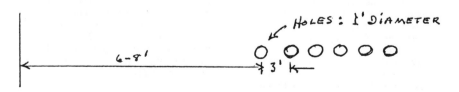

HOLES: 1' DIAMETER

6-8'

3'

Variation: *Indoors Bowline*—Same game can be played indoors by using small boxes and balls that bounce (into them), or by laying boxes on sides and rolling balls into them. If boxes are set on sides, they must be offset from a straight line so players have access to the openings.

60. Bowling Bounce

Aid for smaller children in learning simple addition. For others it's just a simple game that can be played almost anywhere.

Age level: 8 and up
Organizational level: Low
Number of players: Any number in rotation
Supervision: None
Playing time: About a half-hour per player

Space needed: Any area about 10′×10′, inside or outside
Equipment: 5 small boxes of various sizes, 3 rubber balls (small playground balls) that will fit into all the boxes

Directions: Number boxes with number of points awarded if bowler puts a ball in them, smaller boxes being worth more points.

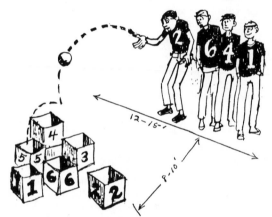

Bowlers take turns bouncing three successive balls into the numbered boxes. Then they repeat for ten turns.

Winner is one who has most total points in 10 turns.

Variations: *(1)* Small children can play in smaller area by using smaller boxes, like oats or cereal boxes cut down to half size, etc., and smaller rubber balls, like a jacks ball. *(2)* Either game may be made more difficult by playing from a seated position on the floor. *(3)* The boxes may be set up 2–3 feet from a wall. Then the wall may be used to carom the ball. They may also be set up in front of a corner, with double caroming used. Caroming the ball may be a requirement, before a score will count, or can be a bonus point or two.

61. Anty-In

Carnival type game

Age level: 6 and up
Organizational level: Low
Number of players: 1–6
Supervision: None
Playing time: Open ended
Space needed: 10′×10′ area, or carnival booth setup
Equipment: 20–25 paper cups set up in ran-

dom design on floor. Use pencil or marking pen to mark the number of points each cup is worth on its side—the harder to hit ones getting 5, with others rated 4-3-2-1. Cups may be set on blocks of wood, inside a bucket or other imaginative placings, 10–20 table tennis balls.

Directions: Players throw or bounce 5 balls each, from 5–6 feet away from the nearest cup, trying to get the highest score total to top other players.

Variations: *Midway Anty*—Same as above, but with more cups and all of them arranged in a semblance of order or design. Instead of point-numbers on the sides, they will be marked in random order, on the *bottom*, telling which type carnival prize has been won: 1 for best prizes (topshelf), 2 for lesser (2nd shelf), etc. *Team Anty*—Choose 2 teams. One team throws all the balls—each player throwing an equal number—then the other team throws. Each gets a 2–5 minute time limit (depending on ages and skills of players). Team with most points is winner. (Or team with most balls in cups, if preferred.) *Cup Baseball*—Set cups on a baseball diamond drawing, each labeled: single, double, triple, home run, walk, stolen base. Have these surrounded by: fly out, ground out, sacrifice bunt, strike out, double play, etc.

Batting team is throwers; fielding team shags and returns balls. Play 7 innings.

Play may be speeded up by calling every ball that doesn't land in a cup, a strike. Any 3 strikes during a team's at-bat in one inning is an out, even if runs are scored in between strikes.

62. Puck Pitch

*Simple hand shuffleboard game that can be played informally
almost anywhere by any number of players, with simple equipment.*

Age level: 8 and up
Organizational level: Low
Number of players: 2–10 ideally
Supervision: None
Playing time: Short term game that can be played over and over as long as wished

Space needed: 5′ × 22′ hard floor or paved area
Equipment: 4 pucks for each player when 2 or 3 play; 3 pucks each for 4–5 players. Pucks can be made by sawing wooden discs the size of screw-on jar lids, or jar lids can be used, or even cut-in-half old tennis balls

Directions: Play may be by individuals or teams. Player sequence or rotation may be determined by lag-offs. One puck is played by everyone before second one is.

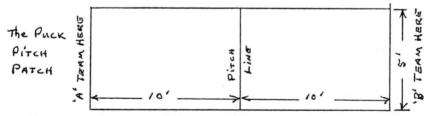

Individual players, or teammates, skid their pucks from opposite ends of the court toward the pitch line. They may knock opponent's pucks away and their team's pucks closer.

Winner is person or team with puck on or nearer pitch line than any other team's. Ties may be lagged off by tied teams.

Game source: Modified from Tom Ronsaino, who innovated it at U.S. Navy Special Services Training School, 1972.

63. Box Score
Carnival type game

Age level: 8 and up
Organizational level: Medium
Number of players: Open
Supervision: None
Playing time: 15 minutes

Egg Carton

4	2	1	1	2	4
6	4	2	2	4	6

Numbers in egg pouches.

Space needed: 3′ × 5′ area, or tabletop
Equipment: Egg carton, 5 soda pop bottle-caps per player (marked for identification), marker pen

Directions: Mark the egg cups with values as shown in figure 1, after removing the carton top. Place egg carton one inch from a wall or other backstop.

Players take turns tossing 5 bottlecaps into the egg carton — caromed off the wall into the carton, if wished, from a throwing line 5′ away. High score wins.

Variations: *Winks* — Same game, except Tiddley-winks are used in place of bottlecaps, from one foot away. Winks must be snapped, as in Tiddley-winks. *Marble Box Score* — Same game, except top is left on egg carton and is bent down to the playing surface to form a ramp. Then each player rolls 5 marbles, in turn, into the carton.

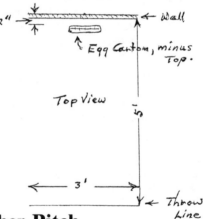

Wall

2″ →

Egg Carton, minus Top.

Top View

5′

← 3′ →

← Throw Line

64. Washer Pitch
Target throwing game relating to horseshoes

Age level: 8 and up
Organizational level: Low
Number of players: 1 on 1, 2 on 2
Supervision: None
Playing time: 50 point game, about 25 minutes average

Space needed: 6′ × 30′ area
Equipment: 6 3″ washers (3 plain, 3 painted), 4 6–8″ stakes (such as pieces of broomstick), 2 tin cans (with tops removed cleanly)

Directions: Players toss washers (3 each) into sunken tin cans, 25′ away, which are protected by two stakes in front of each. Take turns as in horseshoe pitching.

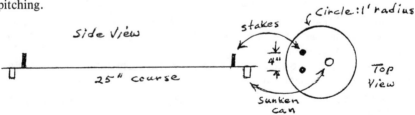

Side View

Circle: 1′ radius

stakes

4″

25″ course

Sunken can

Top View

A washer landing, and staying, in the circle counts one point, hitting a stake counts 2 points; leaning against a stake, 3 points; in the can, 5 points. Opponents may try to knock leaners away to take points away. Highest point scores on each throwing series throws last on the next round.

Game winner is first to 50 points. If tied, after the same round of throws, one more round of throws is held, or as many as necessary to break the tie.

Variation: *50 points or break* — A player must score exactly 50 points to win. If he goes over 50 on a round of throws, he loses 10 points.

65. Backyard Bocce

Teaches basics of an Italian game, bocce, that is very old

Age level: 8 and up
Organizational level: Low
Number of players: 2 or more, individually or as teams
Supervision: None
Playing time: Games are very short, so a number can be played in a half-hour
Space needed: 4' × 12' long area, in dirt fairly well packed

Equipment: Center ball, 2 balls for each player (all same size and composition), croquet balls can be used, with the center ball being a baseball, for example, or softballs can be used, with the center ball a rubber baseball or a golf ball; or golf balls could be used, the center ball being a large steel ball bearing (commercial bocce sets can be secured from General Sportcraft Co.)

Directions: Basic bocce rules. Players throw their balls, trying to hit, or land closest to, the center ball. If only one hit is scored, that person is winner. A hit on the fly is rated over a hit on the bounce. If more than one player scores a hit, they throw until a winner is declared.

A thrower may knock an opponent's ball away or another of his balls closer or into the center ball.

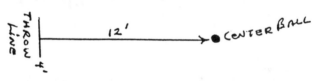

If no center ball hits are made, the winner is the one with a ball closest to it.

Game source: Modified from very old, still popular Italian game of bocce, and a similar Spanish game where players throw at exploding caps, instead of a center ball.

66. Bocce Pole

Teaches hand bowling skills and strategy inherent in many similar games such as bowling on the green, Italian bocce and Canadian curling.

Age level: 10 and up
Organizational level: Low
Number of players: Up to 5
Supervision: Judge-scorekeeper for tournaments, none for free play
Playing time: 50-point game

Space needed: Clear carpeted area inside or grass or dirt area outside, minimum 20' × 25'
Equipment: 1 croquet-type stake, old croquet or pool balls (even baseballs can be used) — up to 15, pencil and paper for scoresheets

Directions: Idea is to hit stake while keeping opponent from hitting stake, or get higher score if no one hits stake.

Each player should get 3 balls if 4 or 5 people are playing, 4 balls each if 2 or 3 are playing.

Each player throws or rolls one ball at a time, in rotation. Balls may hit other balls, knocking opponent's balls out of scoring areas and own into higher scoring areas. Ball must remain with over half itself inside a line to count at the finish of the throwing round.

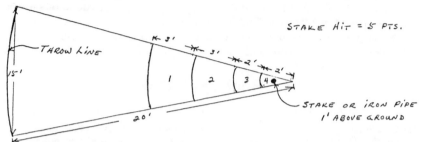

A stake hit does not have to remain inside any area to get its 5 points, but the ball earns bonus points if it does remain inside a numbered area. Unintentional stake hits, caused by carom hits, also count 5 points (for the team whose ball hits the stake).

Each team must have at least one stake hit per round or all players' count on that round will be cancelled for that team.

Variations: *50-or-Break* — Player or team must score exactly 50 points to win. If more points than that are scored, the player or team must start over.

67. Target Bowling

Informal game, based on Italian game of bocce, to be played almost anywhere, with very simple equipment, by mixed ages and handicapped

Age level: All
Organizational level: Low
Number of players: 1 on 1, or by teams: 2-person teams, 4–6 teams per court
Supervision: None
Playing time: Depends on how many players in game or tournament, but 2 2-person teams can play a game in about 20–30 minutes
Space needed: 9′ × 60′ length
Equipment: 2 stakes (like croquet stakes), tape measure, 2 balls per player (croquet, softballs) marked with team's number, Magic Marker pen

Directions: Single players bowl from both ends, in turn. Doubles play has one teammate at each end, bowling toward the opposite end.

Bowl from behind the foul line. Stepping over it is a foul, with any points for that roll taken away, and the ball removed from the field of play for that round, with any balls it has moved put back into their original positions.

Flip coin to decide which team rolls first. Then, the first roller of each round is the player or team with the highest score in the previous round. Teams take turns rolling one ball, then the second ball.

A ball cannot be bowled until the preceding one

stops. A ball bowled out of turn is removed from the field of play, all balls it has moved are put back into original positions, and any points scored by it are taken away.

Any ball may hit any other ball during play.

The score is counted by the positions the balls are in after all players at one end have bowled. A stake hit (even if the ball has been caromed off an opponent's ball) is five points for the team whose ball it is. That ball is removed from the field of play immediately after the hit. The other team may nullify that stake hit and its five points by also scoring a stake hit in the same round.

If any balls belonging to the same team that got the stake hit — and the other team didn't get a stake hit — are closer to the stake than the other team's, they are awarded the points of the circle they are in. If no other balls are closer than the other team's, no more points are given. If no pin hits are scored, then the team with the ball closest to the pin gets all the points from all its balls closer than the other team's closest ball. The "away" team gets no points.

A "round" is defined as the period needed for all bowlers at one end of the court to roll all their balls once.

Game is 15 points. Championship matches can be best two of three or three of five games.

Variations: Younger children, who may have trouble understanding the above scoring rules may play with all balls in the target area counting. The game is then played to 50 points. *25-or-Break* — Either of the above games can be played with the rule added that the winner must score *exactly* 25 points or he "breaks the bank" and has to start over. *50-or-Break* — Same as above, except if exactly 50 points aren't scored, the number of points over is subtracted from 50 and players keep rolling.

68. Potty

*Variety of horseshoe pitching, but
using inexpensive, safe materials so children can play*

Age level: 8 and up
Organizational level: Low
Number of players: 1 on 1, 2 on 2
Supervision: None
Playing time: 15 or 21 point game, about 25 minutes
Space needed: area 10′ × 20′, indoors or out
Equipment: 8 beanbags (4¼″ × 6¼″ pockets of cloth — 4 of one color, 4 of another — each filled with 1 cup of dried beans, then the open side sewn shut), 2 wood boxes or goals (moveable, hinged tops, 21″ square with 7″ diameter hole in it; back 9″ high; sides 3″ high at fronts, 9″ at backs; front 3″ high)

Directions: Basic horseshoe pitching rules, singles and doubles, except beanbags are thrown at holes in boxes set at opposite ends of the court, and each player throws 4 beanbags, taking turns.

Scoring: Bag in hole counts 3 points; on boxtop, 1 point.

Variations: Change rules so *last* person to get a bag in the hole each round of throws gets the score of all the bags scored by both players. If no bags are in the hole, the last one with a bag on the lid gets the total score. (The team throwing last, thus, has an advantage.) But the player getting the total must throw first on the next round.

69. Skid Pins

Introduces rudiments of shuffleboard and bowling into informal activities

Age level: 8 and up
Organizational level: Low
Number of players: Individual, 1 on 1, or teams of 2-5
Supervision: Scorekeeper, pinsetters (though players can take turns doing these jobs)
Playing time: 10 frames per player; time varies greatly

Space needed: 11' × 4' wide area with smooth floor, or shuffleboard court
Equipment: Tenpins (plastic, Pringle potato chip canisters, quart milk containers, or crafted wooden candle pins, made from cut-off 1″×1″ board 8″ lengths or 2″×2″ board lengths), 2 skid discs, bowling scoresheets and pencil

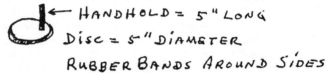

Directions: Basic bowling rules and scoring. Three games is a match. High score wins. Difference is using skid pins instead of rolling balls.

Game source: Modified from Canadian game of curling (ice bowling).

70. Summer Curling

Teaches basics of Canadian game of curling, using equipment that can be made in crafts program or at home

Age level: 8 and up
Organizational level: Low, if players know how to score bowling
Playing time: 10 frames per bowler; time varies greatly
Space needed: Shuffleboard court, or equivalent area in gym, tennis court, parking lot, sidewalk
Equipment: 2 skid pins per player, chalk

and string for marking scoring area, score-sheets and pencil. Target area can be pre-painted onto a paper mat, to be taped to the court for play. This can be used over and over, and also assures the same size scoring area each time. Corn meal sprinkled on the court will make skidding pins easier. (Even a light sprinkling of clean sand can help.)

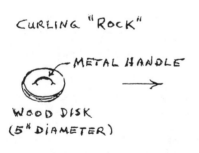

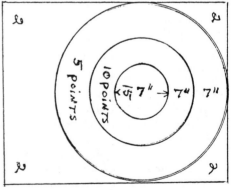

Directions: Players take turns skidding pins into bullseye target area. Players may hit other pins in the target, knocking opponent's pins away or own pins closer to center. The area a "rock" is *most* in determines its score.

Scores for both pins are tallied after each frame is completed, and totaled after ten frames.

Variation: *Bullseye Bowling*—Same setup except different target bullseye, with scoring done as in regular bowling, with strikes and spares. Bowling scoresheets can be used.

Bullseye is marked with 1″ radius circle in middle (which, when completely covered by a "rock," is a strike if on first throw; is an automatic spare if on second throw, regardless of how many pins were left up after the first throw). The next circle is 8-pins-down, the back two corner spots are 9-pins-down, the next circle is 7-pins-down, next circle is 6-pins-down. Then the front extension is divided into sqaures for 5-pins-down (in middle), 4-pins (to left of middle), 3-pins (to right of middle), 2-pins (left corner) and 1-pin (right corner).

Bowler must get exact number of pins needed to score spares.

71. Skittles

Teaches throwing for accuracy

Age level: 8 and up
Organizational level: Low
Number of players: Any number in rotation, but 2–12 is best
Supervision: Chasers, to retrieve thrown sticks
Playing time: 50-point game
Space needed: Minimum 100′ × 5′, inside or outside

Equipment: 5 pins (wooden stakes, candle-pins, Indian clubs or potato chip cans) at least 4½″ high and 2″ thick, 3 throwing sticks (14″ long, 2″ thick, such as sections of a cut-off broomstick), paper and pencil for scoring

Directions: Each player in turn throws three sticks, trying to hit the scoring pins. First to reach 50 points wins.

Pins are set in a diamond shape, the nearest pin counting 1 point for a hit, the next two pins counting 3 points, the farthest pin counting 5 points, and the middle pin counting 10 points. If a throwing stick caroms from one pin to another, points are counted for all pins hit.

Variations: *25-or-Bust*—Winner must score exactly 25 points to win or start over. *Frisbee Skittles*—Same game, but using Frisbees instead of throwing sticks.

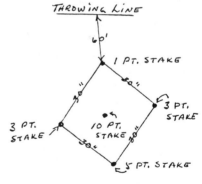

72. Putt Pins

*Combining putting and bowling to teach
fundamentals of golf putting and bowling scoring*

Age level: 8 and up
Organizational level: Low

Number of players: 1 on 1, or teams; limit six per layout for best play

Playing time: 10 bowling frames per player
Space needed: Shuffleboard court, or equivalent area
Equipment: Golf putter (or croquet mallet), 2 golf balls (or croquet balls, softballs, Whiffleballs), 10 candle pins, made from sawing 8″ long sections of 1″×1″ board (or quart milk cartons or Pringle potato chip canisters), score sheets and pencil

Directions: Score as in bowling. (Instruction booklet can be secured at any local bowling lane.) Each player gets two putts to try to knock down all ten pins. Opponents re-set pins for each other. To save time and trouble, either chalk mark the tenpin spots on the court, or make a paper mat with the tenpin spot formation on it beforehand, so it can be taped to the playing surface. This assures the pins will be set the same each time.

Two putts per player is a frame, 10 frames constitute a game, three games make a match. Winner is one having high total score for match.

Variations: *(1)* Smaller children or novices at putting may play by giving each player as many putts as necessary to knock over all pins. Score is number of putts it takes in ten frames, one game. *Low* score wins. *(2)* Set pins in front of a corner, with the head pin facing the corner. Then putts have to be caromed off the wall before they can contact pins to count.

73. Box Carom Bowling (Mini)

Informal playground bowling where bowlers learn to use angles

Age level: 8 and up
Organizational level: Low
Number of players: 1 on 1, or 2–3 person teams
Supervision: None, if players know how to score bowling
Playing time: Two players will take from 30–60 minutes; most time is consumed in re-setting pins

Space needed: Inside corner of room, with flat area 20′ × 20′
Equipment: 10 bowling pins (plastic, or quart milk cartons as substitutes), 2 balls (rubber playground ball, volleyball, or 16″ softball), bowling score sheets and pencil, chalk to mark 10 points positions (or make a paper mat with the positions already marked that can be taped to floor)

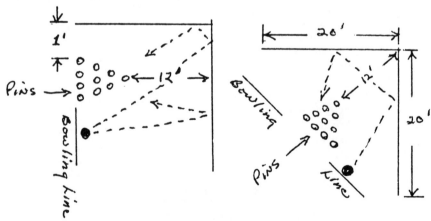

Directions: Basic bowling scoring. (Booklet can be secured at local bowling lane.) Each bowler rolls 10 frames, 2 balls per frame. (All pins knocked down on first ball is strike and allows bowler to add total of next two balls to that frame.

All pins knocked down with two balls is a spare and allows him to add the total of the next ball to that frame.)

Bowlers must carom the ball off one or two walls before it contacts pins. Opponents re-set pins for each other.

Variation: *Box Bowling*—Make box court from boards or plywood. Use small candle pins, which can be made by sawing 3–4″ high sections off 1″ × 1″ board, and shoot glass marbles at them.

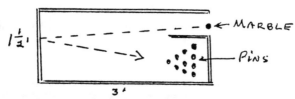

74. Control Bowling

Teaches how to control bowling ball to pick up spares

Age level: 8 and up
Organizational level: Medium
Number of players: Singly, 1 on 1, or by teams of 2–5; good parent-child activity or tourney
Supervision: None, except bowling teacher
Playing time: Free structured

Space needed: Bowling land (or any of the several bowling setups in this section of the book using substitute equipment)
Equipment: Bowling ball, scorecard and marker, bowling shoes (if at commercial lanes)

Directions: Try to avoid knocking down head pin on first ball. No score if you do, for either ball. Try to pick up spare left, with second ball, when you may hit the head pin. Score is 10 for a spare on the second ball (if the head pin hasn't been hit on the first ball), or the number of pins actually knocked down with the two balls. Winner is high scorer after ten frames.

Variation: *Control Bowling 2 (or Spare Bowling)*—Bowl regular, except strikes don't count. First ball rolled must leave one or more pins up. A spare counts 10, but anyone not getting a spare scores only the number of pins downed. A bowler scoring a strike on the first ball may, however, take the second ball for count. If a second strike should result, this would still be a 10-point spare.

Game source: Modified from the idea by Charles Moat at U.S. Navy Special Services Training School, 1972.

75. Carom Bowling

Unique bowling variation, actually tried out by Brunswick Company in 1965. Shows how easily one rule change can revolutionize a game.

Age level: 8 and up
Organizational level: Medium
Number of players: Individual, 1 on 1, or teams of 2–5
Supervision: None, if bowlers can keep scores
Playing time: 10 frames per bowler; time varies greatly
Space needed: Shuffleboard court, or equiva-

lent area, with 2″ × 4″ boards along sides to form railings (anchored with stakes in ground)
Equipment: Tenpins (plastic, Pringle potato chip canisters, quart milk cartons), 2 balls (large Whiffleball, softballs, croquet balls, small playground balls), (Bowlite plastic pins and rubberized ball available from Cosom Company), bowling scoresheets and pencil

Directions: Basic bowling rules and scoring, except extra points are awarded for caroming ball off one or both sides of side railings before contacting pins.

Variation: Tournament might be set up at bowling lanes. Gutters could be fitted with boards wide enough to stick up over lanes, so balls could be caromed off them.

Game source: Modified from both Table Shuffleboard and Brunswick Company's Carom Bowling instruction booklet, 1965.

FOOTBALL, SOCCER AND OTHER KICKING TYPE GAMES

76. Kick Golf

Teaches basics of golf—except for use of clubs— without needing an expensive golf course

Age level: 8 and up
Organizational level: Low
Number of players: 1 to 4 at a time, as in golf
Supervision: Scorekeeper in each group
Playing time: Par 52 strokes, 18 holes for four players

Space needed: Ball field, playground or park area, or beach
Equipment: 18 #10 tin cans, tennis ball for each player, paper and pencil for scorekeeping

Directions: Set up 18-hole golf course by placing #10 cans on their sides at various spots around the selected area of play. Vary the distances between the holes. Number the cans to keep the order straight. The usual course has 2 3-kick holes, 2 5-kick holes, and the rest 4-kick holes. Trash cans, trees, etc., become hazards and cannot be moved or removed by players. A player may drop his ball one yard from such a hazard, but *not* closer to the next hole, by taking an extra (penalty) stroke. Balls are advanced by being kicked.

A can may be turned with the open end toward each putter in turn, though it may not be moved from its spot.

Lowest scorer for each hole plays first on the following hole, second low plays second, etc. One player keeps record of strokes taken on each hole by each player, and totals all individual scores at the end of the 18 holes. Low total is winner.

Variation: *Beach Kick Golf*—Same as above, except that cans can be buried—open ends up—in the sand.

77. Hole-in-One Kickball

Simple game for unstructured play

Age level: 6 and up
Organizational level: Low
Number of players: Any number, in rotation
Supervision: None
Playing time: Open ended
Space needed: Area approximately 30′ × 15′ wide

Equipment: Ball that can be kicked (soccer, playground), box (or wastebasket or trash can, if clean) large enough for ball to fit into easily, numbered tags for each player and safety pins to attach them with, with second set of numbered tags attached to wooden pegs

Directions: Place box, basket or can on side at one end of area. Players stand at other end. In numbered rotation, they try to kick the ball into the goal. Three rounds is a game, winner being player with most goals in three tries. Ties can be kicked off, sudden death.

Until a goal is scored, pegs with the kickers' numbers on them are placed on the spot where balls end up. If no goals are kicked, then the one closest is winner.

Variation: Older players can play the same game, but placing the box upright, so an aerial or bouncing kick is needed for the ball to enter it.

78. Hop-Kick Golf

Pastime for anywhere, anytime, with minimum equipment

Age level: 8 and up
Organizational level: Low
Number of players: Any number, in sequence
Supervision: None

Playing time: 30 minutes
Space needed: 25′ circle
Equipment: 9 pieces of string 12–14″ long, 3″ square block of wood for each player

Directions: Lay out a circle 25′ in diameter and at equal distances around it anchor nine loops of white string. Each player has a small wood block. Starting in the center, the first player, hopping on one foot, attempts to put his block in the first loop with the fewest number of hop kicks. When all have made the first loop, they proceed to the second. The player wins who completes the circuit of nine holes in the fewest kicks.

79. Codeball-on-the-Green

Developed to therapeutically use the large muscle groups of the body

Age level: 10 and up
Organizational level: Medium
Number of players: 2 on 2
Supervision: Referee and scorekeeper
Playing time: 30–60 minutes per round
Space needed: Golf course set up around an entire playground or schoolyard
Equipment: Pneumatic rubber ball (6″ diam-

eter, 12 oz. wt., or equivalent) for each player, 9 cone-shaped holes (about 41″ diameter at bases and 7″ high, with 18″ diameter openings) which can be made from strips of innertube rolled into cones and cut to fit, or more permanent ones from welded tin

Directions: (Rules available through NAAU Codeball Committee.) Place cone "holes" around playing area, like for a golf course. Number them 1–9. Walk players around so they will know where they are, if all can't clearly be seen upon approach.

Basic golf rules, except ball must be kicked, never touched with hands or other parts of the body while it is in play after each kick, except to lift it out of a hole and set in beside the hole for the next "tee off" kick toward the next hole.

Referee keeps track of number of kicks each player takes to put ball into each hole. Winner is low total for the 9 holes.

Variation: *Codeball in the Snow*—Same game may be played with snow on the ground.

Game source: Modified from game developed by Dr. William E. Code, a Chicago physician, and presented in November 1929 at the 41st NAAU convention in St. Louis, MO. *Time* magazine reported the first national champion as Bert Gates, at Forest Park in St. Louis, July 1, 1935. At that time, 50,000 players claimed to play the game.

80. Crab Soccer

*Uses a lot of muscles not commonly used in other
games, especially in hands, wrists and arms*

Age level: 10 and up
Organizational level: Medium
Number of players: 2 teams; 5–7 each
Supervision: Referee-scorekeeper
Playing time: 4 quarters, 5 minutes each,
  2 minutes between

Space needed: Grass or smooth floor (like gym) area about 20′ × 40′
Equipment: Ball (soccer, volley, playground or beach ball), 2 goals (chairs or boxes set on sides), gloves may be worn by players

Directions: Basic soccer rules, except players play from a "crab" position: backside to ground, moving by scuttling around on palms of hands and feet.

Ball can be moved by hitting it with any part of body, except hands and arms.

Penalty free kicks, taken from point of infraction by fouled player, are given for player touching ball with hands or arms, player raising off a three-point contact with ground. Three-point contact can include two feet and seat of pants (when necessary to rest hands and wrists). Fouls also awarded for unneccessary body contact and unsportsmanlike conduct. Fouls kicked by nearest opponent.

Scores are made by putting ball into opponent's goal. Ties played off "sudden death."

81. Soccer-Tennis (or Court Ball)

*Teaches rudiments of handling soccer ball for novices, and refines
ball handling skills for those who already play the game. Small,
controlled area of play means players get more practice in shorter
time than they would on large field, with more players.*

Age level: 10 and up
Organizational level: Medium
Number of players: 2 teams; 2–6 each
Supervision: None informally, referee-score-
  keeper otherwise

Playing time: Best two of three game match, approximately 30 minutes
Space needed: Tennis court, or gym with net installed
Equipment: Soccer or playground ball

Directions: Start service with half-volley kick, like a football drop kick.

Basic tennis rules, except soccer ball is kicked over the net. It can be done on the volley or on one court bounce. Ball can also be played back and forth between/among teammates three times before returning it, so long as it is kept moving and touches the court only once.

Any number of "body hits" (juggling of the ball on head, torso, knees or feet) are allowed per player before playing it to another teammate or kicking it back across the net.

Fouls: *(1)* If ball bounces on court more than once during one team's play, *(2)* ball is touched by arms or hands during play, *(3)* ball is held without moving it, on any part of the body, for over 10 seconds, *(4)* ball is hit out of bounds, *(5)* ball does not get across net on return, or serve, *(6)* players serve out of turn, *(7)* player advances toward the net while controlling juggled ball. Penalty for all these is point award to opponents.

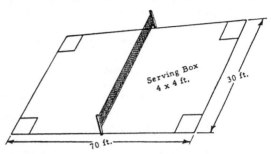

Variation: *Lacrosse-Tennis* — Same basic game can be played using lacrosse sticks and ball. Only three plays of ball per side, no walking with the ball in possession, ball cannot touch court once it has been played by a side. A return is allowed to bounce once before being played by a side, however.

82. Volley-Soccer

Combination of soccer skills with volleyball game,
good practice for soccer ball control

Age level: 10 and up
Organizational level: Medium
Number of players: Singles, doubles or mixed doubles
Supervision: None informally, referee — scorekeeper otherwise
Playing time: 15-point game, approximately 30 minutes

Space needed: 4 wall handball court with 6′ high volleyball net, or 20′ × 20′ space between two buildings, or two walls, that can be enclosed by net (or chickenwire) at least 10′ high

Directions: Serve by dropping ball to floor and kicking it on the bounce over the net.

Ball is kept in play by body blocking, heading, volleying with shoulder or knee, or kicking. It may be kicked into the net or walls or ceiling to keep it alive and set it up for a good return, so long as it touches the floor only once before putting it back across the net. Thus, ball may be juggled or kicked as many times as wished, so long as it is not touched by hands or arms. It may also be caromed off the walls or ceiling as it is sent over the net.

Server continues as long as he makes points. Only server can score. Point is scored when player *(1)* allows ball to bounce twice on floor before returning it, *(2)* doesn't get a return over the net, *(3)* kicks the ball past the line under the net, touches the ball with hands or arms, *(4)* traps the ball without playing it for over 10 seconds.

Server-out is caused by *(1)* not serving ball over net, *(2)* touching ball after the drop, with hands or arms while ball is in play, or any of in-play fouls mentioned above.

Game source: Adapted from game innovated for play aboard the University of the Seven Seas shipboard college in 1963 by students Gene Tinnera, Bill Fowler, John Scudder and Jim Morse.

83. Kicker's Ball

Easy-to-learn team sport for all seasons, teaching positioning
and strategy and giving much action in small space with short
time period. Also trains lateral agility.

Age level: 8 and up (can be played by older and heavy-set players since there is little bending over)
Organizational level: Low
Number of players: 1 on 1 or 2 on 2
Supervision: None

Playing time: About 30 minutes per game, depending on age and skills
Space needed: 3-walls handball court or cleared area of basement or garage, about 8′ × 8′
Equipment: Ball (racquet, tennis or any soft rubber ball, the "deader" the better)

Directions: Basic handball rules, played on three walls, except feet are used instead of hands.

Start game with ball resting on floor at serving line. Server kicks it with side of foot. Server continues so long as he makes points.

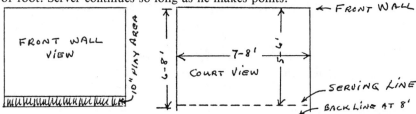

Point, or serve, is lost anytime a ball gets past a player across the back line. (Points scored only by server.) Any ball kicked above the 10″-line on the front wall is an out/fault.

Server must hit the front wall, but may then carom off a side wall. Returns may hit front or sidewall first, but must be returned below the 10″ line on the front wall. Shots may bounce any number of times.

Shots must rebound, in air or bouncing, at least five inches from the front wall, or it is a fault. Balls that roll to rest against the wall are also faulted. Other

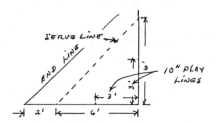

balls must be kicked before they stop rolling, or that is a fault. Ball cannot be stopped and set up to be kicked.

Players who kick and miss the ball are faulted. No second try.

Blocking or interfering with opponent's kick is a replay.

Variation: *Corner Kickball*—Same basic game can be played in a corner, with two walls. Ten inch play line then has to be on both walls, and a lot more carom shots will be made. The court size will also be smaller.

Game source: Modified from game reported played as a youngster by Keith Mano, Blooming Grove, N.Y.

84. Kick Carom Volleyball

Play a Russian innovation that combines soccer and volleyball

Age level: 10 and up
Organizational level: Medium
Number of players: 2 teams, 5 each
Supervision: Referee-scorekeeper-time-keeper

Playing time: 4 8-minute quarters plus 3-minute rest periods between
Space needed: Area 30′ × 30′ adjoining a wall
Equipment: Soccer ball, 2 4′ posts, 30′ long net 3′ high

Directions: To start play, ball is kicked against the wall and over the net from an "open corner." Thereafter, each team attempts to move and return the ball via body blocking, heading or kicking it. Each side is allowed three such "touches" of the ball—hands and arms can't be used—and one floor bounce, before they must return the ball over the net. After every score, ball is kicked again from open corner, by team scored upon.

Fouls: Touching ball with hands or arms, stalling the game (not playing ball within 20 seconds), kicking ball from wall out of bounds through opponent's court, not kicking the serve into opponent's court. *Penalty:* opponent's possession and kick in from open corner.

Scoring: 1 point for opponents if a team kicks the ball out of bounds in its own court (but it re-

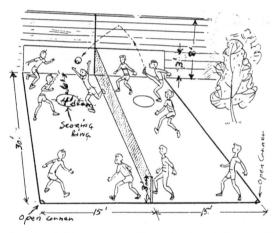

tains the ball, kicking it into play at point it went out of bounds within 10 seconds); 2 points for kicking team if it can bounce the ball from wall to opponents court, so it goes out of bounds and touches the ground there; 5 points for kicking team if it can bounce the ball from the wall into the "scoring ring" (4′ diameter). It is possible, for example, to make both a 5-point circle score and a 2-point out-of-bounds score on the same kick. Defense may body block, kick or head the ball to keep it from bouncing in the scoring ring or out of bounds. Players may not step out of bounds to play the ball, however, except for open-corner kicks.

85. Field Pool (or Kick Pool)

Stretches the game of pool so it can be played on an outdoor field

Age level: 10 and up
Organizational level: Medium

Number of players: 2 or 2 teams of 2 each

Supervision: None informally, referee otherwise
Playing time: About 45–60 minutes per game
Space needed: Smooth, even area about
  15′ × 25′ (or larger, if wished)

Equipment: Ball (soccer, volley or playground type), six small boxes (that ball will
fit into), 15 other balls (smaller than the
kickball), like small sponge rubber balls,
marking pen, six wooden pegs, hammer

Directions: Peg the boxes cornerwise on their sides, open side toward the court,
in each of four corners of field, and at midpoint of each long side of court. These
are the pool "holes." Court should also have sidewalls so balls can't leave court.
These may be boards layed along the court lines, or rocks outlining them, or dirt/
sand ridges, bricks, or even onlookers, standing at spots where it appears balls
will be hit out, with their feet placed so balls will carom off them back into court.

Basic pool rules. Soccer ball is cue or kick ball. It is placed on the cue spot
at one end of the court to start the game. Other balls are numbered 1 to 15 and
placed in triangle at other end of court.

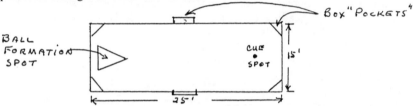

Kick ball is kicked at the other balls, trying to break up the formation and
put one of them in a box. Players take turns kicking, though any player putting
a ball in a box with a carom shot from the kick ball, keeps kicking until he
misses. Balls are taken out of boxes immediately (so that box may be used again).

Game may be played so players can play *any* ball in any hole, or balls must
be played in numbered rotation (unless caromed in off the numbered ball being
shot), or making the #8 ball last, with it having to be put into one of the side
"pockets."

Variations: Softball bats can be used as cue sticks, instead of kicking balls.
Billiards may be played with only three balls, no holes on field.

86. Kick Baseball

*Easier to play than softball for smaller
and less adept children, as well as handicapped*

Age level: 8 and up
Organizational level: Medium
Number of players: 2 teams, 9 each
Supervision: Umpire-scorekeeper
Playing time: About 45–60 minutes

Space needed: Playing diamond 45′ long on
  each side (see sketch on next page)
Equipment: Ball (soccer, volley or playground ball)

Directions: Basic softball rules, except ball is rolled to batter, who kicks it into play.
Ball must be kicked beyond 8′ foul line to be fair ball, otherwise it is a foul ball.
Player positions same as softball. Fielders catch and throw ball as in softball.

Runners cannot lead off base. They may try to steal, but can be put out by
being hit with a thrown ball or having the ball beat them to the base (if caught
by the baseman and the base tagged). (Stealing bases may be outlawed, too, if
wished.)

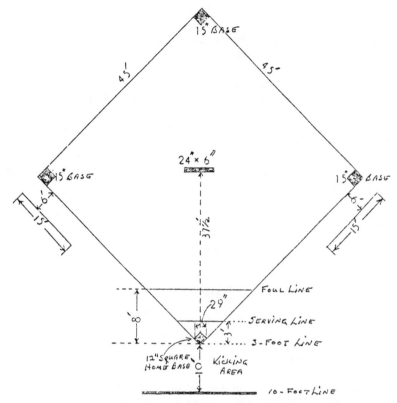

Strike is called when pitched ball is kicked at and missed, when a fowl hit is not caught (an out if caught), and when a pitched ball crosses the legal pitching area and isn't kicked at. Three strikes are out, except foul hit on third strike not caught. Four balls is a walk.

Baserunners cannot interfere with hit or thrown ball. Penalty: out.

Three outs per side. Five innings is game. Ties played off, if wished, or ties may give each team a half-win (in tournament play).

Game source: Modified from Jacksonville, FL Recreation Department game.

87. Cannonade

Informal street game

Age level: 8 and up
Organizational level: Low
Number of players: 2 sides, 1–10 each
Supervision: None
Playing time: Varies greatly; time limit or 21-point game

Space needed: Section of closed-off street, or equivalent outdoors area
Equipment: Tin can (can be wrapped with tape)

Directions: Start game with can in middle of street. On "go" signal, two teams' opposing centers race to play it first.

Teams try to kick the can across the opponents' goal line. Distance of playing area can vary with number of players and space available. The can cannot be caught or held. The can or players may be blocked, but not grabbed or held. No tripping, hitting or intentional kicking of opponents. Penalty for infractions is free kick by the fouled player from point of infraction.

Street curbs serve as sidelines and any can kicked over a curb is out of bounds. It is kicked in by team opposite one touching can last before it went out of bounds.

Game is 21 points. Ties (if playing to a time limit) can be played off "sudden death," first team scoring.

Variation: *Can-Across*—Same basic game, except a no-man's land section is installed between the two opponent teams—a strip 5' wide. (Or, in limited space, the street divider line can be used, with teams playing *across* the street.) No players may cross the strip (or line). Length of playing area—30'.

Alternate teams get kickoffs from their side of no-man's land after each goal.

Game source: Modified from old street game.

88. Line Soccer

Many people can play in relatively small area

Age level: 10 and up
Organizational level: Medium
Number of players: 2 teams; 10-30 per team
Supervision: Referee-scorer

Playing time: 30 minutes; 2 15-minute halves
Space needed: Field 120-150' wide by 240–300' long
Equipment: Soccer ball

Directions: All the players on each side line up in a single line across the field on their own goal line. The first four or six players (as indicated) at the left of each line come out as the whistle is blown and the ball is rolled out into the middle of the playing area. These players attempt to kick the ball across the opponent's

goal, not higher than the height of the shoulders. They continue playing until one side has scored a goal. All the remaining players on each side guard their goal. After each goal, a new set of players advance to the center, usually in successive order from the goal line. When the ball is kicked above the heads of the goal defenders, a free kick is given to the defensive team. The ball is placed on the goal line for this kick. When the ball goes out of bounds over the side lines, the opposite side puts it back into play with a throw-in from the spot where it crossed the side line. On all free kicks the opponents must be at least 5 yards away from the ball at the moment it is kicked. No goal may be scored directly from a free kick. No one is permitted to use their hands or arms below the elbow. When this rule is violated, the opposite side is given a free kick at the spot of the foul. However, when the defending team uses their hands within their own penalty area (the 10 yard area in front of their end line) a penalty kick is awarded. The penalty kick is executed by placing the ball on a line 10 yards from the goal line and attempting to kick it over the goal line within the proper height. The ball is in play immediately after the kick if the goal is not made.

Scoring: Each goal scores one point. A goal from a penalty kick also counts one point. The game is decided by the team with the most points after a specific period of time.

Variation: *Punch Soccer*—Same game, except arms and hands are used to play the ball, instead of the feet, by the group of players in the middle court area. Penalty for illegal use of hands by players on goal line remains same.

Game source: Modified from U.S. Navy games booklet, out of print.

89. Melee (or The Attack Game)

Unique multi-attack game for many players

Age level: 10 and up
Organizational level: Low
Number of players: 2 teams; 10–40 each
Supervision: 2 referees-scorekeeper

Space needed: Field 60' by 120'
Equipment: 2 soccer balls, 2 volleyballs, 2 basketballs

Directions: Place the balls in the center of the field. The teams are lined at opposite ends of the field, behind their own goal. At a signal, they rush for the balls. Soccer balls must be soccer kicked, volley balls hit with the hand along the ground, and basketballs passed. When a ball goes out of bounds on the sideline it is put in play by a "throw-in" from the point where it crossed the sideline by the team which did not touch it last on the field of play. The team advancing the largest number of balls over the opponent's goal line is the winner. Any player guilty of unnecessary roughness is

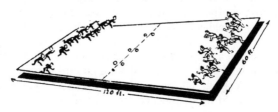

eliminated from the game. After a ball goes over the goal line, it is out of play. When all balls have crossed the goal lines, they are returned to the center and on a signal the game is resumed as at the start.

Scoring: One point for every ball advanced over opponent's goal lines.

Game source: Modified from U.S. Navy sports booklet, now out of print.

90. Dog Fight

Rugged, yet injury-free, game stressing teamwork, using a minimum of space, equipment and supervision

Age level: 12 and up
Organizational level: High
Number of players: 2 teams of 10–15; 12 is ideal
Supervision: Referee-scorekeeper

Playing time: 4 quarters 5 minutes each, 1 minute rest between quarters, 3 minutes between halves
Space needed: Soccer or football field, or

field 40 × 60 yards minimum, with football type goal posts. Yard lines eliminated.
Equipment: Soccer ball, contrasting shirts for teams. (No spiked, cleated or hard-toed shoes.)

Directions: Each period starts with referee tossing ball up in center circle (10′ diameter circle in center of field). Players must remain outside this circle until the referee's toss and whistle signal. Toss-ups are also used for "held" balls.

Teams exchange goals each quarter.

Ball may be kicked, headed or batted with hand or fist in any direction at any time by any player. On all fly balls, the player gaining possession may run with the ball, throw it, bat it, kick it, in any direction, or dribble it.

Ball going out of bounds, or over the end zone, is thrown in by team *not* touching it last, at point it went out.

Any ground ball may be kicked or scooped one-handed into the air, converting it into an air ball. But that player cannot then catch that ball until it has first touched another player. Falling on the ball is prohibited.

If pass is incomplete, the ball is played then as a ground ball, not a "dead" ball. A complete, or incomplete, pass out of bounds gives the ball to the opponents where ball went out.

A player legally running with the ball may be stopped by a two-handed touch, after which the ball is tossed into the air 10′ by the touched player, where it becomes a free ball.

Blocking is legal, but only by using hands, and only above the waist, with no "flying" blocks allowed. Any other body contact — pushing, tripping, holding clothing, or other unnecessary roughness — is a foul also. Penalty: Ball out of bounds to fouled team at nearest point to the infraction.

A touchdown is scored by running or passing over the goal line. If the ball is run over the goal line and touched down between the goal posts, it counts 2 points. A field goal (2 points) is scored by a drop-kick over and between the goal posts.

When a team is scored on, it takes possession of the ball at the goal line and puts it into play as though it were an out-of-bounds ball.

A "ground ball" is one that is stationary, rolling or bouncing — even if it is in the air, if it last touched the ground, not a player.

Game source: Modified from a naval aviation cadet training game from World War II called "Navy Ball."

91. Fieldball

*Develops speed, agility and endurance by combining
features of basketball, soccer and lacrosse*

Age level: 14–17, 18 and up
Organizational level: High
Number of players: 2 teams, 9 each
Supervision: Referee, scorekeeper, and timekeeper
Playing time: 4 quarters, 6 minutes each,
1-minute rest between; overtime: 2-minute period; second overtime: "sudden death" scoring
Space needed: Area 120′ × 180′ (see drawing on next page)
Equipment: Soccer ball

Directions: Playing positions are 4 attackers, 4 defenders and 1 goalie.

Start game, and second half, with a kickoff from any point along the mid-field line. Start second and fourth quarters with possession by the team having possession of the ball when the previous period ended. No player can be closer than 15' to the ball as it is kicked off. Goal areas are exchanged each period.

The ball may be advanced by kicking, passing or running with it. If running, the ball must be carried in both hands in front of the body, but not touching the body. (Penalty: loss of ball at that point.)

"Held balls" between opposing players are jump balls at that spot.

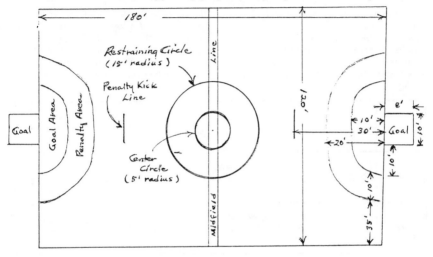

Official Fieldball Layout

Fouls: *(1)* Attack or defense players in wrong half of field at kickoff (loss of ball and 30 seconds in penalty box for that player or players), *(2)* intentionally roughing a player, pushing, tripping, blocking, pushing opponent offside (1 minute in penalty box, with no substitution allowed).

Out of bounds ball is kicked inbounds by team not touching it last before it went out. Exception: shots on goals. Then ball belongs to the player nearest the ball when it passed the boundary lines. (A deflected shot does not alter this rule.) All players must be 15' from the ball for kick-ins.

Scoring: Kicked, 2 points; other than kicked, 1 point.

The goalkeeper, outside the "crease" (goal area), is ruled as any other player. Any player replacing the goalie, even temporarily, is subject to all goalkeeper regulations (can't use hands in playing the ball, arms can be used only when in contact with his body). Penalty: loss of ball or, if foul prevented a goal, score counts.

An attack player, entering the opponent's crease, is penalized loss of ball. A defense player entering the crease, with the goalie present, is given 30 seconds in the penalty box. If an offensive player has scored, then his body enters the crease in following through his throw, he is not penalized, unless he also roughs the goalie.

After a goal is scored, the ball goes to the team scored on at a point even with the face of the goal at the sideline. All other players remain in front of the goal, no closer to the sideline than 10 yards. After a goal, all players in the penalty box may re-enter the game.

Game source: Development can be traced to World War II military training camps.

92. Soccer Shoot

Test or practice soccer kicking accuracy

Age level: 6–7, 8–9, 10–11, 12–13, 14–15, 16–17, 18 and up
Organizational level: Medium
Number of players: Any number, in sequence
Supervision: Judges, timers, recorder, ball shaggers

Playing time: About 10 minutes per person
Space needed: Any open area about 24′ wide against a wall 24′ wide by 8′ high
Equipment: Cardboard 24′ × 8′ with goal wall marked on it (see sketch), several soccer balls, clipboards, scoresheets and pencils for recorders

Directions: Each contestant gets two kicks from each of the five positions marked on the field (see sketch). Score is total points recorded from where kicked balls have struck the target.

(Note: To determine improvement, give a second test later, and subtract the first score from the second.)

93. Circle Soccer

Alternate soccer game taking much less playing area. Advantageous for practices, since coaches can watch all players much easier than on a regular soccer field. More congested area requires much passing and footwork finesse and teamwork.

Age level: 10 and up
Organizational level: High
Number of players: 2 teams, 6, 7 or 8 players per team. More can play, depending upon size of area available, though no more than 8 "strikers" or scorers should be allowed inside the mid-circle line, since the small area becomes too congested for good play

Supervision: Referees (2), scorekeeper
Playing time: 4 10-minute quarters, with 3-minute rest period between; play to a designated score, such as 4 goals
Space needed: Circle 60' radius, or 60' square area
Equipment: Soccer ball, goal post (7' pipe or wooden 4-by-4")

Directions: The main difference is that the game has only one goal, thus play swirls all around it. Since there are no goalies, players must learn to help block shots.

Select two teams and decide which has first possession. That team takes the ball to any of the four "out docks," where it puts the ball into play by the usual soccer throw-in (two hands, overhead, feet not leaving the ground).

Basic soccer rules are followed. Goals are scored by kicking or heading the ball into the scoring pole. After every goal the ball is given to the team scored on in the out dock nearest where the ball ends up.

All fouls result in turning the ball over to the oponent in the out dock nearest the infraction.

Fouls: Touching the ball with illegal parts of the body, causing the ball to go out of bounds, any body contact with an opposing player that hinders his play in passing, receiving or handling the ball, stepping into the goal zone to kick or block the ball, throwing the ball in from out of bounds illegally, and unsportsmanlike conduct.

Flagrant, repeated or dangerous fouls, at the discretion of the referee, may remove players from the game for a part of the game or all of it.

Variations: *(1) Double Trouble*—Same game but using two balls instead of one. The idea is to spread out the players more in the small area of play. *(2)* Different games result from using different types of balls, from tennis balls to beach balls. *(3)* Adding one goalie, who works independently, against both teams, adds another element.

94. Scrambleball

Teaches ball control and passing skills in congested playing area.
Good soccer goal kicking training game, since area is small and
many goal attempts can be made, while, at the same time, working
four goalies. Lots of exercise in a short time period.

Age level: Age group play: 9–11, 12–15, 16–18
Organizational level: Medium
Number of players: 4 teams, any even number of players, depending on size of playing area. More than six players per team, however, and the game becomes a bit congested.

Supervision: Referee, scorekeeper
Playing time: 4 10-minute quarters, with
  3-minute rest periods between
Space needed: 40 yards square, indoors or
  outdoors

Equipment: Soccer ball or similar sized playground ball, 4 goals made of large cardboard boxes

Directions: Divide players into four teams, each protecting a different goal. Idea of the game is for each team to advance the ball into the goal opposite its goal, without allowing the ball in its own goal. Each goal counts 1 point.

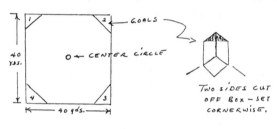

Each quarter is started by giving the ball to the team controlling the goal with the corresponding number, #1 team to start the first quarter, #2 team for the second quarter, etc. After every goal the ball is given to the team with the least number of goals. If more than one team has the same low score, they will take turns, until the tie is broke.

Basic soccer rules, ball being played only with feet, legs, chest or head.

Ball going out of bounds will be put back into play by the player *closest the ball when it went out,* throwing it back into the field *over the back of his head without looking.*

Penalty for violations is sidelining the offending player for one minute. Violations include: ball touching illegal part of body, intentional contact with another player, unsportsmanlike conduct.

Variations: *Volley Scrambleball* — A volleyball is used instead of a soccer ball. It can be moved only by bouncing it off the body above the waist and the arms or hands as in volleyball. It cannot be caught or thrown.

If the ball drops to the floor, it can be hit-bounced to another player, or hit along the floor, or picked up and tossed into the air between the two clenched fists. At no time may the same player touch the ball twice in a row. Penalty rules same as above. *Double trouble* — Either soccer or volley scrambleball may be played with two balls at the same time. A second referee should be added, however, to keep order.

95. Scramble Soccer

Teaches basic soccer skills, alertness

Age level: 10 and up
Organizational level: High
Number of players: 4 teams: 6–8 each,
  though number can vary
Supervision: Referee-scorekeeper-time-
  keeper
Playing time: 4 quarters of play: 5-minute

ones for elementary and junior high ages,
10-minute ones for senior high and up
Space needed: 50' × 50' square area, indoors
  or outdoors
Equipment: Ball (soccer, playground type), 4
  goals (which can be large boxes set on sides)

Directions: Name comes from unusual idea of four teams playing, each moving toward a different goal. Basic soccer rules. Except no guarded goal areas.

Points can be scored by teams only in goals at opposite side of field from theirs: Team A in C goal and vice versa, and Team B in D goal and vice versa. But any team can try to get and keep ball away from any team that is ahead of them in goals, or for any other reason.

After each foul, the fouled player gets the ball for a free kick at the spot of infraction. Fouls include usual soccer rules: touching ball or catching it with hands or arms, kicking or tripping an opponent, using arms or hands to push, hold or otherwise impede opponent.

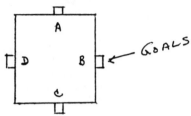

After each goal scored, the ball is given to the team with the lowest score. If two or more are tied, it goes, successively, to the teams to the right of the high score team. That team then starts play by kicking off from the mouth of their goal, with all other players standing no closer than 10 feet. Teammates may stand anywhere else on the court, even in other teams' areas.

Ball going out of bounds is merely tossed over player's head (while standing faced away from playing field) into the center of the playing field.

96. Football Skills Tournament

Test the basic football skills

Age level: 9-10, 11-12, 13-14, 15-16, 17-18, 19 and up
Organizational level: High
Number of players: Any number, taken in sequence
Supervision: Judges, recorders, field measures, ball shaggers
Playing time: All day usually

Space needed: Football field
Equipment: Several footballs, clip boards, score sheets and pencils for all recorders, tape measure, markers (every 10 yards), material for line marking, pegs and paper strips with competitor's numbers on them (for marking distances)

Directions: Four rounds of contestants: first round, punting for distance and accuracy; 2nd round, place kicking for distance and accuracy; third round, passing for distance and accuracy; 4th round, center snap for accuracy.

Accuracy distance is measured as distance from edge of throwing circle to ball's landing spot *minus* the distance from that spot to the accuracy line.

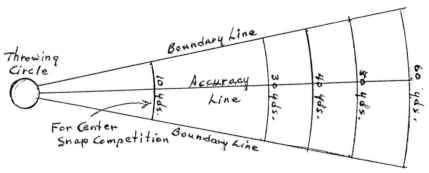

Winners are greatest total overall yardage gainers.

Note: A second tournament may be given later (six months, a year) to test improvement. First scores of contestants can be subtracted from second ones to show amount of improvement (which can be put on a curve or graph to show overall improvement of a group).

97. Speed-a-Way

Originally introduced as a lead-in game to girls field hockey.
It combines elements of soccer, basketball, speedball,
fieldball and hockey, but retains a simplicity of rules.

Age level: 11 and up
Organizational level: High
Number of players: 2 teams, 11 each
Supervision: 2 umpires (one for each length-wise half of field), scorekeeper-timekeeper, 4 linesmen (stationed at 4 corners of field to aid umpires in calling line plays)
Playing time: 4 quarters, 8 minutes each, 2-minute rest periods between quarters, 10 minutes between halves, 3 1-minute time outs are allowed each team per game

Space needed: Minimum size field: 75 yards by 45 yards; regular size: 60 yards by 100 yards

Equipment: 2 goals (field hockey cage, or can make-do with soccer or football goals), Speed-a-Way ball (or soccer or speedball), shin-guards may be worn, different colored shirts for teams (with added distinction for goalkeepers, like stripes), (equipment available commercially through W.J. Voit Corp.; rules through Burgess Publishing Co., 1426 S. 6th St., Minneapolis, MN)

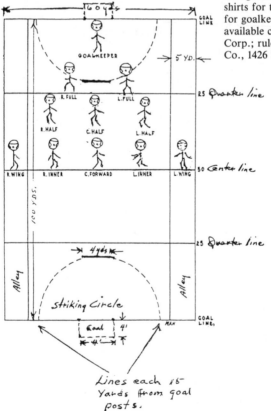

Directions: Player positions are 5 forwards, 3 halfbacks, 2 fullbacks and goal keeper.

Combines running, throwing and kicking, one or two-handed underhand, overhead, chest and hook throws, and punt, drop and place-kicks, as well as dribbling. (Differs from Speedball in that ball here can be caught on one bounce.)

Start game, and each quarter, with kickoff of stationary ball on ground at center line. Must be kicked forward, but does not have to be kicked so opponents recover it. Teams change sides at halftime.

The ball is moved by drop kicking, kicking the stationary ball (place kick), punting, dribbling with the feet soccer style, throwing with one or two hands, juggling (a series of aerial passes to oneself), or running (after catching an aerial ball, or ball on first bounce, after a kick). A thrown ball cannot be caught on one bounce, but must be converted to an aerial by a kick, although it may be kicked up to oneself, or trapped between the feet and kicked up to oneself.

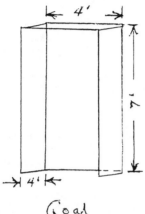

Goal

The ball may be blocked, or volleyed, by any part of the body except hands and arms. Players may guard an opponent, but not touch them. If player in possession of ball holds it over 3 seconds or moves his pivot foot, he may be tagged (two hands on the back) by an opponent. Penalty for these acts is loss of ball at point of infraction (offense), free kick at point of infraction (defense). Free kicks are place kicks and no defensive players may block or guard the kicker.

Substitutions may be made any time the ball is dead, though the "out" player must be off the field before the sub goes on.

Goalies may handle the ball with hands and block with arms at anytime, anywhere on the field (which is why their team shirts must be discernible from teammates).

An intercepted forward pass over the goal is considered out of bounds and is thrown into play from the goal line. Other out-of-bounds balls are thrown in from point where ball went out by team not touching it last.

Personal foul (pushing, hitting, tripping, body blocking in motion), or other unsportsmanlike conduct, gives the fouled player a free shot on goal from the outer rim of the striking circle.

A successful field goal shot earns 5 points; a penalty free shot, 2 points; a run or pass across the goal line, 3 points.

Any offensive player stepping into the defensive striking circle, or interfering with the goalie as he tries to protect his goal, loses any goal scored and the goalie gets the ball for a penalty corner kick.

Game source: Marjorie S. Larsen, chairman, Girl's P.E. Dept., Edison High School, Stockton, CA, experimented with it 10 years in girl's P.E. classes before introducing it into Canada, and ultimately into England, India, Australia and West Germany. The original rules committee included Loretta Stallings, Thelma Lagerberg, Dorothy Marshall and Kathryn Maloy. Rules were copyrighted 1950. This is a modified version.

98. Speed Football

*More exercise than regular football, since
action doesn't stop for incomplete passes, etc.*

Age level: 12 and up
Organizational Method: High
Number of players: 2 teams, 11 each (though game can be modified for 5, 6, or 8-person teams)

Supervision: Referee, lineman and score-keeper
Playing time: 4 quarters, 10 minutes each; time can be varied accordingly to age and fitness of players
Space needed: Football field (though smaller areas can make-do)
Equipment: Football (can be sponge or Whiffleball types for younger ages)

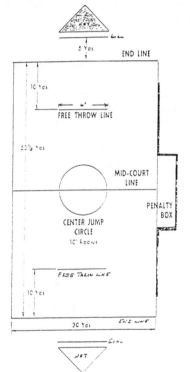

Directions: Basic flag/touch football rules. No time outs.

Ball must be snapped (from center) within 15 seconds after it is put into play.

On a forward pass, ball remains in play even after it has hit the ground. Either team may recover it. The offensive team, however, cannot make more than half the distance to the goal on a forward pass that strikes the ground within 20 yards of the goal line.

On a lateral pass, the ball is dead as soon as it hits the ground.

On a kick, the ball may be recovered by the kicking team within 5 seconds after it hits the ground, even if an opposing player has not touched it.

Variation: Same game can be played with a soccer ball.

Game source: Modified from game by Edwin H. Paget, Professor of Speech, North Carolina State, and director, the Institute of Direct Clash Thinking, Raleigh, NC.

99. Touch Rugby

Teaches rugby, but without the tackling and rougher play

Age level: 12 and up
Organizational level: High

Number of players: 2 teams; 6–9 each
Supervision: Referee-scorekeeper

Playing time: 4 quarters, 8–10 minutes each
Space needed: 40 yards by 80 yards field, or larger, with 5-yard endzones; goalposts can be eliminated, if wished

Equipment: Rugby ball (or football, or sponge or Whiffleball-type football)

Directions: Basic Rugby, except two hand touching on back is designated a tackle. (Or detachable "flags," used in touch football, may be used.)

Kickoffs at start and half of game taken from roughly 40-yard line. It can be drop or place kick. (With sponge or Whiffle-type balls, it may be a punt.)

Teams line up with linemen's shoulders in contact. Center heel-kicks the ball back to any member in his backfield. Positions are center, right and left guards, right and left halfbacks, and a safety back. If using more players in a larger area, add right and left tackles and ends, and/or right and left quarterbacks and safety backs. Backs run forward or lateral to advance the ball, no forward passing.

Kicking allowed only on larger fields, and ball must be dropkicked.

Each team gets three downs to advance the ball 10 yards. If it doesn't, or the ball is intercepted, the other team takes over the ball immediately. If by interception, play continues. If by recovery of grounded ball or unsuccessful three downs, a scrum (scrimmage lineup) is held immediately (without referee calling a pause in the action or having to touch the ball).

Defensive team members may block and tackle (touch with two hands on back) any player with the ball.

Out-of-bounds balls are thrown inbounds, by team that didn't touch ball last, by having both hands on ball, overhead, both feet on the ground. Teams line up opposite each other at 90° angle to the sideline where the ball is to be thrown in.

Fouls are called for unsportsmanlike conduct, defensive holding, passing the ball forward, either team jumping offside before the ball is centered. Off-side penalties are 5 yards, all others 10.

A score is made when team with the ball touches it down inside the goal area, for one point.

Game source: Modified from game of Rugby football.

100. Hocker

Five athletic journals extolled this game as a great physical conditioner—fast, easy to learn, simple to score, suited to all ages, sexes, sizes, skills, with minimum expenditure and equipment, played almost anywhere

Age level: 6 and up
Organizational level: Medium
Number of players: 2 teams, 10 each
Supervision: Referee

Playing time: 2 15-minute halves
Space needed: 60 yards × 100 yards
Equipment: 16″ soft rubber playground ball, 2 Hocker goal posts

Directions: Play starts with the ball placed at midfield by the referee. On "go" signal, opponents race for it.

Player positions are goalie, 3 back-court "defensemen," 3 mid-court "attackers," 3 fore-court "strikers."

Ball may be moved via basketball-type dribbling, soccer-like footwork and body contact, volleyball punching and football-type kicking with any part of the body.

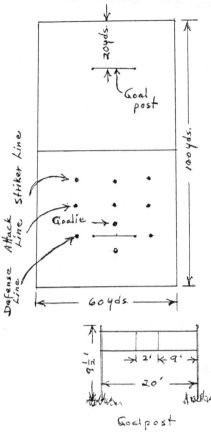

No tackling or tripping. One armed pushes allowed in guarding the ball only. Foul penalty: free kick at goal from point of infraction.

Held balls are bounced on the ground between the two opponents holding it by the referee, so it bounces overhead before being played.

Scores are made by guiding the ball through the goal posts *from either side*. Under both crossbars—1 point, over both crossbars—3 points, between the two crossbars in the end sections—5 points, between the crossbars and through the smaller middle section—8 points.

Variation: *Circle Hocker*—Use only one goal post, at center of field. Each team can score only from it's field side, however.

Game source: John Morton, a Fairfield, CT lawyer and real estate developer, innovated Hocker about 1957. A similar game, called Sockey, was played as a league under lights in the P.S. 26 school yard in Queens, N.Y. in 1966. Hocker was reported by *Sports Illustrated* 8/77 being played at the University of Bridgeport, the school systems of California, Connecticut and Florida, and 1100 affiliates of the National Boys Clubs of America, with clinics given at Miami-Dade JC and Southern Connecticut State College.

101. Flicker Ball

Originated as a game to replace touch football in college intramurals and classes to cut down on injuries to players. Inventor wanted to have a game to develop ball handling and team-work to a high degree.

Age level: 10 and up
Organizational level: High
Number of players: 2 teams, 7 each (or 5 each, if played indoors)
Supervision: Referee-scorekeeper
Playing time: 2 20-minute halves
Space needed: 90' × 159' (see sketch), three fields may be layed out across a football field. (Can be played on indoor basketball courts, with goals mounted on basketball backboards and lines across the court 15' in front of each goal as free throw lines. These

are designated as "no-score" zones. Play may take place there, but no goal shots.)
Equipment: Football, 2 goals (4' × 5' board, rounded corners, with 2' × 3' holes in centers and weighted, heavy duty netting behind the holes to stop and drop the ball) mounted on posts or pipes so board bottom is 8' above the playing surface. (Net may be hung from snap hooks, fastened to sliding rings in the hanging brackets.) (Made available commercially through John L. Lynch Enterprises, Phoenix, AZ.)

Directions: Players have no special positions or names, thus player positioning and styles of offense and defense can be varied. Center jump starts each half.

Object of the game is to advance the ball, by passing, to a position from which a goal throw may be attempted. Any player can handle a loose ball, including a fumble, at any time, so long as the ball is carried rearward or laterally, and not forward. Ball must be passed forward. (Penalty: place ball on ground and nearest opponent plays it from there.) No body contact is allowed. (Penalty: free throw.) Body contact during throw on goal is an automatic 3-point goal. Time outs (2 minutes each) are limited to 3 per team per half. Technical foul is called for more. (Penalty: loss of ball, or free throw.) Time is out whenever ball is dead, and substitutions may be made then.

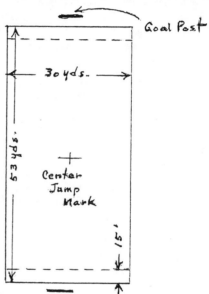

Out of bounds ball is thrown in laterally, not forward, by team not touching it last before it went out, at point where it went out.

Points are scored by passing the ball so it hits the board (1 point) or goes through the hole (3 points). Penalty free throws count the same. No goal tending is allowed in the goal area.

Kicking a loose ball, or diving on it is a foul. (Penalty: free throw by nearest opponent from that spot.)

One of the novel features of this game is that *any* attempted goal throw results in loss of possession of the ball, since the goals are situated out of bounds. The reason is to make players work together to get ideal positioning before attempting goals. Defense puts the ball back into play by throwing inbounds from behind its goal line.

Variation: Goals may be used in holding pass accuracy and pass for distance tests and/or competitions.

Game source: Modified from the game originated in 1948 at the University of Illinois' College of Physical Education, Urbana, IL by Dr. H. E. Kenney and Dr. Armond H. Seidler. They demonstrated it at a Illinois State high school football clinic and at halftime of a Illinois-Indiana basketball game. It eventually became an intramural sport at 10 colleges and was paced up and adapted by the U.S. Army Adjutant General School (Booklet CS 2903 SS [U], HO-6 [8121]).

102. 5-Man Football

For when limited number of players, or limited space, is available

Age level: 12 and up
Organizational level: High
Number of players: 2 teams – 5 each
Supervision: Referees-timekeeper-scorekeeper

Playing time: 4 quarters: 6 minutes each for elementary and junior high ages, 8 minutes for senior high, 10 minutes for college and other

Space needed: 80 yards long by 25 yards wide, with 5 yard wide end zones; no goal posts.

Equipment: Football, "flags" for all players which can be commercial ones or nothing more than bandannas stuck into the belts in back (commercial belts and velcron-backed "rip" flags can be found at several sports equipment companies)

Directions: Basic flag football rules.

On the kickoff, at least two members of the receiving team must be within five yards of their restraining line (kickoff line). Others may be behind this. Opponents must be 10 yards from ball.

On scrimmage plays, offense and defense both must have three players on line of scrimmage, though defense line will be one yard away from offense line. On snap of ball players may go anywhere on field, however, and any player is eligible for lateral and forward passes.

Touchdown is 6 points, conversion is worth 2 points. No place-kicks allowed.

Game source: Modified from game set up by James J. Rafferty, League Director of Greater Johnstown Parochial Schools, PA. (In 1950 he had 4 teams with an 18-game season; in 1951, 14 teams.)

COMBATIVE SPORTS & GAMES

---

103. Dueling

Play-acting shows how historical dueling was carried out

Age level: 8 and up
Organizational level: Low
Number of players: Any number, with shootoffs by twos; can be individual or team game
Supervision: Referee
Playing time: Approximately 15 minutes per duel

Space needed: 5' wide by 25' long, inside or outside; several areas, if tournament is held
Equipment: 2 blowguns (made from neon tubing, copper tubing or rolled cardboard), 12 "darts" (6 per player) (made from 1½-inch pieces of clothesline rope with taped ends)

Directions: Contestants stand back to back, in middle of area. Referee says "Go," and counts as they slowly take six steps.

As soon as referee says "Six," contestants may turn and fire at opponents until their ammunition is exhausted or the referee says, "Hit!" and awards that duel to the winner scoring the hit.

Variation: *Water Gun Dueling*—Same as above, except water guns are used instead of blow guns. Duelists must wear poster paper hearts pinned over their actual hearts. To win, a hit must be scored on a heart.

104. Playground Sumo

Lead-in for teaching concept of Japanese Sumo wrestling, so the culture behind it can be understood. Good playground game for letting off steam also.

Age level: By age groups, 9-10, 11-12, 13-14, 15-16, 17 and up
Organizational level: Low
Number of players: 2
Supervision: None

Playing time: Free play
Space needed: Area 10' square, indoors or outdoors
Equipment: Chalk or rope to mark off a ring with 3' radius

Directions: Lay out 3' radius circle. Two competitors enter circle. Idea is to make the opponent lose balance or to force opponent out of the ring.

Bumps-a-Daisy Sumo—Contestants hold their ankles with their hands, then try to bump each other out of the circle with their bottoms. Anyone letting go of his ankles or falling to the ground loses, as well as anyone touching any part of his body outside the circle.

Rooster Fight Sumo—Contestants hold ankle of left leg behind them in right hand. Then try to bump each other out of the ring with their left shoulders. They cannot use their hands or let go of their legs. The loose hand must remain on the hip at all times. Any fault gives win to opponent.

Leg Hook Sumo—Contestants balance on one foot, extending the other out in front. Arms must remain behind the back, and cannot touch the ground. On signal contestants hook ankles of extended legs and try to wrestle opponent off balance or out of the ring.

Crab Sumo—Contestants sit on ground inside ring, then raise selves on hands and feet with the seat off the ground. On signal they try to wrestle or push opponent off balance or out of the ring. If any part of the body but the hands and feet touch the ground, it is a loss.

Tournaments in any of the above may be set up by holding elimination matches in the age groups mentioned.

Free-for-all tournaments may also be held, taking a lot less time. Up to 20 contestants are put into a large ring (about 25' radius) and everyone tries to upset all the others or push them out of the ring. A different contest is held for each type Sumo, of course. Winner is the last one legally upright inside the circle. If a contest goes 5 minutes without a winner, the contestants should be given a 3-minute rest period, then moved to a smaller circle (size depending upon how many contestants are left).

105. Push Duel

Strength contest

Age level: 8 and up
Number of players: 1 on 1, though teams can compete against each other, too
Supervision: Referee
Playing time: Approximately 10 minutes per

contest; if teams are competing, several can go at same time
Space needed: Area 10-12' × 4-6', with end boundaries marked
Equipment: None

Directions: Opponents face each other from an arm's length away. Put arms out in front of body, hands so palms face opponent. Opponents place palms of both hands together and, on signal, try to push each other back over an end line.

Variation: *Pool Push* — As a water game, this can be played with flutterboard, or other piece of wood that will float, between contestants. They put their hands against this and kick their feet, trying to push the opponent back over preset boundary line.

This may also be played by two-person teams, both teammates pushing the flutterboard, side by side, or one teammate holding around the waist of the other and kicking.

106. Indian Dueling
(or Where Are You, Moriarity?)

Rowdy variation of Blind Man's Bluff

Age level: 10 and up

Organizational level: Low

Number of players: 1 on 1, though tournaments can be held by elimination

Supervision: None informally, referee otherwise

Playing time: 10 minutes per duel

Space needed: Area 10' × 10' indoors or outdoors

Equipment: 6' length of rope, loosely rolled-up newspaper (six pages)

Directions: Combatants lay side by side, feet to heads, with the hands next to each other tied with the ends of the six-foot rope.

Decide who is "It." He is blindfolded, after being given the "swat," the rolled-up newspaper.

On "Go" signal It tries to swat his opponent (getting six tries), while the opponent can move anywhere the rope will let him to keep away from the swats. He must make a sound, like a grunt, after each swat, however, to aid It.

Players change places after a hit or after It has missed six times. Match can go three or five games, with winner being the one with the most hits total.

Variations: Same positioning, but both players blindfolded and given rolled-up papers. Both may move about to avoid hits, while at same time trying to hit opponent. First hit is winner.

In another variation opponents, both blindfolded but standing up, are tied together. Each gets a rolled-up newspaper, and they try to swat the opponent as many times as possible, while keeping from getting swatted themselves, over a three-minute time period. Referee-scorekeeper needed here.

Game source: Modified from an 18th century game.

107. Swat the Dancing Bear

Adds an active fun bit to the old game of tag

Age level: 6 and up

Organizational level: Low

Number of players: 6–10 ideal, more possible

Supervision: None

Playing time: 20–30 minutes

Space needed: 20-foot circle, inside or outside

Equipment: Section of rope 10–12' long, rolled sections of newspaper (6–8 pages) for each player except "bear" and "keeper"

Directions: "Bear" and "keeper" are selected. Bear has rope tied around waist, Keeper holds other end. Both must stay inside 20' circle (more players, larger circle), the other players can leave circle.

Players try to swat bear with paper rolls, while bear tries to dance out of their way and keeper tries to tag swatters.

Tagged swatters are out of game. Last one to remain is winner.

Start over with first one tagged becoming the bear and last one in the game the keeper.

Game source: Adapted from game of grandpa's day.

108. Horse Hassle

Method of making a pillow fight into a game

Age level: 8 and up
Organizational level: Low
Number of players: 1 on 1, elimination
Supervision: None informally, referee in competition
Playing time: About 5 minutes per contest; elimination tournament depends on number of contestants
Space needed: Soft ground area 20′ × 20′

Equipment: 2 large pillows (or commercial Pillo-paddles available from U.S. Games Co.), kitchen stepladder (for mounting horse), tumbling mats (if played inside), 1 oversize competition sawhorse (4–6′ tall, long enough to hold two riders, with smooth 6′-long saddle piece securely fastened by tape)

Directions: Two opponents sit astride the sawhorse facing each other, each with pillow in hand. On "Go" signal, each tries to knock the other off, using only the pillows. No personal contact is allowed. If both go off, the one touching the ground last is the winner.

Variation: *Mud Bath*—Same game, but held with sawhorse over a mud bog or in shallow water. Pillows would have to be foam, cleanable after each dipping in the mud. *Elimination Rodeo*—Two groups, such as scout troops or playground groups, may compete by matching age-group competitors, as in a boxing tournament, in an elimination "rodeo." Each match winner would earn his group a point.

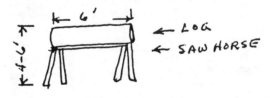

Game source: Adapted from Scottish Highland Games.

109. Push-O-War

Age level: All ages
Number of players: Any number that can be equally divided

Space needed: Field or large gym
Equipment: Several large surplus weather balloons

Directions: Divide group into two equal teams.

Referee places balloon in center of field. Teams line up at opposite ends of playing field.

On command by referee, teams rush to balloon and try to advance it to the opposition's goal line, while at the same time keeping their opponents from advancing it toward their goal line. The balloon may be advanced by pushing, punching, heading, etc., but cannot be kicked or carried. (Several balloons are necessary, since they don't stand up too well under this type use.)

Winning team is the one to be ahead on goals at the end of a pre-decided time limit, or to reach a pre-specified number of goals.

110. Pushball

Team strength game

Age level: 12 and up
Organizational level: Low
Number of players: 2 sides, 10–50 per side
Supervision: Referee
Playing time: Varies greatly, 20–60 minutes before teams will tire; or 4 10-minute periods
Space needed: Field 40–50 yards wide by 80–100 yards long; does not have to be

smooth or free of hazards, like trees, small ponds, etc.
Equipment: Large pushball, standing 5′ or more in height when inflated (weather balloons can be used, but they break easily, so several have to be kept on hand, and they must be used in area free of impediments that will puncture them)

Directions: Objective is for one team to propel the ball over the other team's goalline, by pushing, rolling, passing, carrying, etc., (no kicking), after it has been placed at midfield.

If using quarters, ball remains dead where it ended up at end of first period, and same at end of third period. Second half starts again at midfield.

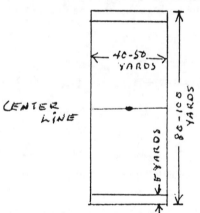

Players may interfere with opponents by getting in front of them, bumping with shoulders, etc., but no hitting, clutching, clipping or other potentially dangerous actions.

If ball goes out of bounds, teams line up at right angles to the sideline, 10 feet apart, and the referee rolls the ball inbounds. On his whistle, teams again commence play.

When a ball, any part of it, crosses a goal line, it is a 3-point score. Then scoring team may try for extra point. Ball is placed on the five-yard line and, on referee's signal, play resumes for one minute. If score is made, it counts one point more. Defending team cannot score during this extra-point period. (Only one offensive team player may have hands on the ball to start an extra-point period. Defending team must be one yard back from the ball.)

Game source: Modified from U.S. Navy Recreation & Welfare sports booklet, out of print.

111. Team Bar Wrestling

Strength game, with strategy involved, and teamwork

Age level: 10 and up, by age and size
Organizational level: Low

Number of players: 2 teams, 2–6 per team
Supervision: Referee

Playing time: Varies widely; can set up time periods, from 10–15 minutes

Equipment: Strong wooden bar about 2″ diameter, (softball bat will do for 1 on 1, and cut-off broom handle for more players)

Directions: Team captains line up over the center line, with other teammates 15 feet behind them. On referee signal, the two captains wrestle the stick, trying to pull it, and the opposing player, back over his goal line. Twenty seconds after the first signal, the referee signals again and the other players may help their captains.

All players must either keep their hands on the bar or on a teammate, as they tug, push, twist the bar. The team wins that can maneuver its opposing team back over their goal line, or has the bar  TEAM BAR WRESTLE. furthest in their territory at the end of a given time period.

Player letting go the bar or a teammate to interfere with an opponent is banished from the contest, and his teammates must continue without him.

Game source: Modified from U.S. Navy Recreation & Welfare Sport booklet, out of print.

112. Hot Spot

Variation of tug-of-war where
everyone competes against everyone else

Age level: 8 and up
Organizational level: Low
Number of players: 4–12
Supervision: None, referee for formal contests
Playing time: About 15 minutes per contest

Space needed: Any space 30′ × 30′ or so, indoors or outdoors
Equipment: Circle of stones, sticks or whatever is available, number depending on number of players, thus size of ring formed

Directions: Players form ring around the mid-stone, or mid-ring of stones, clasp hands tightly with players on either side. On "Go," players try to pull, push and otherwise maneuver other players—without unclasping their hands—so others' feet touch the mid-ring "hot spot."

Player who touches the hot spot is "burned-out" of play. Person who unclasps hands from circle is also out of play.

Players may join with others, ganging up on one or more, to get them out. But the last player left is the winner.

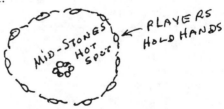

Variation: *Bumper Hot Spot*—Same game, except players bend over, grasp their ankles and, on go signal, try to use backsides to bump opponents out of a circle.

113. Tethered Dodgeball

A unique new game to try

Age level: 8 and up
Organizational level: Low
Number of players: 2 teams; 2–6 each
Supervision: Referee
Playing time: Avg. 15–20 minutes per game

Space needed: Space for a 50′ diameter circle, indoors or outside
Equipment: Tetherball with rope on it, (or football, basketball or plastic Whiffleball with laces attached to 2′ rope), two 8′ ropes

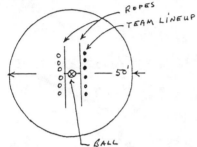

Directions: Attach both rope lengths to tetherball so ball dangles from middle of each rope length.

Teams line up opposite each other, facing the ball in the middle, with one rope held by one team, the other held by the other team. Team members hold the ropes along their lengths, holding them taut so ball is suspended.

On "Go" signal, both teams try to manipulate their rope—by pulling, releasing quickly, turning, etc.—to make a member of the opposite team come in contact with the ball. The team which the ball touches loses.

114. Arm Wrestling

Strength contest

Age level: 8–10, 11–13, 14–16, 17–19, 20 and up
Organizational level: Medium
Number of players: Two at a time
Supervision: Referee
Playing time: 5 minutes per contest, tournament can take all day

Space needed: Area large enough for special table equipment and chairs, about 20′ × 20′
Equipment: Table, arm wrestling platform (commercial [made by International Arm Wrestler Co., 228 N. Garfield, Box B, Monterey Park, CA 91754] or crafted), 2 armless chairs (for sitting competition)

Directions: Two contestants face each other from opposite sides of the table. They grip arm wrestling platform as shown in illustration.

If either contestant releases grip on the upright bar or base handle, he loses. If he moves his elbow out from between the elbow strips during the competition, he loses. If he lifts his elbow off the base, he loses. If one contestant forces the other's hand down to the base, he wins.

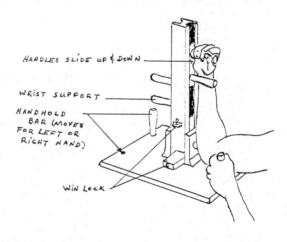

115. Greek Tug-of-War

Test of strength between two people. Spinoff from standard tug-of-war.

Age level: 14 and up
Organizational level: Low
Number of players: 2
Supervision: None
Playing time: Varies, free play

Space needed: Circle with 20' radius
Equipment: 15' pole (at least 6" radius), 40'
length of rope (preferably unbreakable
nylon), gloves (for participants with tender
hands)

Directions: Pole must be securely anchored in ground, as in cement. (It is usually a permanent piece of game equipment mounted on a playground, schoolground or in a picnic area or park area.) Either a notch is cut in the top of it or a hole is bored through the end about 8" down from the top, large enough so the rope slips easily through it. Rope is threaded through the hole with an equal length hanging free on each side.

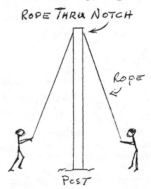

Contestants hold opposite ends of rope and on "Go" signal they try to pull each other until one either lets go or is dragged right up the pole.

Variations: *Tug-on-a-Bend* — Smaller, younger contestants may compete by bending the rope around the side of the post, rather than putting it over the top, as a safety factor. *Blind Tug-o-War* — Rope is bent around a corner of a building so two groups of pullers can't see each other. This allows strategic jerks and releases in trying to unbalance the opponents. *Surf Tug-o-War* — A tug-of-war in waist deep water is a novel experience. The buoyancy of the water makes footholds hard to establish.

116. Pony Jumping (Pony Express)

Rowdy, let-off-steam type activity for hardier children

Age level: 10 and up, depending on size and
fitness
Organizational level: Low
Number of players: 2 teams; 3–5 each, or
elimination team tournament
Supervision: None informally, umpire otherwise

Playing time: 20–30 minutes per contest
Space needed: Area 10' × 20–30', preferably
on soft ground or tumbling mats
Equipment: None

Directions: Flip coin for which team becomes "pony" first, and which the "riders."

Pony team lines up, single file, with each one holding around the hips or waist of the one in front, with the front person bracing against a wall.

Riders take turns running at the ponies and vaulting or leaping onto their backs, trying to break them down by their combined weights. If "pony" is forced to its knees at any point, or any part of it has to break its hold on another, the riders win the "half." If the pony withstands the riders, it wins the half.

Then teams exchange places. If each team wins a "half," game is a tie. If one team wins both halves, it is the winner.

Variation: *Pony Vault* — Pony does not brace against a wall, but can brace or lay over a small table or vaulting horse. Riders, instead of trying to break down the pony, take a run, put their hands on the hips of the last player in the pony, and try to vault over as many of the pony players as possible. He doesn't remain on top of the pony. He earns as many points as the number of players he vaulted over. Team's total is number of players all members of the team vaulted over. Teams change sides. Winner is team with highest score of vault-overs.

Game source: Adapted from old children's game originally called "Johnny on the Pony," popularized at English prep schools.

117. Gang Rush

Rough-house conditioning game, useful for
football, rugby, lacrosse, etc., team conditioning

Age level: High school and over
Organizational level: Low
Number of players: 2 sides; 4–50 each
Supervision: Referee
Playing time: Varies with number and skills
of players. Best to play to a time limit, or
2 halves of 15–20 minutes each.
Space needed: Field 75′ × 100′ or larger
Equipment: None

Directions: Decide attack and defense teams. Attack team lines up along its goal line. Defense team lines up across the center line.

On referee signal the attack team attempts to get its players past the defenders and over their goal line. One point is scored for every person across. (A player is across if most of his body is across the line.)

At halftime, teams exchange roles.

Winning team is one with most points at end of contest.

Defense players may catch, hold, block out-of-bounds or push attack players back over their own goal line. Those pushed out of bounds or back over their own goal line are out of the game at that pont, until the half.

Attack players who score cannot re-enter the game, until the half. They cannot help teammates from the sidelines or end zone either.

Variation: *Two-Way Gang Rush* — Both teams line up across their own goal lines. On "go" they both try to push, pull, carry or otherwise get opponents back over their own goal line. Other rules same.

Game source: Modified from U.S. Navy games booklet, out of print.

118. Battleball

Helps throwing accuracy; good active game for "letting off steam"

Age level: 8 and up
Organizational level: Low
Number of players: 2 teams; 4–20 each
Supervision: Referee
Playing time: Average 30 minutes per game
Space needed: Small gym or multipurpose room, or even a cleared hallway. If outside, should be between two buildings (to use walls as backstops).
Equipment: 6 volleyballs or beachballs or large Whiffleballs, 12 plastic bowling pins or Indian clubs (or gallon plastic milk or juice jugs, or wooden blocks 4″ × 4″ and 14″ high).

Directions: Select teams. Line equal number of pins along each opponent's wall, two feet out from the wall. Line balls up midway between teams.

On "go" signal, players race for balls and try to throw them to knock over opponent's pins. But they can't cross midline. Balls can be blocked and caught, and recovered and thrown again. Winner is team knocking all opponent's pins down first, or one with least of its own pins down at the end of time limit.

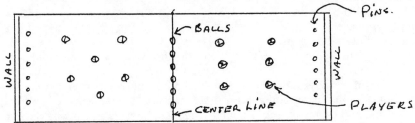

Variation: *Knockout* — Eliminate pins. Players, after racing for balls, try to hit opponents with thrown or bounced or caromed-off-wall balls. Hit players are out of the game and must go to the sidelines. Team with last player or players on court is winner.

Game may be made to last longer by putting in a rule that any two opposing players on the sideline may rejoin the game at the same time. This makes it much harder to win.

Game also may be changed with a rule that players hit have to join the side that hit them, every time they are hit. This also makes for a longer game.

Game source: Adapted from Watts, CA, High School P.E. Department, early 1960s. Other modifications from Jim Dyer, while at Navy Special Services School.

119. Battleball II

Good game to "let off steam," with lots of exercise in a relatively short period of time. Many people can play in relatively small area with minimal equipment and supervision.

Age level: 8 and up
Organizationl level: Low
Number of players: Depends on how many balls are available, 2 players to a ball; 2 teams, even number to a side
Supervision: Referee-scorekeeper, pin setters
Playing time: Varies with ages and skills of participants and number playing

Space needed: Indoors or outside, 25' × 50' minimum
Equipment: 6 pins (Indian clubs, 16"-high blocks of 4-by-4 wood, or quart milk containers), 2 posts 5' tall (badminton net or high jump standards or just wooden poles driven into the ground), 26' length of string, old volley balls or playground balls of like size, 1 for every 2 players

Directions: Divide players into two teams, decide which team will bowl first. Teams go to bowling areas opposite each other for play.

Players on bowling side, in turn, throw or bowl balls at the center goal line. Points are scored thus: 1 point for a ball going across the line and under the 5' string-line without hitting a pin, 3 points for hitting a pin (and an extra 3 for a carom into a second pin), and 5 points for going over the line above the pins but under the 5' string-line. Team's points are totalled after each player has had a turn. Then the other team bowls. Team with highest total after both have had their turns wins.

Fouls: Throwing a ball twice in the same turn, going over the safety line while bowling, or bowling from outside the bowling area boundaries. Each foul subtracts a point from the team's total, and the throw does not count and is not allowed over.

Variations: *(1)* Same game, except that bowlers must call what they are aiming at before they bowl. If they score other than what they called, they earn only half value. *(2)* If playing area is not large enough, both teams may use the same playing court, taking turns. But the waiting team must then serve as ball chasers and pin setters. *(3)* Game variation #2 may also be changed by playing with the goal line 2' out from a wall, with the pins set on the line. The 5' restraining line could be marked by chalk on the wall. Wall caroms would be part of the acceptable play. Same rules otherwise. *(4) Blocking Battleball* — Played against wall as above. Team not bowling, however, stands between bowling team members and the pins and tries to block balls thrown or bowled. Game can be played allowing each ball only one turn, or rebounding balls may be played over as often as the bowling team members can reach them without going into the safety zone. When all the balls have been removed from play the game would be over. Game may also be played to a time limit (10 minutes per side) with balls thrown as often as bowling team members can regain them and take them back into the bowling area for replay. *(5) Bonkers Battleball* — Eliminate the pins from game variation #4. Bowlers try to hit other team members standing in the safety zone. Every hit is a point. Balls may be recovered and reused, but not thrown from inside the safety zone or from outside the bowling area. Play to 5 minutes, then change sides, with bowlers becoming the dodgers. *(a)* Variation of the above is to have hit players leave the game, until only one remains as the winner. Time is

kept for how long it takes to put all team members out. Then teams switch, with
bowlers becoming dodgers. Winning team is one taking least time to knock out
the other team's players. As an added attraction, the champion from each team

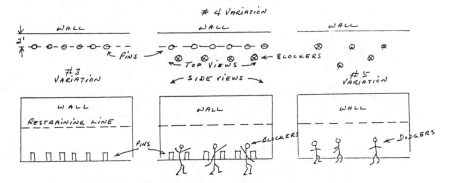

can go into the zone, with everyone throwing at them, to see which is the overall
champion. This should be two out of three tries.

Game source: Basic game invented by Dr. D. A. Sargent of Harvard, according to G. A. Gipe
in "Yesterday," *Sports Illustrated* Magazine, January 1976. A modified version was played in
Watts, CA high school phys ed department about 1957–8.

120. Blindfold Smoker

Boxing event for novices

Age level: 6–7, 8–9, 10–11, 12–13, 14–15,
16–17, 18 and up
Organizational level: High
Number of players: 1 on 1, or teams, elimination tournament
Supervision: Referee, 3 judges, timekeeper,
seconds for all boxers, doctor in attendance
or on call
Playing time: Varies greatly: 3 1-minute
rounds for 6–11 ages, 3 2-minute rounds for

12–17, and 3 3-minute rounds for others, all
with one minute rests between rounds
Space needed: Small boxing ring for 15 and
under, larger one for 16 and up
Equipment: Large size padded boxing gloves
for all contestants, headgear and mouth-
pieces for all, athletic cups for all, 2 corner
stools, bell, stop clock, boxers wear tennis
or boxing shoes, 4 blindfold cloths

Directions: Boxers blindfolded. On bell, they try to hit opponents, with seconds
trying to give them directions where and how to find them. Basic boxing rules
followed.

If a knockdown is scored, it's a point for the winner's team. If a boxer
swings so hard he falls down, he loses and a point goes to opponent. Judges
decide winners on points otherwise. Winning team is one with most wins.

Variation: *Gang Bang (or Free-for-Brawl)*—Four to six boxers in ring
at same time, blindfolded, with each trying to be the last one standing in the
ring. Two team seconds are allowed to call directions, from diagonally opposite corners. As boxers are downed or disqualified, they must leave the
ring.

Variation on this, would be team gang-bang, where seconds try to give
directions so teammates don't hit each other. Boxers may give identification

calls, while boxing, for same reason. Once all members of one team have been
eliminated, the other team becomes winner.

HAND STRIKING & THROWING GAMES

121. Bird-on-a-Rock

*Variation of the simple target game of throwing stones to
knock a tin can off of a rock, adapted to a game using marbles*

Age level: 8 and up
Organizational level: Low
Number of players: 2–6 per ring
Supervision: None
Playing time: 20 minutes per game

Space needed: 3′ radius ring, on ground or
carpet
Equipment: 1 distinctive marble for target,
1 golf tee to put it on, 3′ length of string to
mark circle with, and shooting marbles for
each player

Directions: Players take turns shooting from behind the edge of the circle trying
to knock the target marble off the tee so it rebounds outside the circle. It is
replaced on the tee after ever unsuccessful try.

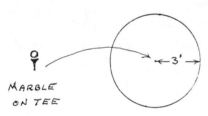

MARBLE
ON TEE

First person to accomplish this 5
times (with 2–3 players), or 4 times
(with 4–5 players), or 3 times (with 6
players), is winner.

In campout situations, small pebbles may be used to play this game.
Make it a treasure hunt to find the
nearly round ones that can be used.

Game source: Adapted from an old game from Granddad's childhood.

122. Two-Up

A gussied-up coin-matching game; good as a money raiser

Age level: 8 and up
Organizational level: Low
Number of players: Any number
Supervision: Banker
Playing time: Quick games, so play may be
open-ended, continuous

Space needed: 10′ × 10′ area
Equipment: 2 coins (same type), wooden
spatula-shaped coin holder ("kip") (or
kitchen spatula will work)

Directions: Both coins are tossed overhead at the same time from the "kip" by
one person (the "spinner"), who may be anyone, but changed every few tosses.

Participants bet play money (or chips, or pebbles) on how the coins will come down—2 heads or 2 tails. If they show 1 head and 1 tail, the "bank" wins. Otherwise, the bank pays winners the amount they bet (and they get their bet amount back, too).

Coins must be placed on kip showing one head, one tail before each toss. Tosses must rise 3' over the head of the spinner, turn completely over at least once in the air and fall free to the floor without touching anyone before coming to rest. A blanket may be layed down to keep the coins from rolling.

Game source: Unofficial national game of Australia, according to *Sports Illustrated* of May, 1981. It's believed to have been taken by the first European settlers there—British convicts transported there at the turn of the 19th century. It was carried into World War I by Australian troops and became a common soldier's game, playing for "smokes" and coins.

123. Ring-a-Balloon
Carnival type game

Age level: 10 and up
Organizational level: Medium
Number of players: Any number, in sequence
Supervision: Play leader
Playing time: 10 minutes

Space needed: 4' × 7' area, or carnival booth
Equipment: 10 long balloons (plus extras for breakage), 10 clothes pins, marking pen, 12 cardboard strips 20" long × 1" wide, glue

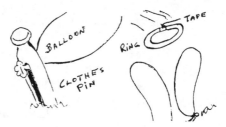

Directions: Glue rings, blow up 10 balloons and number them as shown in figure 1, then anchor them in the ground as shown in figure 2 (for design and method).

Each player tosses 6 rings while standing at the foul line. Numbers on the balloons are how many points are awarded for ringing them. Winner has highest total score.

124. Ring-Tac-Toe
Active variation of the paper-and-pencil game of tick-tac-toe

Age level: 6 and up
Organizational level: Low
Number of players: 2–4, play individually or as teams
Playing time: About 5–10 minutes per game

Space needed: 6' × 6' area, indoors or out
Equipment: 4 sticks 3' long each, 6 cardboard cutout rings (about 4" diameter) and 6 cut out crosses (same size)

Directions: Lay out sticks across each other to form tic-tac-toe formation. One player (or team) gets the circles, the other gets the crosses. Players, or teams, take turns tossing from 4–5' away, one at a time, trying to toss their pieces so as to form 3 in a row in any direction (a tic-tac-toe).

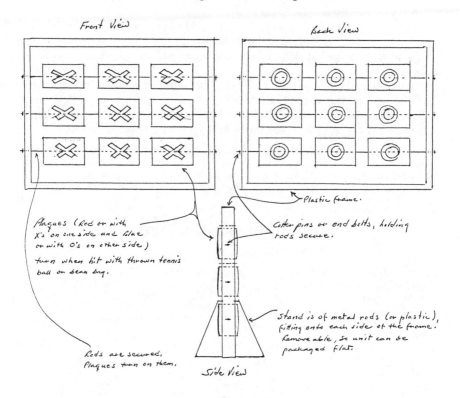

Front View

Back View

Plastic frame.

Plaques (Red or with
X's on one side and blue
or with O's on other side)
turn when hit with thrown tennis
ball on bean bag.

Cotter pins or end bolts, holding
rods secure.

Rods are secured,
Plaques turn on them.

Stand is of metal rods (or plastic),
fitting onto each side of the frame.
Removeable, so unit can be
packaged flat.

Side View

Diagram 1

If a player tosses his piece into the same square with an opponent's piece, both are removed. Turns are continued, using unsuccessfully thrown pieces, over and over until a tic-tac-toe is made.

Variations: *Peg-a-Tac-Toe* — Stick 9 pegs into the ground, each one representing a square for tic-tac-toe. Each player has 6 or more rings (cardboard cutouts, or twisted wire), colored differently. Players take turns trying to ring 3 pegs in a row in any direction. *Toss-a-Tac-Toe* — Same basic game, except an upright board is constructed with nails or L-shaped picture frame holders nailed in center of each tic-tac-toe square. Players try to throw rings (Mason jar rings, cardboard cutouts or twisted wire) to form a tic-tac-toe in any direction on the board from 5' away. *Sock-a-Tac-Toe* — Same basic game. Players throw beanbags, or tennis balls, at a target board with flip-flop sections (constructed as shown in diagram 1.)

Game is played by two persons (or two teams, with individuals taking turns) throwing tennis balls or bean bags from about 15' away and trying to score a tic-tac-toe (three reds or Xs against three blues or Os in a row in any direction).

All plaques on the board are turned crosswise to board, so only ends are seen to begin game. Balls and bags may be thrown to come "down" onto a plaque to turn it. Balls may also be bounced before contacting the plaques.

If ball or bag misses the board, or only partially turns a plaque, the throw still counts and the plaque remains as it is until another throw by anyone, in turn, changes it.

Opposing players may throw at and turn each other's plaques as often as they can while maintaining turns. If a player turns his own plaque by mistake, benefiting his opponent, that is still his turn and the hit stands.

The winner is the person, or team, getting three red plaques (or X marked ones) or three blue plaques (or O marked ones) in a row in any direction. They must all be clearly visible, turned past the halfway mark between plaque colors.

125. Ring-a-King-Tac-Toe

Age level: 8 and up
Organizational level: Low
Number of players: 2–4
Supervision: None
Space needed: 6′ × 6′ area, indoors or outdoors

Equipment: 12″ × 12″ board, 18 nails, hammer, 16 rings (jar rings, cardboard cutouts, or twisted wire), 8 each of 2 different colors, wire for hanging up board

Directions: Prepare your playing board (see fig. 1).

Play Tic-Tac-Toe by ringing *four* nails in any direction from 6–10′ away, depending upon age of players.

Game can be played by two-person teams, with partners taking turns on each side.

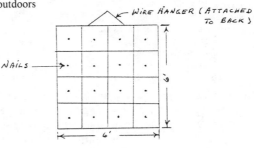

FRONT VIEW

126. Super Ring-a-Tac-Toe

Action variation of tic-tac-toe paper-and-pencil game;
has advantage of allowing players to handcraft their playing materials

Age level: 6 and up
Organizational level: Low
Number of players: 2–4, playing individually or as teams
Supervision: None
Playing time: About 10 minutes per game
Space needed: 6′ × 6′ area or larger, in or out

Equipment: 2 egg cartons, 18 pencils or used ball point stick pens (or all identical wooden pegs, or large nails), 18 or more 4″ diameter rings, 9 of one color and 9 of another color (cardboard cutouts, twisted wire or rubber bands cut from an innertube), glue

Directions: Glue the two egg cartons together at one side, as they lay upside down, lids removed. Then push pencils, or pegs, into the bottoms of the container's egg pouches as shown in figure 1 (on next page), but arrange them in the design shown by dots in figure 2. The advantage of this design is that more than one game may be played, with 2 or 3 completed tic-tac-toes required for a game win.

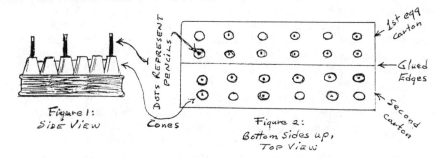

Figure I:
SIDE VIEW

DOTS REPRESENT PENCILS

Cones

Figure 2:
Bottom Sides up,
TOP VIEW

1st egg carton

Glued Edges

Second carton

Pouches with pegs in them may be colored to make them more visible.

Larger egg cartons may be used (18-egg pouches), if wished, with pegs continued in the same order.

127. Ring Scrabble

Turns action into word-play

Age level: 10 and up
Organizational level: High
Number of players: 2, or teams of 2–4
Supervision: Referee-recorder
Playing time: 10–20 minutes
Space needed: 6′ × 8′ area
Equipment: Playing board. (Cut plywood

piece to size for 4 lines of seven 3″ squares. In random order, print each letter of the alphabet in the squares. In the 2 extra squares, print "Free Letter." Stick L-screws into the middle of each square.) Supply of 50 Mason jar rings (or rings cut flat from innertubes), paper and pencil.

Directions: Players take turns throwing rings from 5′ away, each trying to ultimately spell a word by ringing the necessary letters on the board. The referee-recorder keeps a running account of letters rung by each player. A player may change the word he's been attempting to spell at any time (in case he rings wrong letters). Player ringing the first word, at least 6 letters long, is winner. Referee is final judge on words and spellings.

128. Poker Toss

Teaches a card game while also playing a targeting game

Age level: 10 and up
Organizational level: Low
Number of player: 2–10
Supervision: Umpire-ring caddy
Playing time: 10–15 minutes per game
Space needed: 6′ × 8′ area, indoors or out
Equipment: Pack of old Bridge playing

cards, 52 nails, 5 rings (rubber canning washers, drape hanging rings, wire loops 3–4″ diameter), piece of plywood or corrugated cardboard large enough to hold 52 playing cards exposed face up (about 3′ × 3′), hammer

Directions: Lay cards on board in haphazard order. Nail each one through the center, leaving the nail sticking up at least 2″. Board can be layed flat or hung on a wall, fence or chair.

Players stand 6–8′ from the board and take turns tossing five rings at the board, trying to ring the nails in the cards that will form the best possible poker hand—3 or 4 of a kind, full house (3 of one denomination, 2 of another), a "run" (cards in sequence order), a "flush" (5 cards in same suit), "royal flush" (a 5 card run in same suit).

129. Dart Baseball

*A target game that can be handcrafted and
teach the basics of baseball to novices*

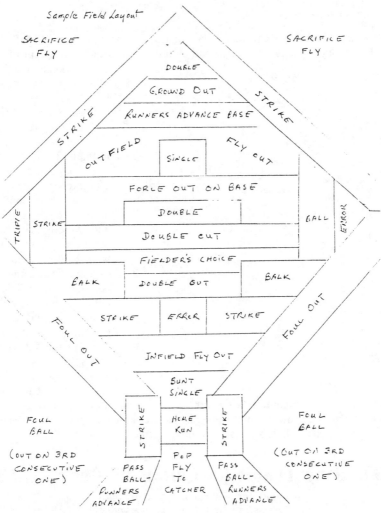

Sample Field Layout

Age level: 10 and up
Organizational level: Medium
Number of players: 1 on 1, or 2 teams with members taking turns throwing darts
Supervision: Play leader (to oversee making and use of darts), scorekeeper

Playing time: Depending on skill of dart throwers, 30–90 mins.
Space needed: 6′ × 8′ area with a wall (or fence, or picnic table or other place to hang target board)

Equipment: Baseball dart board (made from large sheet (3′ × 3′) of corrugated cardboard), baseball diamond (marked on another piece of cardboard, 1′ × 1′, scoresheet (see diagram 2), 4 buttons, 4 or more darts (commercial, or made from wooden match sticks and needles, scotch tape and paper strips (see directions), 1′ length wire as hanger), knife

TEAM	SCORE BY INNINGS									TOTALS		
	1	2	3	4	5	6	7	8	9	R	H	E
HOME												
VISITOR												

Figure 2: Scoresheet

Directions: Mark 3′ × 3′ cardboard dart board as shown in figure 1. Mark 1′ × 1′ cardboard playing field with a baseball diamond, showing 4 bases. Buttons will be to keep track of players on base by scorekeeper.

Make scoresheet as shown in figure 2.

Make darts as shown in figure 3.

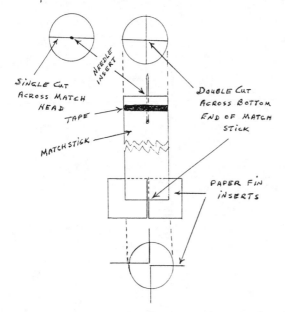

Figure 3: DART MAKING

SINGLE CUT ACROSS MATCH HEAD

TAPE

MATCH STICK

NEEDLE INSERT

DOUBLE CUT ACROSS BOTTOM END OF MATCH STICK

PAPER FIN INSERTS

To make darts, scrape off match tip, then make one cut from that end about ½″ lengthwise, and two cross cuts in the other end, also lengthwise. Insert the hole end of a needle into the head cut and tape around the match tightly to hold it securely in place. Insert the edges of two 1″ × ½″ slips of paper into the tail cuts so they form "fins."

Game is played with one team at bat (throwing the darts at the game board) and the other team in the field (keeping the scoresheet and the buttons on the playing field board according to what the darts indicate). Use basic baseball rules, 9-inning game.

130. Ring Tennis (or Quoits or Deck Tennis)

Invented for play aboard decks of ships . . .
no ball to bounce or roll overboard.
Involves very subtle and entirely different
throwing skills from any other game.

Age level: 10 and up
Organizational level: Low
Number of players: 2 or 4, singles or doubles

Supervision: Umpire-scorekeeper for competition, none for free play

Playing time: Game of 21 points

Space needed: Badminton court, though court size can be varied to suit area available, and size and skill of players. Inside or outside. Can also be played in shallow water.

Equipment: Rubber ring (though a rope quoit can also be used), badminton net (or string with newspaper folded over it), and net standards (commercial equipment is available from U.S. Games Co., General Sportcraft Co., and the Voit Company)

Directions: Idea is to throw the ring back and forth over the net, trying to place it so the opponent cannot reach it or cannot return it fairly into the opposite court.

The main rule that makes this throwing game different from all others is that the ring must be caught and returned in the same continuous motion, *without direct reversal of the arm* (breaking of the elbow).

This leads to such returns as catching the ring on the right side of the body, continuing to pivot the body and releasing the ring, while backwards to the net, from the rear of the hand, or catching the ring with the heel of the hand forward and returning it by flipping the hand in a U-motion so it leaves the hand from the front of the hand.

The ring must be thrown so it does not wobble unnecessarily, in order that it cannot be caught by the opponent. It may be thrown either vertically or horizontally, though. It can be played with either hand, but only one hand at a time. It must be caught cleanly, not juggled, before returning. It cannot touch any other part of the body except the hands.

Faulting any of the above rules gives the point to the opponent. Points are made by legally throwing the ring into the opponent's court so it cannot be returned, or so it touches the opponent before it goes out of bounds.

The net should be high enough so neither player may throw the ring over the net at a downward trajectory (a slam). This height varies with the size of the competitors, though 7 feet is usually adequate.

Only the server can score (or the server's team in doubles). If the server makes an error, the serve goes to the other side. Game is usually 21, though it can be varied to suit circumstances.

Variations: *Frisbee Tennis*—A type of Frisbee called a Whiz-Ring, which has a hole in the middle, may be used instead of the regular ring. Since it hovers longer and sails greater distances easier, the court area may be enlarged.

These may also be used for a team game—4, 5 or 6 to a side—if played on a volleyball court with a volleyball net. Rules stay the same.

Game source: Old English origin under the name Tenequoits (from tennis and quoits).

131. Flying Rings

Discover an unusual scientific principle
of flight— the gyroscopic action of spin-induced airflow—
by folding a sheet of paper "aerodynamically," or
using other common materials

Age level: 10 and up
Organizational level: Medium
Number of players: 1–20, individual or class
Supervision: Craft leader or teacher
Playing time: 15 minutes to craft; play, open
ended

Space needed: Table for crafting, 20′ × 20′
area for "flying" rings
Equipment: 8½″ × 11″ sheet of paper

Directions: For crafting rings, start with a fold of about ½″ on an 8½″ × 11″ sheet
of paper.

Continue folding in same direction until approximately 2½″ are left (approximately 8 to 10 folds give proper wing length).

Holding folded portion, bend A to B so that folds are on inside of cylinder.

Push one end between fold and top of paper at other end until proper
diameter is reached. Tape resulting seam with plastic tape. Round cylinder
out.

There is a clockwise spin and the cylinder is falling. The air flow is up.
Greater airflow on left (subtraction of flow on right side) causes lower air
pressure on left side. The cylinder moves left.

To throw, grasp in
hand as you would a
football and throw
overhand or sidearm,
or, grasp in hand with
front part (foldover
side) forward and toss
it underhand, with spin.

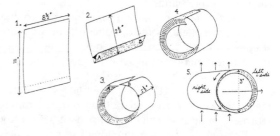

Game source: The first patent for a cylindrical flying
wing was granted in the 1920s, and another, in 1956, was licensed for "a full-scale rotary cylindrical wing" aircraft development. Toobee Toy Company, Berkeley, CA., in 1978 marketed a
toy "ring wing" made from the top 2″ of beer and soda cans.

132. Flying Horseshoes
Interesting variation on horseshoe pitching

Age level: 8 and up
Organizational level: Medium
Number of players: 2 on 2
Supervision: Referee—scorekeeper
Playing time: 21-point game, about 20
minutes

Space needed: 20′ × 30′ area (larger for older
players)
Equipment: 2 Whiz-Rings (commercial game
set available from General Sportcraft Co.),
4 2′-long round sticks with cross-pieces
(to delineate handles from rest of sticks)

Directions: Players must remain inside goal areas when catching and throwing
rings. If any player steps, or falls, outside these boundaries, a point is counted
for the opposing team.

Rings are thrown only from, and caught only on, sticks. No hand touching
of rings.

Rings are thrown between teammates. Opponents must each throw an equal
number of times to complete a game. If a throw by one player isn't caught on
the stick of his partner before it touches the ground, or either player moves out
of the goal zones in throwing or catching, a point is counted for the opposition.

Each caught ringer (Whiz-Ring on stick) counts 2 points for the team making it.

Variation: *Crash*—Same game, except player must score *exactly* 21 points to win. If he "crashes" (scores over 21 on one catch), he loses 10 points.

133. Flying Saucers

Target game good for picnic or campout situation, since materials used are available even there. Game is simple and any number may play.

Age level: 8 and up
Organizational level: Low
Number of players: 1–8, or more, depending upon availability of "saucers"
Playing time: 24–48 point games, about 20–30 minutes

Space needed: 8′ × 12′ area, or larger
Equipment: 8 paper or tinfoil plates or pie tins per player, 2 poles (7′-8′ long), 3 8′ lengths of string, ruler or tape measure

Directions: Set up playing field as in sketches.

Players write their names in their plates (or team names, if playing by teams). Establish order of play by flipping a plate. Players take turns throwing, skidding or skipping a plate (flying saucer) like a Frisbee, between one of the three scoring areas between strings (as designated in sketch). Winner is person, or team, with the highest point total for 8 throws, or, throw until one player reaches designated score (24 or 48).

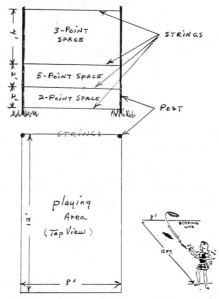

Variation: *Skidding Saucers*—Same basic game, except that scoring area is drawn out on the ground beyond the end of the 12′ throwing area, instead of being marked vertically by strings on posts.

Plates must be more than half inside an area to be counted. Opponent's plates may be "covered" for 1 bonus point (by tossing a plate so it covers more than half of an opponent's plate in any scoring, or non-scoring area). If a player's thrown plate knocks another onto a plate, the bonus point goes to whichever team's plate covers the other, regardless of the thrower's team. *Breaking Saucers*—Same game except to win a player, or team, must score exactly 25 points. If he goes over, he loses 10 points and must start from that new score. Or he can go on to 50 points (but, to win, he must then reach 50 before the others reach 25).

134. Pie-Pan (Frisbee) Horseshoes

Modified horseshoe-pitching game, substituting materials that can be found around the home so children can play it safely

Age level: 8 and up
Organizational level: Medium
Number of players: 1 on 1, 2 on 2
Supervision: None
Playing time: 15 or 21-point game, about 30 minutes

Space needed: 6' × 46' area
Equipment: 2 ring posts (commercially available through several mail order houses, such as Miles Kimball of Osh Kosh, WI, or made by bending wire coat hangers to shape), 4 Frisbees, or tinfoil pie plates

Directions: Stick wire hoops into ground at spots designated in sketch. Basic horseshoe pitching rules.

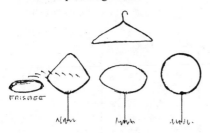

Fig. 1: Bend wire hangers as loops.

Players take turns throwing, skidding, or skipping 2 pie pans from one end of the court through the rings at the other end. A pie pan going through a ring counts 3 points, a pie pan that ends up leaning against a ring counts 2 points and a pie pan that ends up as close or closer to the ring than a pie pan's width away counts 1 point. First person to 15 or 21 points (pre-set) is winner.

Variations: *Bat Hunt*—Hooks are left on wire hangers so they may be hung from tree branches, clothesline, etc. Players pretend they are bat hunting in a forest, for example. A pie pan thrown through a ring is a "hit." Each player can carry 4–6 pie pans, and 6–8 hanger-loops may be hung at different places, and different heights around a yard or playground, to simulate a real hunt. *Miami Vice*—Same idea as above, except players are Miami Vice officers at a shoot out. Instead of hangers, cardboard faces or entire bodies of gangsters are placed around yard on playground, to be hunted and shot with pie pan Frisbees.

135. Frisbee Baseball

Age level: Elementary, junior and senior high age groups
Number of players: 9 to a team

Space needed: Outdoors, any open space the size of a small softball field
Equipment: Set of softball bases, 1 Frisbee

Directions: Game is played as in softball, except there is no pitcher. That position remains as an extra infielder, to field short throws.

Batter stands adjacent to home plate and uses the cross-chest throw of the Frisbee into the playing field. He then runs the bases as in softball.

In addition to the regular softball outs, two foul throws by a batter in succession will constitute an out. Leading off base is also an out.

Variation: For skilled players, the pitcher may be reinstated. The batter then would catch and return the Frisbee to the field in one single motion. Other play would remain the same.

136. Ring Tag

Learn eye-hand coordination in use of game implements

Age level: 10 and up
Organizational level: Low
Number of players: 2 teams, 2–12 each
Supervision: None informally, referee-score-keeper otherwise
Playing time: 15-point game
Space needed: 50 × 50 yards for 6 or more per side

Equipment: 3-foot length of broomstick (or equivalent) for each player, Whiz-Ring (Frisbee with hole in middle [commercially available from North Pacific Products, Inc., of Bend, OR; Olympic ring set, from General Sportcraft; Hoop-X and Fling-It from other companies])

Directions: Teams line up facing each other on opposite sides of the midline.

On signal, starting team player "throws" the Whiz-Ring across the midline into the opponent's court. All throws must be at least waist high. Penalty: on serve, re-serve; during play, point to opponent. Ring is thrown by whipping it off the end of the stick with a cross-body motion, to impart spin to it. All catches and throws must be made from sticks. No hand help.

Scoring: If ring is thrown out of bounds or doesn't get across the midline or is thrown below waistline to opponent, the thrower loses a point. The catcher loses a point if he doesn't catch the ring legally on his stick before it touches the ground, if he touches it with his hand while it's in play, if he (or his stick) touches it in fair territory, but catches it with his body out of bounds.

Variations: *Double Ring Tag* — Same game, using 2 or 3 rings at the same time. *Elimination Ring Tag* — Same game, but with rule that a player who makes an illegal throw or misses a catch is eliminated from the game. Last player on the field is the winner. (The player closest to a missed catch that hits the ground inbounds is out, whether he actually plays the ring or not.)

Game source: Based on an old Italian game.

137. Frisbee Volleyball

Adapts Frisbee-flying skills to volleyball

Age level: 10 and up
Organizational level: Medium
Number of players: 2 teams, 6 each
Supervision: Referee and scorekeeper
Playing time: 21-point game, about 30 minutes

Space needed: Volleyball court (or basketball court with net or rope tied across mid point at 8′ height)
Equipment: Frisbee, volleyball net and posts

Directions: Basic volleyball rules, except Frisbee is used in place of ball. It must be caught and released again in one continuous motion, being passed to a teammate or back over the net. Three people can handle it before it must be returned over the net.

If playing singles on a smaller court, only one touch per player is allowed before the Frisbee must be returned.

138. Flying Saucers Skill Tournament

Tests Frisbee throwing skills

Age level: 8–12, 13–17, 18 and up
Organizational level: High
Number of players: Open
Supervision: Referee, sign-up clerk, field judges, recorders (to keep distances, placings and points) and Frisbee shaggers
Playing time: Depends on number of participants, can take all day
Space needed: Baseball, or other large field, with bleachers for spectators and waiting competitors

Equipment: Public address system, lime liner (to mark field), string (for marking circles), whistles for referee and field judges, clipboards, paper, pencils (for all recorders and sign-up clerk), 3 measuring tapes, 20 or so Frisbees (for practice and competition) and large nails and name tags for every contestant

Directions: Set up competition area shown in figure 1.

Contestants in each age classification draw numbers from a hat to establish order of competition. If enough space and officials are available, 4 different areas may be made up for competition at the same time in different events. If not, one event at a time can be run, or a different event each of 4 days or weekends. Contestants must be ready to throw when their names are called.

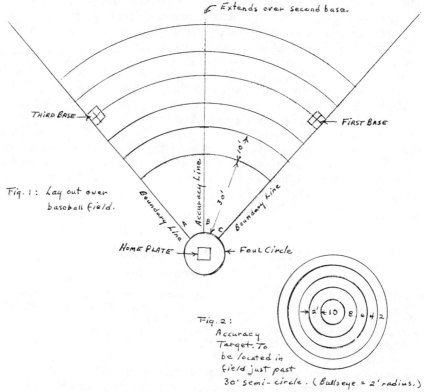

Fig. 1: Lay out over baseball field.

Fig. 2: Accuracy Target. To be located in field just past 30' semi-circle. (Bullseye = 2' radius.)

Sailing Directions: Hold saucer with open curled edge down with thumb on top, index finger along the curled edge and the other fingers underneath. Hold saucer in right hand (if right-handed), bringing saucer in arc from the left side of the body, letting go when the arm is pointing straight forward in front of the body. Be sure the hand and the saucer are parallel with the ground at release or it will tip and curve.

Event #1: Sailing for Distance ... *"Blast off" Event*—Saucers are sailed from inside a circle. Measurement is taken for maximum distance from the front center point of the circle to the point of the saucer contact with the ground. Each contestant is allowed three trials. Score is total distance for the three trials.

Event #2: Sailing for Accuracy... *"Bull's Eye" Event*—Saucers are sailed from inside a circle toward a bullseye target on the ground at a pre-determined distance away. The target should have five rings; center ring, 2' radius, and each ring being at least two feet apart. Points are awarded 10-8-6-4-2, from the inner-most circle out. Three trials are allowed each pilot-contestant. Each pilot's score is the sum of the three rings in which he has landed his saucer. The Clerk-of-the-Course decides in which ring the saucer has landed by determining which one the saucer is *most* inside when it stops moving.

Event #3: Sailing for Both Distance & Accuracy ... *"Into Orbit" Event*—Saucers are sailed along a straight line. The place where they first strike the ground is marked. The Clerk-of-the-Course checks distance, then how far to the right or left of the line that mark is. This distance is subtracted from the first distance. The remaining distance is that score for that trial. Three trials are given each pilot and his total score is the sum of these three trials.

Event #4: Sailing Tricks ... *"Aerobatics" Event*—There are five basic stunts. Each pilot is allowed only one chance to do each stunt. He is judged by the Clerk-of-the-Course standing either directly behind or directly in front of the thrower, on a basis of 1 to 10 points on each trick, depending on skill, accuracy and beauty of execution. Score is total of points awarded on all five stunts.

Stunt #1 is the "right-hand curve" to a pre-determined target. *Stunt #2* is the "left-hand curve" to a pre-determined target. *Stunt #3* is "settling" the saucer on the top of a pre-determined target. *Stunt #4* is the "boomerang." Sail the saucer up into the air at such an angle it will return to the sender, without moving. *Stunt #5* is the "skipper." Sail the saucer into the ground in front of you so it skips back into the air and continues on to a pre-determined target.

139. Crosscatch

Teaches young novices the skill of catching a ball correctly in a game situation

Age level: 6–8, 9–12, 13–16
Organizational level: Medium
Number of players: 2 teams, 4–10
Supervision: Instructor

Space needed: 20' × 40' area
Equipment: Softball (12–16") or rubber/ plastic baseball

Directions: Choose teams. Line them up facing each other 10–20 feet apart, depending on their throwing skill. One team is selected to lead off.

The members of the two teams throw the ball back and forth between their lines. Players must catch two-handed with wrists nearly together and palms facing each other.

When the end of the line is reached, that player immediately reverses the field, throwing to the opposing player as shown in the sketch, #10 to #7. If play had ended with player #9, he would reverse to #8.

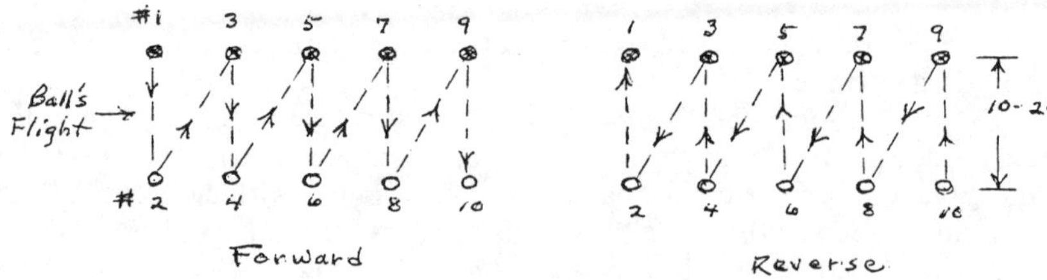

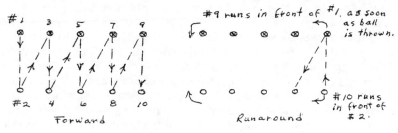

Fig. 1: Cross Catch

Every fumble gives the fumbler's team a −1 (minus-point). Players throw as quickly as possible, trying to catch opponents not ready and force a fumble. But throws must be easily catchable and not thrown hard. A bad throw into the dirt, over the receivers head, or more than 2 steps away from receiver, gives a minus-point to the thrower's team. Game can be to a time limit, or to pre-set point total that is double the number of players.

Variations: *Cross Bounce*—Team players must *bounce* the ball back and forth, to teach catching of ground balls. *Moving Catch*— As each player throws, he must run to the far end of his line of players and get ready to catch and throw

Fig. 2: Moving Catch

again. He can catch on the run, but if he doesn't get in position before the ball gets there he gets a minus-point.

Same rules about throwing.

The line can curve to follow playing area boundaries so as not to run out of space.

140. Star Ball

Adds interest to game of catch.
Can be played by wheelchair-bound players.

Age level: 6 and up
Organizational level: Low
Number of players: 5, but could be adjusted for more
Supervision: Referee-scorekeeper and time-keeper

Playing time: 10 minutes per game
Space needed: Start with 10–15′ diameter circle for novices. Enlarge area for older, better players
Equipment: Ball for each player (any kind, all the same, or all different for more fun)

Directions: Players form a circle, each holding a ball. On "go" signal by referee or designated player, each, at the same time, tosses his ball to another player, the second player on his left (see diagram). With five players, the throwing trajectories form a star, thus the name of the game.

Any ball collision in the air signals starting over, so the game idea is, through teamwork, to avoid hitting other balls in the air by throwing balls at different heights. Referee calls "go" for each new round of throws. Ball fumblers are allowed to recover their balls without penalty.

Note: If 7 players play, each person would throw to the 3rd person from his left, so balls are less likely to collide in the air. Ball trajectories will form a 7-pointed star.

Even 9 or 11 players can participate, though the circle must be enlarged, which means a longer throwing distance.

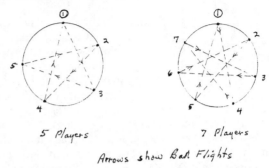

5 Players   7 Players

Arrows show Ball Flights

Each player would throw to the 4th (9 players) or 5th (11 players) person to their left.

Variations: *Count Out* — Same game, except every fumble of a ball that touches the ground, and every mid-air collision of balls, counts a minus-point for the fumbler or throwers. Winner is player with least penalty points after 10 minute playing period. *Count Out II* — Same game may be played with players seated in circle on floor, throwing wadded-up paper balls. *Count Out III* — Same game may be played by enlarging the circle, outside, and using Frisbees instead of balls. *Crash Out* — Same game for 7, 9, or 11 players, except when two balls collide in air, the two players ending up with no balls are out of the game. They must step back out of the circle. The other players must immediately adjust their throws to 2nd person from their left (7 players), 3rd person (9 players) or 4th person (11 players). This sequence is repeated for every mid-air collision of balls until only 2 players are left in the game. They are the winners. *Star Socko* — Star Ball may also be played by adding a target, like a tin can on a post or atop a stack of boxes (6-7' high) in the middle of the circle. This is merely a "hazard" and counts nothing if hit, unless playing a Count One version of the game.

Game source: Modified from game innovated by Elmer E. Heft, owner of Uncle Elmer's Restaurant in Daytona Beach, FL, June 1952, from warm-up exercises and formations used by soccer and volleyball players for many years.

141. Wind Up

Teaches hand-eye coordination in an active, competitive game situation

Age level: 8 and up
Organizational level: None
Number of players: 2
Supervision: None
Playing time: 10-20 minutes per game
Space needed: 20' × 20' area including an overhead crossbar, 8-10' high

Equipment: Overhead crossbar (football goal post, or swings frame may be used), 2 Whiffleballs (or sponge or tennis balls inside a plastic grocery bag), and 2 8' lengths of light rope, and a rake

Directions: Basic Tetherball rules, except played on a vertical plane in place of the usual horizontal plane. Tie or tack up ropes 2' apart on crossbar. Balls should hang about shoulder level with players.

Players play both balls, using either or both hands, trying to wind the ropes around the crossbar, so the ball is out of reach of the players.

Winner is player whose last hit results in both balls hung up. If neither player gets both, it is a tie.

A garden rake (or ladder) is kept on hand to un-wind the ropes after each game.

Variations: *Double Wind-Up I*—Doubles teams may play this, by starting out with each team member on one of the balls. But they may switch back and forth at anytime and once one ball is hung up, both may double up on the second ball. *Double Wind-Up II*—Same as above, except ropes are moved 4–5' apart and each game is played separately, but simultaneously. Teammates may switch places at anytime but not double up on the same ball. *Double Tetherball*—Ropes are placed each only 1' from the side posts. Players then play regular Tetherball around the side posts, instead of the overhead crossbar. Teammates switch places anytime, as above, but cannot double up on the same ball.

142. Squares

*A game simple enough that anyone can play, but with skills
and strategy involved that can take experts some time to master too*

Age level: 6 and up
Organizational level: Low
Number of players: 1 on 1, or teams of 2, 3, or 4
Supervision: None

Playing time: Varies
Space needed: Sidewalk area with 2 squares
Equipment: Ball (jacks, hand, tennis, racquet, or other small rubberball)

Directions: Players face each other from adjoining sidewalk sections. Teams may use four sidewalk sections, two each.

The dividing line between each team's court is the "over-line," the crack between the two center sidewalk sections. Players bat the ball with their hands back and forth over this over-line. The ball may be undercut, backcut or sliced to put erratic spins on it.

Players may retreat behind their squares, or out to the side of their squares, to play the ball. Serves, however, must be made from inside their squares and served underhand (ball above the palm of the hand when contacted).

Points are made when the serve is not served legally or lands out of the opponent's square, when a player doesn't return a ball before its second bounce, and when a ball lands on the over-line.

Variations: *Penny 2-Square*—Same game as above, except a penny is placed on the "over-line," in the center of the sidewalk. Players take turns trying to throw the ball—from beyond their sidewalk squares—and hit the penny, knocking it into their opponent's square.

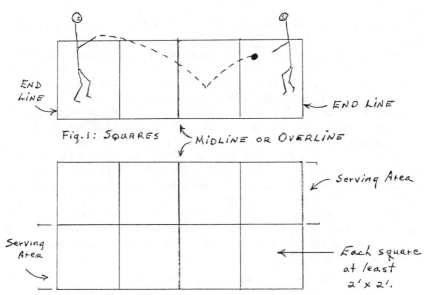

Fig. 1: SQUARES

MIDLINE OR OVERLINE

Fig. 2: FOUR SQUARES LAYOUT

If the penny is knocked off the sidewalk, it is replaced on the over-line. If it is moved, but is not totally off the over-line, it remains where it is. *(Variation #2)*—Same game may also be played where the penny must be knocked completely over one of the opponent's end zones to register a win. No limit is placed on the number of throws this might take. Also, a stone may be substituted for the penny. *Four Squares*—Same game as those above, except each team has a court of 4 squares which can be chalked on a closed street or parking lot.

Singles or doubles may be played. Ball may be hit to any of opponent's 4 squares, after the serve, and either teammate may play it in any order. The serve, however, is done underhand from behind the playing court, from the right hand court into either of the opponent's diagonally opposite squares. Teams alternate serving for six points each, with teammates alternating serving chores each time the serve comes to their team. Game is 24 or 48 points.

Game source: Adapted from old New York street game, which may have had its roots in ancient Egypt, according to historians.

143. Stoop Ball

Adds a baseball fielding element to the simple game of catch

Age level: 8 and up
Organizational level: Low
Number of players: 1 on 1 or teams of 2, 3, or 4
Supervision: None
Playing time: 15–30 minutes per game

Space needed: A set of 3–6 house or other building steps, with a clear, smooth apron in front of them, free of traffic
Equipment: Ball (handball, tennis or other small rubberball)

Directions: Players take turns throwing and catching the ball against the steps.

A catch of an ordinary return ground ball (at least 2 bounces) counts 1 point; an ordinary fly ball, 2 points; a grounder off a point or corner of a step, 3 points; a fly ball off a point or corner, 4 points, and a fly ball the player must take 6 or more steps to catch, 5 points. Game is 25 or 50 points.

Variations: *Ledge Ball* — A more difficult version of the above game is throwing the ball against a first floor window ledge or other similar building projection. (Windows should be protected with a covering.)

The offensive player, or team member, throws the ball and the defensive player, or team, defends the field of play. They play baseball by forcing imaginary runners around the bases with throws the defense misses or making outs with throws the defense catches. Play 7 or 9 innings.

Fielding on one bounce gives the thrower a single; on two bounces, a double; on three bounces, a triple and on 4 or more, a home run. A caught fly ball is an out. A caught fly ball over the end boundary where the fielder has to take 6 or more steps, is a double out.

Game source: Adapted from an old New York street game.

144. Tchouk Ball

Adaptation from the Basque game of Pelota for non-aggressive play in family setting or as a leisure sport

Age level: 10 and up
Organizational level: Medium
Number of players: 2, 4, 6
Supervision: Umpire and scorekeeper

Playing time: 3 periods, 15 minutes each
Space needed: 45–60′ square area
Equipment: Rebound net and ball

Directions: The game is played by throwing a ball (a handball or Wham-O-Superball) against elastically tensioned net on a metal frame of the type trademarked "Tchouk Ball," which rebounds symmetrically.

The playing area begins 10′ in front of the base of the net; thus a 10′ zone is marked directly in front of the net and is extended across the front of the playing area. This zone is "out of play;" neither the ball nor the players may touch this "Forbidden Zone." The playing area is marked out directly facing the net 45′–60′ in length and width. The two teams mix freely on this area. The size of the playing area governs the amount of physical effort exerted; the smaller the area, the smaller the effort. (Note — For match play the straight 10′ restricting line is replaced by a semi-circle centered from the base of the frame.)

To create team play, up to three passes between members of the same team are authorized (but are not obligatory). No player may hold the ball more than three seconds.

To be "in play" the ball must not touch the ground inside the playing area thus delimited. It must not be caught outside these limits.

The ball changes sides each time it rebounds from the net.

After each point lost, the ball is brought back into play by a member of the team which lost the point.

A player may not walk with the ball in his hands. (This is known as "Ball-stop.") A player may pivot on one foot and move the other, but, once the pivot foot is lifted, the player has "traveled."

It is a fault when: (a) the ball goes outside the authorized boundaries, (b) a player fails to catch the ball (and it touches the ground), (c) deliberate obstruction occurs, (d) a player takes more than one step, (e) a team makes more than three passes, (f) a player mistakenly takes a pass belonging to the opposing team, (g) the ball returns from the net to hit the thrower himself, (h) the rebounding ball is caught by a player of the same team that has made the shot.

A player must not interfere with anyone, in any way: all obstruction is forbidden (the ball must be allowed unhampered flight). No inappropriate or aggressive gestures are permitted. 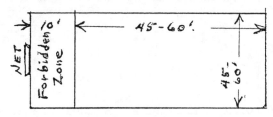 (It is a contest without aggression.) Receiving a pass, and throwing, should be done without any interference (no interception).

Scoring: The ball is in play as long as it passes from one player to another and changes sides by rebounding normally from the net ("normally" means without touching the metal frame) and without touching the ground. Anyone who lets, or makes, the ball go out of normal sequence (by missing a pass, a catch, sending the ball out-of-play, or missing the net) loses a point for his team. Each fault counts as one point for the opposing team.

The winning side is the one which has two sets to its credit. A set can be decided in either of two ways: (a) By the number of points scored, generally 20, 30, or 35 points; (b) The set can last a pre-arranged number of minutes; usually 10 minutes (15 minutes for well-trained players).

Each system has advantages and disadvantages. In the open air, balls which go out-of-play are often lost for several seconds and take time to be retrieved, so it is advantageous to decide the sets by points scored.

All modifiable rules must be decided upon before the start of the game.

Note — For official matches there are three periods of 15 minutes and the team with the most points at the end of this time is the winner.

Game source: The name comes from the sound made as the ball rebounds from the highly tensioned net. The basic principle is taken from the Basque game, Pelota. Dr. Herman Brandt, an eminent Swiss biologist, won the J. G. Thulin Prize in 1970 from the Federacion Internationale d' Educacion Physique when that organization sponsored an "International Competition on the Theory of Physical Education." He won it with his work titled "A Critical, Scientific Study of Team Games," with an associated practical application of this study, a new game he called Tchouk Ball.

145. Crazy Bounce

*Trains quick reactions. Gives a lot
of all-body exercise in a short time.*

Age level: 10 and up   *Number of players:* 1 on 1, 2 on 2
Organizational level: Medium   *Supervision:* None

Playing time: 15–20 minutes for 15 point game

Space needed: Handball court, or similarly sized and marked area with a wall at one end

Equipment: Ball (hand, tennis, sponge, volley or playground ball), handball gloves if wished, curved wall 8'–10' high that can be braced against the wall if moveable, or wood wall (plywood, concrete or other) constructed to form curve. Bottoms could be anchored into ground or bolted to a floor if the court is to be permanent.

Directions: Basic handball rules. Difference in the game comes from the crazy bounces the ball will take from the curved wall.

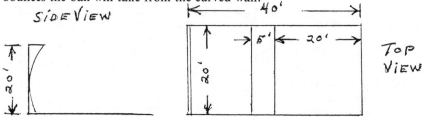

Variations: *(1)* Same game, but using racquetball and racquet. Courts may be enlarged, if wished, for older, better players. *(2)* Same game, except table tennis paddles and balls are used, and the court can be much smaller, like 10' × 20', and the curved wall would not have to be over 6–7' high.

146. Giant Wallball

Handball activity that may be played by children,
and requires no special, expensive courts for play

Age level: 6 and up
Organizational level: Low
Number of players: 2 or 4, singles or doubles
Supervision: None
Playing time: 15-point games, though this may be varied to fit circumstances

Space needed: Any wall with a relatively flat, hard surface fronting it, 20' × 20' minimum, wall preferably 10' high
Equipment: Volleyball or similar sized rubber playground ball, chalk or tape to mark boundaries and court lines

Directions: First server is decided. Thereafter the serve changes hands after every point. A serve is made from behind the service line by bouncing the ball on the floor and hitting it with the hand or fist on the rise. The ball must then hit the

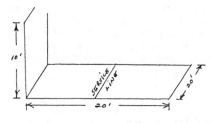

floor, the wall, and rebound back over the service line before the opponent may hit it. The service is the only time the ball must bounce back over the service line before it can be hit. At all other times it may be played anywhere on the court, but the ball must still be hit into the floor before it hits the wall.

After the serve, the ball may be played with either one or two hands clenched together. It is a fault, however, to hit the ball twice, or with two parts of the body successively on the same swing.

Other faults include: (a) stepping over the service line before the ball is hit on the serve, (b) serving out-of-hand, without first bouncing the ball, (c) serving so the ball does not rebound behind the service line, (d) serving or hitting the ball out of turn, (e) hitting the ball against the wall instead of the floor first, (f) hitting the ball out of bounds either before or after it contacts floor or wall, (g) moving so as to block an opponent of his shot in any way.

Faults result in a point for the opponent. Other points are made when one person hits the ball so that the opponent cannot return it.

Variations: *Double Wallball* — Same rules as singles, except that partners on each side take turns serving *and* playing the ball. *Team Wallball* — Two teams line up at the end of the court, with two players from each side on the court. Players take turns, as above, playing the ball. But as soon as one person has played it, he must run off the court and go to the end of his team's line, and the front person in that line goes onto the court for a turn. The rotation keeps going until a game is won. More than six players 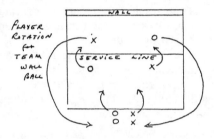 per team are too hard to keep track of. Any out-of-order play results in a point loss. *Team Elimination Wallball* — Same rules as for Team Wallball, except scoring. Instead of points being scored, the 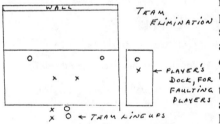 person who makes a fault or missed shot drops out of play. Last team with a player still in the game wins. *Individual Elimination Wallball* — No teams, only one line of players. First two start the game, then proceed as above, as soon as a player hits the ball he goes off the court and to the end of the line, being replaced by the person at the front of the line. A player faulting or missing a shot drops from the game. Winner is last person left in the game.

This is a good game for use when many persons want to play on the only court available. They may also play one point, rather than one hit, before rotating players. *Tournament Workup Wallball* — Individual Elimination Wallball can be used as a tournament format. Instead of players dropping out, however, when they fault or miss a point, their opponent would earn a point. The winner stays on court for the next point, while the loser goes to the end of the line and the person at the front of the line moves onto the court. The first player to get 5 points is the winner, second one is second place, and so on. For tournaments of more than six players, games should be divided into sections, with a playoff among the section champions establishing the overall champion.

147. Rumble Ball

Very fast moving conditioning game

Age level: 10 and up
Organizational level: Low

Number of players: 1 on 1, or teams of 2, 3, or 4

Supervision: None informally, referee for competition
Playing time: 4 10-minute quarters, or to 15 points

Space needed: 4-wall handball or racquetball court
Equipment: Rubberball (sponge, tennis, volleyball, playground or racquetball)

Directions: Players take turns serving. Serve may be taken anywhere in the court, but must carom off either two walls or one wall and the floor and try to hit the opponent. If the ball touches an opponent anywhere before he can hit it with his hand or fist, it is a point. Otherwise, each player hits the ball in turn until one can carom it into his opponent.

Fouls resulting in point awards: catching the ball while in play; physically holding, blocking or hindering an opponent from playing the ball.

Variation: *Human Billiards*—Same game, except players may catch and throw the ball, as well as hit it. But, they may not hold it over 5 seconds and may not move more than one step while holding or throwing it. Penalty: immediate turnover of ball to opponent. Players do *not* have to take turns hitting or catching the ball! Any player may throw the ball anytime he can recover it without fouling another player.

Game source: From informal game played by Bengal professional football players Bob Trumpy and Bob Johnson in hotel rooms on the road to pass the time.

148. Anty-Over

Variation on the old game of Anty-Eye-Over

Age level: 10 and up
Organizational level: Low
Number of players: 2 teams, 2–6 each
Playing time: 1–2 hours
Space needed: A one-story building with a

sloping roof and open space on all four sides
Equipment: Ball (sponge, tennis, playground, Whiffleball or even small plastic or sponge football)

Directions: Select teams. One team is on one side of building, the other is on the opposite side. Players cannot stand in the "no-peek zones."

One team starts play by throwing the ball over the roof of the building to the team on that side. The ball must bounce at least once on the roof. If a member of the receiving team catches the ball off the roof, without it bouncing on the ground, he and his team run around the building and try to "capture" members of the other team. This is done by touching or hit-

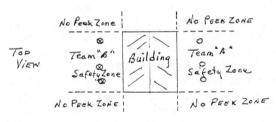

ting an opponent with the ball before he can run around the house to the opposite safety zone.

The ball must be carried in plain sight, though other players can pretend they have it. Once the catcher has thrown it, it may be picked up and thrown again by any of his teammates, as long as any opponents are still outside the safety zone to which they are running. The ball can be passed among teammates to get a shot or give the best thrower a target, as well. No blocking, holding or tripping of players.

All "tagged" players then join the team that tagged them, and that team becomes the ball anty-over thrower for the next session. Play continues until all players are on one team.

Variation: *Double Anty-Over*—Same game, except throwing team members when running to escape the team that caught the ball, must completely circle the building and return to their own safety zone before being tagged with the ball.

149. Balloon Volleyball

How to simulate volleyball play safely indoors on a rainy day

Age level: 8 and up
Organizational level: Low
Number of players: 2 teams, 1, 2, or 3 players each
Supervision: None
Playing time: 15-point games

Space needed: 10' × 10' area
Equipment: Balloon (round), though plastic bread wrappers may be blown up and used as a substitute, a 15' length of string, 2 kitchen type chairs

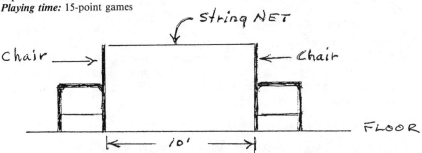

Directions: Basic volleyball rules, with the balloon used as the volleyball being batted over the string "net." Players play the game from their knees.

150. Volleyball Serving Skill Test

*Test activity for volleyball skills
at serving, accuracy, ball control and speed*

Age level: 10–12, 13–15, 16–19, 20 and over
Organizational level: High
Number of players: Any number, in rotation
Supervision: 1 Referee, judge, marker and 2 ball shaggers

Playing time: Open
Space needed: Volleyball court, with net, marked off in sections as shown in figure 1.
Equipment: 4–6 volleyballs, 20 4" squares cut out from an innertube or scrap carpeting

Directions: Each contestant takes 10 serves (or 10 underhand and 10 overhand, if both are being tested. Judges place markers where each serve hits the floor. The marker writes the number of the squares these are in under each appropriate heading on the

8	4	6	10
2	1	1	2
10	6	4	8

Fig. 1 :   Placement value chart

Figure 2: Serving Test Score Sheet									
Placements	Hit Net	Foot Fault	Out-End	Out-Side	Just Over	Over Speed	Placed	Placed-Speed	Ace	Total
Point Values	0	0	0	0	1	4	3	5	10	
Name 1	%	%		½	¼	⅞	⅕		17	
Name 2										
Name 3										

scoresheet (figure 2), as referee calls them.

When the testing is completed, the referee multiplies the number of balls marked in each category by the point value of that column category to get the sub-totals, then adds all column sub-totals across to get a final total, which is the individual's test score.

Highest score denotes best server/winner of the contest.

151. Volleying Football

A diverting game of volleyball with an innovative twist and a good practice for football players in learning to handle the football

Age level: 12 and up
Organizational level: Medium
Number of players: 2 teams, 6–8 each
Supervision: Referee and scorekeeper

Playing time: 21-point games, about 30 minutes
Space needed: Volleyball court with net
Equipment: Football, volleyball net and posts

Directions: Basic volleyball rules, except a football is used in place of a volleyball. The rule against open-handed hitting is relaxed, because of the hardness and nature of the ball. (A sponge or whiffle-type football may be used.)

Variation: *Tip-Up*—A basketball may be substituted for the football for basketball players to practice tipping-up the ball.

152. Three-Way Volleyball

Change-of-pace for volleyballers, especially for beach groups. Teaches the dink and soft touch and finesse game of volleyball.

Age level: High school or over
Organizational level: High
Number of players: 3 teams, 2–6 players per team
Supervision: Referee, scorekeeper, linesman

Playing time: Varies; somewhat longer than usual volleyball game
Space needed: Circle 15' radius, minimum
Equipment: Volleyball, 2 volleyball nets, 4 volleyball standards

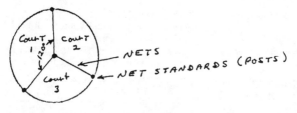

Directions: Serve clockwise, always into the court on server's left. When serve is lost, the serve goes to the team in the left court, and so on around.

After the serve, the ball may be played into either court.

Basic volleyball rules are used.

Variations: *Clock Volleyball*—Same as above except that the ball must be always played into the left-hand court for five points, then into the right hand courts for five points, and so on until the game is over. *Four-Way Volley-ball*—Same as Three-Way, except there are four teams playing on smaller courts. Five volleyball standards are needed instead of four. Court is layed out as shown in figure at right.

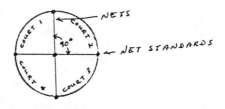

153. Long Volley

Variation on regular volleyball that
especially presents practice in "passing" the ball

Age level: 12 and up
Organizational level: High
Number of players: 2 teams, 4 each
Supervision: Referee and scorekeeper

Playing time: 20–30 minutes per game
Space needed: Volleyball court
Equipment: Volleyball

Directions: Basic volleyball rules, except ball may only be hit over the net from behind the dividing line between front court and back court, on each side of the net. (This eliminates blocking and spiking at the net, thus ensuring longer rallies and more practice in "passing" the ball.)

Back court spiking *is* allowed, providing, as in regular volleyball, the spiker jumps from behind the line. (He may land in front of the line.)

Variation: *Long-Volley Tennis*—Same game, except played on tennis court with tennis racquet and tennis ball.

Game source: Modified from R. R. McKaughan innovation at U.S. Navy Special Services School, 1972.

154. Cage Ball (Gang Volleyball)

Teaches basic volleyball skills. Many can play in relatively small area,
with minimal supervision and equipment. Relaxed rules also
make it good game for older adults and handicapped players.

Age level: 8–12, older adults, handicapped
Organizational level: Medium
Number of players: 2 teams, 10–40 per team
Supervision: Referee
Playing time: 10 point game

Space needed: Level space 30' × 60' for small group of players, 40' × 80' for larger groups
Equipment: Volleyball type net and posts, volleyball, or any 18–30" circumference ball

Directions: Basic volleyball rules, with following exceptions:

With more players, three lines of players may be set up on each side. Rotation, thus, will be from serving position (back row, right-hand corner) across back line, down to middle line and across that line, down to front line and across that line to far left corner, then back to serving position.

Player may hit or juggle the ball as many times as wished, with one or both hands, using fingers or palms, so long as player doesn't improve position by moving toward net.

Only serving team scores. That team keeps serving as long as it keeps scoring, but the players rotate before each serve (so all players are sure to have

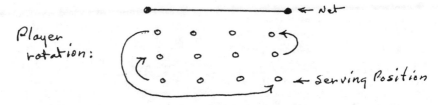

Player rotation:

chance to play all positions each game). Server may hit ball directly over net, or hit it to a teammate to hit over net. (This last rule may be changed to require an assisted service, with direct over-net service being a fault, if wished.)

Game source: U.S. Navy Recreation & Welfare sports manual (out of print).

155. Blind Volleyball

Adds variety to regular volleyball program

Age level: 13 and up
Organizational level: Medium
Number of players: 2 teams, 6 each
Supervision: Referee and scorekeeper

Playing time: 30 minutes per game
Space needed: Volleyball Court
Equipment: Canvas or cloth panel covering net area from top of net to floor, volleyball

Directions: Basic volleyball rules, except the net is covered so players on two sides can't see each other.

Variations: *Beginner Blind Volleyball* — Younger and novice players may institute a rule that the ball is allowed one floor bounce between each person and the net. This is also a good training tool to teach 2-hand "bumps" and high fingertip "sets" for more skilled volleyball players. *Blind-Carom Volleyball* — If an area is available between two buildings, where a net may be put up between them and there are no windows to be broken, the "blind" game may be made more complex by allowing players to carom the ball off the side buildings and over the net.

Game source: Adapted from a Russian game innovation in the 1970s.

156. Peteka Rio

*Good active game with simple rules, needing little equipment
and a small area. Excellent beach or picnic game.*

Age level: 10 and up
Organizational level: Medium
Number of players: 2 teams, 1–6 each (singles and doubles play best)

Supervision: None
Playing time: 15 point game, about 30 minutes
Space needed: 20′ × 30′ area

Equipment: Badminton net (or string with a beach towel draped over it), Peteka Rio shuttlecock (a rubber or leather disc with 3–5 long, large feathers sticking up from it). Gloves may be worn. (Commercial game equipment marketed by Sportcraft Co.)

Directions: Basic badminton rules, except this shuttlecock is hit with the palms of the hands.

Game source: Originated on the beaches of Rio de Janeiro.

157. Gaucho Tennis

Teaches basics of an Argentine game that requires good hand-eye coordination

Age level: 8 and up
Organizational level: Medium
Number of players: 1 on 1, 2 on 2
Supervision: None informally, referee and scorekeeper otherwise
Playing time: 21-point game, about 30 minutes

Space needed: Badminton court and net, or equivalent area 20′ × 44′ (see figure 1)
Equipment: Pato ball (or large Whiffleball with 4 stiff rope lengths inserted through holes and tied to form catching rings [see figure 2])

Directions: Ball is served, thrown and caught one-handed by the rope loops only. Catch and return must be accomplished in the same continuous motion, with no reverse motion of the elbow.

Any miss that lands in the court, including a tick of the net, is a point for the thrower. Any throw failing to get over the net or landing out of bounds, or illegally delivered, is a point for the receiver.

Serve must be underhand from behind the service line, starting in

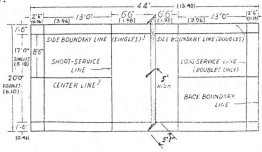

Fig. 1: Court Layout

the right hand court and landing in the diagonally opposite court, over the short-service line. Player keeps serving as long as he makes points for himself (or his doubles team), switching courts to serve each time. When the opponent makes a point, he also wins the serve.

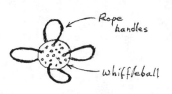

Fig. 2: Pato Ball

Throws other than the serve may be underhand, sidearm or overarm.

Variations: *Gaucho Volleyball—* Same game, played with 4–6 players per team on a volleyball court. Basic volleyball rules, except pato ball will be passed among teammates and over the net by its rope rings.

Game source: Unusual ball is based on that used in Argentine Gaucho (cowboy) game of Pato, a sort of keep-away on horseback.

158. Hoover Ball

A "keep-in-shape" game

Age level: 16 and up
Organizational level: Medium
Number of players: 2 teams, 3 each
Playing time: 15-point game, about 45 minutes with 2 rest periods

Space needed: Volleyball court, 8' high net
Equipment: 6 lb. medicine ball, or sandbag

Directions: Basic volleyball rules, except the medicine ball is hoisted over the net. Each side is allowed 3 catches before returning it over the net.

Faults: ball thrown out of bounds, ball not clearing the net, ball touching the floor while in play, player moving pivot foot from where he caught the ball, and player holding the ball more than 10 seconds before playing it.

Game source: Originally invented in 1929 by President Herbert Hoover's doctor to help our 31st president stay in shape. Hoover played it almost daily on the White House lawn. A modified game was played at the Newport Naval Air Station in 1973. The game was revived in 1988 for a "national tournament" at Hoover Library and Museum. Then Senator Mark Hatfield (R-OR) sponsored the first Hoover Ball Capital Classic, September 29, 1990, holding it on volleyball courts at the mall in Washington, D.C. 50 teams participated.

159. Gorodke

Learn a uniquely Russian sport

Age level: 13–15, 16–18, 19 and up
Organizational level: Medium
Number of players: Any number, in rotation
Supervision: Referee-scorekeeper
Playing time: Depends on number of competitors; tournament can take all day, unless more than one competition area is set up

Space needed: 20' × 50' area outdoors
Equipment: A beta (6-pound throwing stick), 20 or more round tree sections cut in 2-foot lengths, circumferences as nearly equal as possible

Directions: Contestant picks up beta and throws it at variously fashioned stacks of wooden sections, trying to knock over as many pieces in each stack as possible. Those who succeed, in two tries each, in knocking over one stack, go on to successively larger, more complex stackings. Winner is one who lasts longest.

    etc.

There are 15 standard stackings, each of which gets more complex. Complexity of formations depends upon age and skill of competitors. Examples of stackings above. Slight notches in sides of wood pieces will make them easier to stack, since pieces are round.

Game source: Russia has half a million registered players. Translation of the name, Gorodke, is "The City Game."

160. Team Handball
Learn an international sport

Age level: 14–16, 17–19, 20 and up
Organizational level: High
Number of players: 2 teams, 7 each, plus 3 substitutes
Supervision: Referee, scorekeeper-time-keeper, and linesman
Playing time: 2 halves, 30 minutes each, with 10 minute intermission; overtime, 10 minutes each

Space needed: Rectangular field 50–83′ × 100–166′ (international: 126–147′ × 60–73′) (see sketch)
Equipment: Ball (official: men 15 oz. weight for 14–16 ages, 17 oz. otherwise, with 23–24″ circumference; women 11½ oz. and 14 oz. for age groups, with 21–22″ circumference)

Directions: Start game with throw-in by referee at center of court. Teams exchange ends at halftime.

No watches, wristlets, rings, earrings, glasses without safety protection, or any other items that could pose a danger to players allowed.

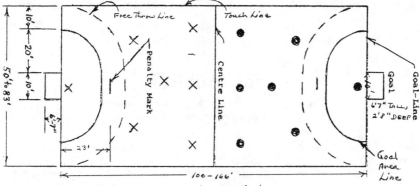

Team Handball Court

Substitutes may enter at any time, after the player for whom they are substituting has left the field. Any player evicted from the game for unsportsmanlike conduct is excluded for the rest of the game, and no substitute is allowed. Penalty for illegal substitution is a free throw by opponent from the point where the sub joined play.

The ball is advanced by throwing, hitting, bouncing, blocking or catching in any manner using any part of the body except the legs below the knees and feet. Ball cannot be carried more than three steps and is dribbled repeatedly with one hand (after 3 steps), but only once with two hands, though there is no limit on number of steps taken between that bounce and the recovery. Ball, also, can only be held 3 seconds before playing it some way. (Penalty for illegal play is loss of ball at point of infraction.)

It is a fault to dive for ball rolling or lying on ground. (Penalty: free throw from point of foul.) Ball cannot be snatched from opponent's grasp.

Held ball, by two opposing players, will be a jump ball at point of occurrence. Referee bounces ball between the two players, so it rebounds at least 10′ in air before players may touch it.

No player except goalies may be in goal area during play. (Penalty: penalty shot on goal from penalty mark by team captain.)

Goalies may use any part of bodies, including legs below knees and feet, to protect goals from the ball. Goalie may leave goal area (without the ball), but then becomes subject to all rules other field players are subject to.

Out-of-bounds ball is thrown in by team not last touching it at point it went out. Ball must be thrown in with both hands holding it overhead, while flat-footed. No opponent may closely obstruct a throw-in.

If the ball is sent out of bounds over the goal line, outside the goal mouth: (1) by defensive player, the attacking team is awarded a corner throw-in from the corner of the field nearest where the ball went out, and a goal may be scored direct from a corner throw; (2) by attacking team, the goalie throws-in from the goal area, with opposing players behind the free throw line.

The penalty for (1) a personal foul on an opponent in one's own half of the court, (2) a player entering his own goal area to help his goalie, (3) intentionally back-passing the ball to one's goalie, and (4) goalie touching ball outside goal area while standing inside it, is a penalty free-throw from the penalty mark. A free-thrower cannot touch the ball after his throw, until it has been touched by another player.

Game source: Adapted from International Handlball rules.

161. Foxball

Includes skills of tennis, handball and basketball;
de-emphasizes sex and size in game play

Age level: 10 and up
Organizational level: High
Number of players: 1 on 1, 2 on 2, or up to 5 on 5 in the expanded court team variation
Supervision: Referee and scorekeeper
Playing time: 4 10–15 minute quarters
Space needed: 9' × 20' area on a hard, even surface, indoors or out
Equipment: Foxball set, which includes 2 5"
inflatable rubber playground balls, 2 9' × 38' tubular steal backstop frames, accompanying nylon backstop nets, goal nets and red outline strips, 4 attaching triangular shaped wooden stands, 2 3 × 19' cotton side nets (commercially available through Game Innovations, Inc., 157 Glenhurst Dr., Verona, PA 15147)

Directions: In "Singles" Foxball two players compete. Each starts with a 4" rubber ball. A mid-court line separates them. The idea is to "Outfox" the opponent by feinting him out of position and bouncing the ball into one of four net openings for a score. First to score 12 points wins.

Singles and doubles game requires only a small playing area (9' × 20'). Each side net opening scores 1 point, lower middle 2 points and upper middle opening 3 points. Side nets attached to each side of both upright goals prevent 85 percent of stray balls from leaving the court.

"Doubles" Foxball is played the same way as the "Singles" game, only four players compete, two on each side of the court.

In "Team" Foxball, two five-man teams compete. Flip of a coin determines which team gets to take the ball out of bounds first. As in "Singles" and "Doubles," the idea is to shoot the ball and have it bounce on the court and into one of the four openings for a score, otherwise, regulation basketball rules are employed including dribbling, passing, double dribble, jump ball and fouls. Played on any size basketball court or comparable area. "Team" Foxball goals

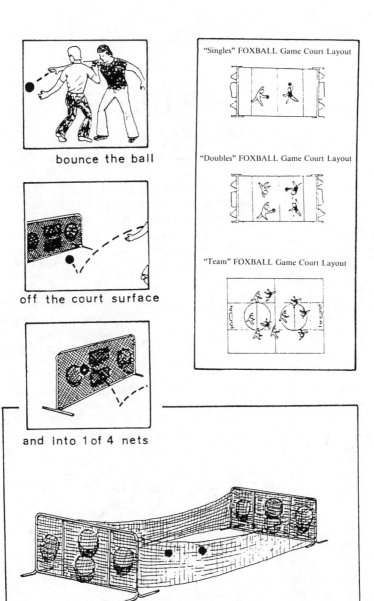

bounce the ball

off the court surface

and into 1 of 4 nets

"Singles" FOXBALL Game Court Layout

"Doubles" FOXBALL Game Court Layout

"Team" FOXBALL Game Court Layout

are set up under each basket and centered in the "key" zone. Only the assigned goalie is permitted in the Key and then only when the ball has hit the backstop.

MALLET-CLUB-STICK GAMES

162. Placement Pool

Fast competition innovation of pool;
good practice activity for lone player, too

Age level: Any
Organizational level: Low
Number of players: 1-6 in rotation
Supervision: None informally, referee-
scorekeeper otherwise

Playing time: 10 minutes
Space needed: Pool table
Equipment: Cue ball and 8 other balls, cue
stick for each player (or pass one stick
around)

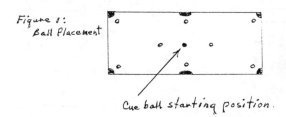

Figure 1:
Ball Placement

Cue ball starting position.

Directions: Place balls as shown in figure 1. Shooter continues as long as he pockets balls, each one counting 1 point. If he runs the table, the balls are set up again.

When first shooter misses, the second shooter takes over. Contest goes on until each player has started one game. Winner is the high total scorer.

163. Cross the Line

Teaches pool skills in a field setting

Age level: 10 and up
Organizational level: Low
Number of players: 1 on 1, 2 on 2
Supervision: None
Playing time: 4 5-minute periods

Space needed: 40' × 60' area, with 3' high goal
posts set 3' apart at each end
Equipment: Field hockey stick for each
player, 3 balls, (croquet mallets and balls
may also be used)

Directions: Start with 3 balls together at mid field. Decide which player hits first. He breaks them. Then opponents take turns hitting. First hitter and his team-mate, if playing doubles, take turns playing one ball between them, called the "cue" ball. The opponent and his teammate, if playing doubles, take turns play-ing two balls, called the "align" balls.

The way to score a point is for the cue ball to go across the (invisible) line between the two align balls. Thus, the align balls should be hit each time so they touch each other or lay in such a way this becomes difficult.

Player, or teams, change which balls they are playing each quarter. Only the player or team playing the cue ball can score.

Five points are scored anytime the cue ball is hit between the align balls *and* goes between the goal posts, on the same shot.

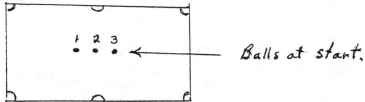

Variations: *Double Crossing*—Same game, but using two cue balls. *Cross-Carom*—One cue ball, 2 align balls. But, instead of crossing the line between them, the cue ball must be caromed off both align balls in the same shot to score a point, *and* go through the goals posts for 5 points. *Cross the Line on Ice*—All these games can also be played on ice, with hockey sticks and pucks, or with plastic sticks and pucks on cement or wood flooring.

Game source: Modified from game idea suggested by Mark Cox in U.S. Navy Special Services Training School session, 1972.

164. Three-Ball Pool

Practice for both pool and billiards in the same game

Age level: 14 and up
Organizational level: Medium
Number of players: 2–12 in rotation
Playing time: 20–40 minutes

Space needed: Pool table
Equipment: Cue ball and #1, 2 and 3 balls, cue stick for each player

Directions: Place #1, 2 and 3 balls as shown in sketch, about 6″ apart. Cue ball can be placed anywhere within 6″ of the #1 ball by the first shooter. It must contact both #2 and 3 balls, or a cushion and one of them, to score and, thus, keep shooting. If he misses, the next shooter takes over wherever the first shooter leaves the balls.

Points: Cushion and any one-ball carom, 1 point; any two-ball carom, 2 points; any cushion and two-ball carom, 3 points; three-ball carom, 4-points; plus bonus points if any ball is put in a hole after completing a carom-1 point for the #1 ball, 2 points for the #2 ball, and 3 points for the #3 ball. Pocketed balls are returned immediately, before another shot is taken, to its starting spot on the table (or as near as possible if that spot is covered by another ball).

If the cue ball or another ball is hit off the table, or a ball is pocketed before completing a carom, the shooter's turn is over and the errant ball is immediately replaced on the table at its starting spot, and the cue ball may be placed anywhere in the "D" area within 6″ of the #1 ball spot.

Game is 25 points.

Game source: Modified from game idea suggested by Steve Bonche at the U.S. Navy Special Services Training School, 1972.

165. Billiard Baseball
Another use for an unused billiard table

Age level: 12 and up
Organizational level: Medium
Number of players: 2 teams, 2–4 each
Supervision: None

Playing time: 1–2 hours
Space needed: Billiard table
Equipment: Cue stick for each player, set of billiard balls, baseball score pad and pencil

Directions: Game starts with cue ball "spotted" at one end of table and the 2 other balls centered one behind the other on the spot at the other end of the table.

Two teams take turns playing (at bat), being allowed 3 outs. Teammates bat in sequence. An out is called for a shooter not completing a legal "billiard" (carom from 2 or 3 balls).

A player may sacrifice an out to place the cue ball in better position for the next batter, or to place the cue ball in an awkward place, so the opposing team will not score on the third out.

A successful billiard counts as a single, and pushes any player already on base, one base ahead. A billiard, plus a cushion touch, counts as a double, a billiard plus 2 cushion touches, a triple, and a billiard with 3 cushion touches, a home run.

After 3 outs, the opposing team starts shooting from where the balls are left on the table. When both teams have completed an at-bat, it is an inning. Game is 9 innings. If score is tied, win goes to team with the most hits.

Game source: Modified from game reported by Myron N. Hendrick, Director of Recreation, Niagara Falls, N.Y. in a 1952 report.

166. Hammer Pool
Kookie variation for playing pool. Saves wear and tear on cue tips and table coverings from novice and careless pool players

Age level: 10 and up
Organizational level: Low
Number of players: 1 on 1; 2 teams, 2, 3, 4, each
Supervision: None

Playing time: 20–30 minutes
Space needed: Pool table
Equipment: Regular set of pool balls, triangle, and rubber mallets (such as used in auto body shops)

Directions: Regular pool rules, except rubber mallets are used in place of cue sticks.

167. Marble Golf

Teaches basics of golf rules before need to
go on a golf course. Good rainy-day inside game.

Age level: 6 and up
Organizational level: Low
Number of players: Foursomes. One is selected scorekeeper.
Playing time: 18 holes of golf, about 30 minutes
Space needed: 15′ square level area of packed dirt (outside) or carpet (inside)
Equipment: 1 marble (as golf ball), 1 pencil (as golf club) for each player, 18 golf "holes" (plastic measurers from powdered drink canisters, which can be sunk in the dirt outside or laid on their sides inside), scorecard and pencil and various imagination-inspired golf "hazards" placed around the golf "course," like plants as forested area, ridges, dishes of water as ponds, sand traps (put on sheets of newspaper inside), etc.

Directions: Lay out 18-hole mini-golf course.

Basic golf rules for penalties, out-of-bounds rulings, order of play in teeing off and continuing.

Players hit marbles with pencils. (Using pencil as a cue stick is not allowed.) Number of strokes for each hole is kept on the scorecard and these are totaled after 18 holes to find the winner, the player with the fewest overall strokes.

Variation: *Hurry-Up Golf*—If more than 4 players want to play, teams can be chosen, then players on each team will take turns hitting their ball.

168. Mini-Golf

Simple game using simple materials that
can be played by almost anyone almost anywhere

Age level: 8 and up
Organizational level: Low
Number of players: 2-4
Supervision: None
Playing time: About 30 minutes
Space needed: Indoors or outdoors, wherever a 10-20′ by 6′ area is free and smoothe
Equipment: 8-12″ stiff squares of paper, 16 marbles, scissors and glue

Directions: Cut into paper center and trim out a circle 2-3″ across. (See Fig. 1.)

Roll paper into a cone with opening at top and glue along overlapped edges. Hole at top should remain large enough so marbles can drop through easily. (See Fig. 2.)

Game is to roll the marbles up the incline of the cone and into the hole at the top.

If players compete, each may take 4 rolls, counting a point for each hole-in-one made. First to reach a set score is the winner.

Variations: *(1)* Cardboard can be used to make the cones on larger scale, so tennis or golf balls may be used in place of marbles. *(2)* Several holes, either paper or cardboard, may be put out in a golf course layout. Players may then play an actual game of mini-golf, rolling their ball from hole to hole and counting up the number of rolls needed for each hole. Lowest total for entire course is the winner.

169. Handicap Golf Driving

For golf driving practice in distance and accuracy under pressure

Age level: Teens and up
Organizational level: Low
Number of players: Any number, in sequence
Supervision: Scorekeeper, 2 judges, 2 ball shaggers
Playing time: Open
Space needed: Golf driving range or open soccer or football field, free of traffic

Equipment: 1, 2, or 3 golf "woods" (club), enough golf tees for all contestants, 9–12 golf balls, 3 paper slips with each contestant's number/name on them (as markers), enough large nails to mark ball landings of contestants, tape measure

Directions: Each contestant takes 3 tee shots, trying for distance and accuracy. Each is measured and marked, the average of the 3 taken and the contestant's *average* distance marked (removing the other 3 markers). This average is given to the scorekeeper.

When all contestants have average markers displayed, each will take 3 more tee shots. These are marked, measured and averaged, then marked with the "average" distance marker, same as before. When everyone is done, the referee subtracts this second average from the first average if it is less, or the first from the second, if it is more for a "score differential." If the second average is more, a plus-point differential results, and if the second average is less, a minus-point differential. But the winner is the player with the *least* differential (showing consistency). If two are tied, the win goes to the plus-point differential.

Game source: Modified from an innovation by U.S. Navy Special Services officer McGowan at Navy Special Services Training School, 1972.

170. Putter Pool

Combines golf putting and pool in a patio or backyard setting

Age level: 8 and up
Organizational level: Medium
Number of players: 1–4
Supervision: None
Playing time: 15–20 minutes

Space needed: Enlarge pool table dimensions to fit available playing area
Equipment: 15 golf balls (marked with numbers like pool balls, 1–15), golf putter for each player, scorecard and pencil

Directions: Basic pool rules, but using putters and golf balls in place of pool cue sticks and balls.

Game source: Tom Tarbox of Phoenix, AZ invented Putter Pool in 1960, using painted golf balls on a pool "table" made of cement and covered with a carpet of high resiliency.

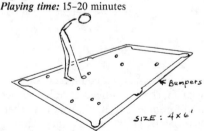

SIZE: 4×6'

171. Wall Golf

*Homemade golf practice range
made more fun with a game tied in*

Age level: 12 and up
Organizational level: Medium
Number of players: 1-4 taking turns, one of
which is designated scorekeeper. Players
shag own balls.
Playing time: 18 holes, about 60 minutes
per foursome

Space needed: Baseball batting cage (or similarly net enclosed area for safety), 10′ × 20′
Equipment: Basic set of golf clubs, bucket of
balls, package of tees, rubber mat, scorecards and pencil

Directions: Draw target design (figure 1) on 8′ × 10′ piece of canvas and hang it
as end drop at the end of the batting cage. It can be sewn or safety pinned (figure
2) to be hung on a stretched rope and to catch balls that hit it.

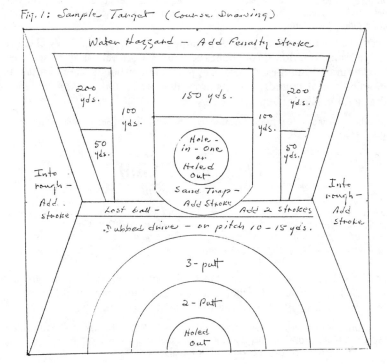

Fig. 1: Sample Target (Course Drawing)

Set the rubber mat at the opposite end of the cage, with the clubs, balls and
tees. Players tee off and continue hitting in order according to what section of
the target their balls hit. A miss of the target is a stroke penalty and a second
ball to hit.

Players who "hole out" do not have to wait until all players hole out that

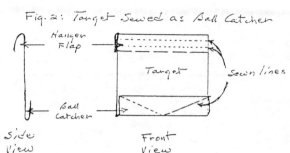

Fig. 2: Target Sewed as Ball Catcher

Hanger Flap

Target

Sewn lines

Ball Catcher

Side View

Front View

hole. All play ahead as fast as they can make holes, keeping the strokes records, however, for each person on each hole on the scorecard. Low total strokes is winner.

Players may use any variety of clubs available.

172. Team One-Ball Golf

A golf tournament in a much shorter time than regular golf

Age level: Teens and up
Organizational level: Medium
Number of players: 2 teams, 4 each
Supervision: Referee
Playing time: 45–60 minutes

Space needed: Miniature or regular golf course
Equipment: Basic set of golf clubs and 4 balls each foursome

Directions: Each foursome plays as a team, using a single ball. They play in strict rotation, same rotation throughout the match. Lost balls may be searched for a maximum of 5 minutes, before dropping another ball at the point it was last seen going out of bounds. It costs a penalty stroke. Otherwise, regular course and general golf rules apply.

Game source: Adapted from an innovation by U.S. Navy Special Services base director Charles Leahy, 1972.

173. Speed Golf

A different approach to golf

Age level: 14 and up
Organizational level: Low
Number of players: Foursomes, in sequence, with one member of each serving as score-keeper

Supervision: Tournament referee and starter
Space needed: Golf Course
Equipment: Golf clubs and balls for each player

Directions: Basic golf rules, except instead of counting strokes, the time used to play each hole is counted. One watch in each foursome should be used, and either everyone, or no one, in the tournament uses golf carts.

Game source: Formalized for tournament by Edwin H. Paget, founder and national director for Speed Golf and professor, Department of English, North Carolina State, Raleigh, N.C. The first annual Speed Golf Tourney was held in Raleigh in 1966.

174. Croquet Bowling

Teaches basic rules of bowling, in a game situation,
without having to be on the lanes

Age level: 8 and up
Organizational level: Medium
Number of players: 2–5

Supervision: Scorekeeper, players pin-set for each other

Playing time: About 60 minutes, depending greatly on speed of pin setters

Space needed: 6' × 20' smooth floor, cement, grass or packed ground area, like shuffleboard court

Equipment: Croquet mallet, 2 croquet balls, 10 bowling pins (Indian clubs, plastic pins, half-gallon milk cartons, tennis ball cans or Pringle potato chip canisters filled ⅓ with sand or dirt), bowling scoresheets and pencil, scoring instruction booklet, if needed, from bowling lane

Directions: Either make a spotting chart for tenpins to tape to the court, or chalk the triangle design on the court, so the pins will be set the same each time.

Basic bowling rules, except balls are struck with the mallet instead of being thrown. Ten frames constitutes a game, 3 games, a match. Winner is high score.

175. Target Bowling

Practice speed-distance element of bowling a ball

Age level: 8 and up
Organizational level: Low
Number of players: 2, 3 or 4
Supervision: None
Playing time: Variable, to point totals decided
Space needed: Grass or field area 60' × 10'

Equipment: 2 croquet-type stakes, 1 tape measure, 8 croquet balls, 52 yards of kite string, and four tent-peg-type stakes (or lime and liner for outlining playing area), enough flour or chalk dust or lime to outline the target areas

Directions: One side uses dark colored balls, other side uses light colored ones. Two players may use either three or four balls each, or three players may use two balls each, and four players use two each. A doubles game may be played with one member of a team at each end (as in horseshoes), with both members counting their scores cumulatively.

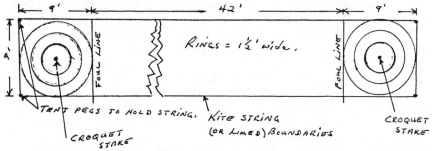

Singles players take turns bowling from one end to the other and then bowl back. Doubles players are stationed at one end throughout the game, bowling only one way.

The first turn doesn't count, but merely determines the order of the first roll. Person closest to stake rolls first, next closest second, and so on. On succeeding turns the person scoring highest score with all his balls goes first, next highest, second, and so on. If there is no score, the order remains the same as in the previous turn.

Bowl from behind foul line. Stepping over the line is a foul and points of that throw are lost, the ball is removed from the field of play, and any balls hit by it are replaced in their previous positions.

No ball is bowled until the one preceding has come to a stop.

Anyone bowling out of turn loses the next turn, loses points scored on that roll, has the ball taken from the field of play, and any balls that were hit are replaced in their previous positions.

Any ball may contact any other ball during play. The positions of balls after all have bowled in the round determines the count for that round. A ball knocking an opponent's ball into the pin scores those points for the owner of the ball that hits the pin. Ball position is determined by over half of it being inside.

Game is 15 points, but can be made any amount players agree on before starting play.

Scoring: Pin hit is 5 points. It can be nullified if opponent also hits pin in same round. If pin hit is not nullified, all other balls belonging to the pin-hitting side *which are higher placed than the highest placed opposition ball* may also be counted as points for that turn. (If an opposition ball is in the smallest circle, for example, and the pin-hitting side does not have one there, the pin-hitting side scores for the pin hit only, all other balls in lesser counting circles of the target are cancelled. The opposition, however, gets no points, because the pin hit cancels all opposition balls in lesser circles too.) The inner circle counts 4 points, the middle circle, 3 points, the outer circle 2 points and any of the four corners, 1 point. If there is no pin hit, the side with the highest placed ball or balls that are not cancelled out scores points, as indicated by placement, for that round, and the other team scores none. (As in horseshoes.) Ball hitting pin is counted only for pin-hit, not for position also.

A "round" is the period taken for all bowlers at one end of the court to roll each of their allotted balls once. A "game" is defined as that period taken for completion of a regulation game of 15 points.

Variations: For small children or other players who might have trouble understanding the "cancelling out" idea in point scoring, the game can be played with *all* balls in the target area counting. Game would then be 50 points. *Bowl or Bust*—Played as above, all balls in target area counting, except that winner must score *exactly* 25 points. If player scores more, he or she must start over agan. Other players maintain their scores, unless they ultimately "bust" also, in which case they, too, would then have to start over. *50 or Break*—Also played with all balls in target area counting, except that winner must score *exactly* 50 points to win. Instead of starting over if a player "busts," however, the number of points scored over 49 is subtracted from that person's previous score, and he or she continues play. *Club Bowling*—All the four above described games may also be played by using croquet mallets instead of hand-bowling the balls.

176. Hole-in-One Croquet

Makes use of croquet sets which may be missing the mallets through breakage. Trains eye-hand coordination for speed and distance in bowling a ball.

Age level: 8 and up
Organizational level: Low
Number of players: As many as there are balls available, 8 usually

Supervision: None, unless tournament play is planned. Tournament would require judge-recorder
Playing time: One to three rounds of play

for contestants. Varies with number and skills of players.

Space needed: 65' × 20' or larger, grass or dirt

Equipment: 1 croquet-type stake, 3 wire croquet-type wickets, equal number of balls for each contestant, some material such as flour, chalk or lime to outline the throwing circle

Directions: Decide first roll by any method agreeable to all contestants. One way is to roll-off, one ball each, with the person whose ball is closest to the stake then rolling first in each round, the next closest rolling second, and so on.

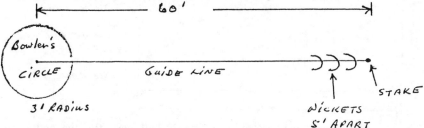

Divide balls so each competitor has an even number. Decide before starting how many turns will constitute a game. (Three or four balls per person gives a fair chance to everyone usually.)

Roll from inside the circle, trying to roll the ball through all three wickets and hit the stake. A stake-hit is 5 points. A ball getting through all three wickets, but not hitting the stake earns 3 points; a ball getting through two wickets earns 2 points, and a ball getting through one wicket earns 1 point. Game is 15 points.

Each ball is removed from field of play after it has stopped rolling, so each player has a clear field to the stake.

Stepping outside the circle while bowling is a foul. The ball does not count and cannot be taken over.

Variations: *(1)* A game may be to 15 points or won by a stake hit, whichever comes first. *(2) Hazard*—Same as basic game, except that all balls remain on the field of play instead of being removed after each person has bowled one. This game is only played if each player has two or more balls to use. Knocking other players' balls out of the way is allowed. Game can be 10 or 15 points. (The more players, the lower the point total should be, since it becomes progressively harder to score.) *(3)* All the above described games can be played also by using croquet mallets instead of hand-bowling the balls.

177. Croquet Field Pool (or Croquet Pool)

Teaches pool rules and playing basics without having pool equipment ruined by young children or beginners. The outside action aspect is more pleasing to children, too. Good change-of-pace game when regular croquet begins to pall.

Age level: 8 and up

Organizational level: Low

Number of players: Best game is with 2; however, 3 to 6 may play if turns are taken in rotation

Supervision: None

Playing time: Free play, games depending on skills of players

Space needed: Minimum 30' × 10', field or turf

Equipment: Croquet mallet for each player (or take turns using what are available), 8 balls (or 16, if two sets are available), 6 wickets (as "pockets"), 2 strips of plastic, plywood or other useable material 9' × 4", plus four strips 14' × 4" (as sides of playing area), spare wickets or wooden pegs (at least 18) to anchor and hold up these sides. Triangle (for formation of balls to start each game) can be formed from a metal hanger (equipment is now available commercially at some large department stores, such as the Woodward and Lothrop chain in Washington, DC)

Directions: Follow basic rules of table pool — rotation, eight-ball and other variations.

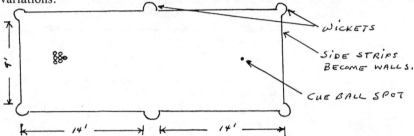

The mallet head must be used in striking the ball, never the stick end, as in using a cue stick.

The highest numbered ball is used as the cue ball. If using two sets of balls, the pairs (as both #3s) must be played consecutively.

Variations: *Field Billiards (or Croquet Billiards)* — Same equipment, except no wickets are used as pockets — they are eliminated, and only three balls are needed (one as cue ball and two as billiard balls).

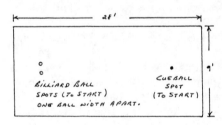

Basic table billiards rules followed. Game, however, can be pre-decided for any number of billiards or points. Suggested: 10 or 15.

A point is scored by making a "billiard." A billiard is performed by hitting the cue ball so it strikes both the billard balls before it stops rolling. A player keeps taking turns until he or she misses a billiard.

178. Super Croquet

Greater challenge for expert croquet players. Also good change-of-pace for when regular croquet begins to pall

Age level: 8 and up
Organizational level: Low
Number of players: Any number for which balls and mallets are available
Supervision: None
Playing time: About same as regular croquet
Space needed: Same as regular croquet, variable
Equipment: Same as regular croquet, except that 11

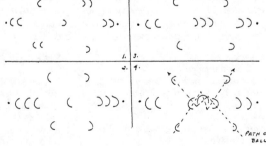

wickets are needed. They may be placed as shown on the previous page for four variations

Directions: Same as for regular croquet, except there are more wickets to go through.

179. Snoo-Quet

Combines croquet and snooker type pool

Age level: 10 and up
Organizational level: Medium
Number of players: 2, 4, 6, 8
Supervision: Referee-scorekeeper
Playing time: 60 minutes
Space needed: 21′ × 30′ area, or 9′ × 18′ if using side panels
Equipment: Croquet set for 8 players, 12

balls, 6 red, 1 black, white, blue, brown, green, yellow and pink, plus 6 2″ high canvas strips 9″ long, with connector snaps or hooks, or commercial Snoo-Quet set (available from Webber-C.P.J. Ltd., Devon, England), paper and pencil for scorekeeping

Directions: The white cueball is used by all players. It is the only one struck directly with the mallets. It is hit into other balls in trying to put other balls, in correct sequence, through the ground hoops from their front or inward sides. A ball must pass completely through a hoop to score.

Set up balls on court as shown in figure at right. Cueball (white) is set anywhere in the "D" area and hit in any direction to start the game.

Sequence of Play: If a hit (Roquet) is achieved, the Cueball is lifted and placed in contact with the red where it has come to rest after being roquet'd. The cueball is placed in a straight line with the red facing towards the *front* side of a hoop. After lining up the 2 balls, the player hits the cueball so it propels the red toward the hoop (or "pocket") and endeavors to "pot" it, making sure that the cueball does not follow through the hoop.

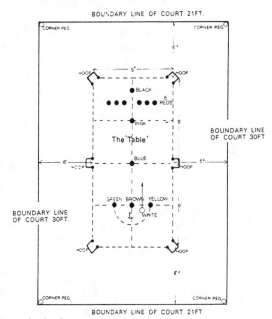

When a red has been successfully "potted" it is taken out of the game and the player hits the cueball from the point where it came to rest towards a color (black, pink, blue, brown, green or yellow), and makes a roquet on it. The cueball is again lifted, placed in a straight line behind the color which is then "potted." When colors are potted they are immediately replaced on their correct positions on the table *so long as there is a red still in the game.*

Having potted the color and replaced it on its correct spot on the table, the player continues the "break" by aiming the cueball at another red, and if successful in potting it, goes on to a color, i.e., alternating red/color/red/color, etc., until all have been "potted." When all the reds have gone, the colors are potted in the following strict sequence — Yellow, Green, Brown, Blue, Pink and Black. As each color is "potted" in correct sequence it is taken out until only black is left in the game.

Scoring: Potting the Red and colors score: Red — 1 point each; Yellow — 2 points; Green — 3 points; Brown — 4 points; Blue — 5 points; Pink — 6 points; Black — 7 points.

Penalties are incurred when a player fails to hit the Cueball on to an Object ball. Penalty points are given away when the Red, Yellow, Green or Brown are missed, but the penalty points are 5, 6, or 7 when the Blue, Pink or Black are missed.

The same scale of penalties applies when the Cueball is hit on to the wrong ball or misses altogether, e.g., if the player selects to aim at the Blue and hits a Red by mistake, or misses completely, the penalty is 5 points (the scoring value of the Blue) as Blue was the ball the player selected or nominated to play next.

Players responsible for sending balls over the boundaries give away the same scale of penalties.

After incurring a penalty shot, the player's turn or break ends, but if the play appears inevitable (as when Snookered) the player concerned should hit the Cueball to the limits of the Court to give the opponent as long a shot as possible, but must not leave a Snooker — see next paragraph.

Snookers: Players who are placed in positions from which they cannot "pot" a ball should propel the Object ball to a "safe" position within the boundaries of the Court or, endeavor to leave a Snooker for the next player, leaving a "wrong" colour between the Cueball and the correct Object ball. Players who are successfully snookered give away penalty points (as above) and cannot leave another Snooker for the next player. If this happens, or on any occasion after penalty points have incurred, the turn comes to an end and the next player may lift the Cueball and move it just sufficiently to give a clear and unimpeded shot at an appropriate Object ball.

Variation: The Snoo-Quet games booklet lists Billiards, clock Billiards, Snooker, Snooker Pool, Slosh Pool, Boules (for 2), Webber-Croquet, Clock Croquet, Conventional Croquet, Garden (9 hoop) Croquet and Garden Bowls.

180. Whopolo (or Pillow Polo)

Good action game with elements of polo and field hockey,
stressing strategy and team play, with minimum of supervision

Age level: 7 and up, including handicapped
Organizational level: Medium
Number of players: 2 teams; 6 per team, plus subs

Supervision: None for informal play, referee-scorekeeper for handicapped and organized competition
Playing time: Pre-set time or score limit

Space needed: 50′ × 100′, indoors or outdoors
Equipment: Foam ball or Whiffleball (7″ circumference), 12 pillow polo sticks (6 each of differing colors), goal net 56″ × 42″ × 24″ in size, (commercial sets available from U.S. Games Co.)

Directions: Basic field hockey rules. But no body contact. Foul gives fouled player a free hit of the ball at the point of infraction.

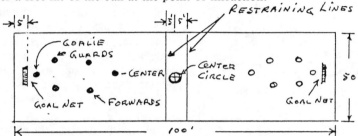

Ball going out of bounds is given to team opposite one last touching it, at out-of-bounds point.

To start game, and after each goal scored, referee places ball on ground in center circle. On his signal, centers from both teams race to play it to their teammates. Then each team tries to hit the ball into its opponent's goal.

Each team's goalie, with the help of his teammates, tries to stop any ball from going into their goal. Goalies are the only players who may use hands to block the ball (though they may not catch or hold it).

Court and player positions are shown in the chart above.

Game source: Modified from Field Hockey and Pillo Polo game.

181. Slalom Hockey

Teaches basic skill of ball control for field hockey in a fun situation

Age level: 10 and up
Organizational level: Medium
Number of players: 2
Supervision: Course judge
Playing time: 4–5 minutes
Space needed: 3′ × 14′ area

Equipment: 2 field hockey sticks (or corn brooms or croquet mallets), 2 balls (field hockey, tennis or croquet balls), 12 1′ long posts (or tin cans) and an ending post with a paper flag on it

Directions: On "go" signal, two opponents start up court, each striking and guiding his ball with his stick only, going slalom style (around stakes alternately to left and right) up the course and back. Each player starts on a different side of the course and crosses at the halfway point as they start back. Each must touch the ending stake with his ball to end his run. First to return with a legal run is the winner.

If balls contact each other, play goes on. But players cannot touch another player's ball with his stick. And no body contact is allowed with balls, like foot stopping, kicking or guiding and hand touching. Penalty: start over. However, if one player drives his ball into the other player, except accidentally, the player hitting the ball will start over.

When a player is penalized by having to start over, he may then pick up his ball and carry it back to the starting point.

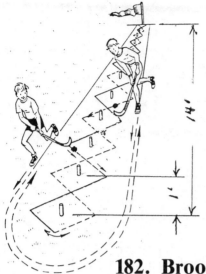

Tournaments can be held by elimination runs or by timing the runs.

Variations: Slalom Hockey Relay— Two teams run against each other on side-by-side courses, 2 opposing players on each course start at the same time. Then, as soon as these first two hit the end-stake, the next two players take over, and so on until all players have had turns. First team legally completing its run is the winner.

These also may be run either by elimination brackets or timed trials.

Game source: Russian game innovation.

182. Broom Hockey

Simple forerunner for learning field hockey

Age level: 8 and up
Organizational level: Medium
Number of players: 2 teams, 6–8 each
Supervision: Referee and scorekeeper
Playing time: 4 5-minute quarters
Space needed: Multi-purpose room or cleared cafeteria, or outside grass, paved or packed dirt area at least 40′ × 40′
Equipment: Kitchen type broom for each player, roll of toilet tissue taped all around, 2 benches (as goals)

Directions: Put benches at two opposite ends of playing field. One team starts play with "ball" (toilet tissue roll) on the floor beside its "goal" (bench). On "go" signal, the ball is hit into the court and then it may be passed from player to teammate, intercepted, or shot for a goal as available by all players.

Brooms may not be raised above waist high in striking or blocking the ball, and they may not be used in blocking or tripping an opponent in any way.

Scores are made by hitting the ball *under* a goal (bench).

PADDLE, RACQUET & CESTA GAMES

183. Roof Ball

For play where usual fields and courts are not available

Age level: 10 and up
Organizational level: Low
Number of players: 1 on 1, 2 on 2
Supervision: None

Playing time: 15-point game, about 20 minutes

Space needed: Small building with sloping roof and no windows on playing wall

Equipment: Ball (playground, volley, tennis or Nerf ball), paddles or racquets (type decided by type ball used) for all players, (Wham-O-Mfg. markets Trac-Ball equipment, a curved plastic racquet and ball)

Directions: Object of game: Bat ball with hand, fist, paddle or racquet (depending on type of ball used) onto the sloping roof. Players take turns hitting it as it rolls off roof.

Point goes to opponent each time a player fails to return a roll-off to the roof or hits the ball so it doesn't return to the pre-selected playing area (about a 20′ frontage).

184. Cup Jai Alai

Informal game to play anywhere with simple equipment

Age level: 8 and up

Organizational level: Low

Number of players: 1 on 1, 2 on 2

Supervision: None

Playing time: 15–21 point game, about 20 minutes

Space needed: Table tennis table (or any other type table) pushed against a wall with one-half of it laid up against the wall

Equipment: Table tennis ball, paper cup for each player

Directions: Basic table tennis rules, except players stand on same side of table and alternate turns receiving the ball, throwing and catching it in the paper cup. Catcher can't move from spot where he caught the ball before throwing it again.

Variation: *Cup Volleyball*—Play volleyball over a net (or a fence) by catching and throwing table tennis ball with paper cup. Several players can play on each side, then each side is allowed to catch, and pass the ball twice, before throwing it back. (If a table tennis ball isn't available, a tightly wadded sheet of newspaper, tightly taped, can be used.)

185. 99

Good informal game with minimal rules and equipment in small area

Age level: 8 and up

Organizational level: Low

Number of players: Individually, in rotation, with scores compared, in tournament play

Supervision: None informally, scorekeeper otherwise

Playing time: Variable, since it is a skill test

Space needed: Area adjacent a wall 6–8′ wide and 10–12′ long

Equipment: Table tennis table (without legs), paddle and ball

Directions: Play table tennis against yourself, hitting ball against top half of table (which is leaned against the wall at a 65° angle) so it drops onto the lower half (resting on the floor or ground). Then it is played on one bounce again, with the cycle repeated until an error is made: (1) the ball bounces more than once on the "floor" before a return, (2) the ball is hit out of bounds (off the table), or (3) the ball hits floor before wall on a return.

Player cannot step onto the table to play the ball. Score is the number of complete returns, paddle to paddle again. When an error/fault is made, turn is over and the next player takes his turn.

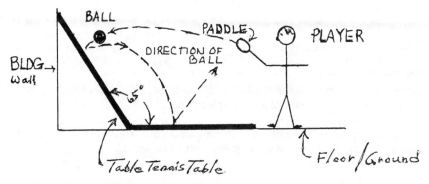

Variations: *(1)* Table tennis table half is propped against the wall at 90° angle (straight up) with other half on the floor or ground. Play one-wall racquetball rules, singles or doubles. *(2)* Set table, on its legs, against a wall and two players can play against each other from the same end of the table, playing ball against wall, so it drops to the table and is played by taking turns returning it.

Game source: Modified. Name came from a record score racked up the first summer it was played on a Cedar Rapids, IA playground, as reported by assistant superintendent of recreation, Nat Hull.

186. Twist Table Tennis

Table tennis variation just for fun

Age level: 12 and up
Organizational level: Low
Number of players: 3
Supervision: None

Playing time: 10-point game, about 30 minutes
Space needed: Table tennis table
Equipment: 3 paddles, table tennis ball

Directions: Table tennis basic rules, except play starts with one player at one end of table and two at the other end.

Single person serves always. Once serve has been returned, players rotate positions clockwise, while trying to keep the ball in play.

The player who makes an error is awarded a point, and the first player assessed 10 points is the loser.

187. Floor Tennis (or Smash)

Eliminates need for expensive table tennis tables and storage
area for them. Good change-of-pace game for table tennis players.
Game can be set up in places a table couldn't be.

Age level: 10 and up
Organizational level: Low
Number of players: 2 or 4, singles or doubles
Supervision: None in free play; competition:
  referee-scorekeeper
Playing time: 4-point games (as in tennis
  scoring: 15, 30, 40, game), six games to a set
  (or more, until one side wins by two games),
  and best two of three sets

Space needed: Gym floor, hallway or other
  inside area, 8′ × 16′ minimum
Equipment: Table tennis ball, paddle for
  each player, net (can be string between two
  chair backs with double pages of newspaper
  hanging over it or commercial equipment
  can be obtained from U.S. Games), chalk
  or line marking tape, rubber-soled shoes
  for players

Directions: Serve by bouncing ball on floor then hitting it over the net. Otherwise play basic tennis rules.

Variations: Scoring may be done as in table tennis instead of as in tennis.

Game source: Origin undetermined.

188. Cornerball

Age level: 8 and up
Organizational level: Low
Number of players: 2 or 4, singles or doubles
Supervision: None in free play, referee-scorekeeper for competitions
Playing time: 15-point games
Space needed: About 15-foot square in corner of gym or room with 7-foot high, smooth walls

Equipment: Table tennis ball, table tennis paddle for each player (commercial Cornerball game [called Cracket], modified and portable, available from Acro Inc.), chalk or line-marking tape (to mark boundaries, etc.)

Directions: Players take turns hitting ball off one or both side walls so it returns to floor inside the playing boundaries. Ball may be played off the wall(s) either before it hits the floor (volley) or after one bounce.

Serve from serving area, by bouncing ball to floor and hitting it on the rise against either or both walls, so it rebounds into the playing area. Opponent stands anywhere except in the serving area to receive a serve.

Serve must first contact the wall above the serving line. All subsequent hits, however, may be played off the walls without regard to the serving line.

Server is the only one who can score, one point for every fault the opponent(s) make(s). Faults include not returning the ball into the court in any way.

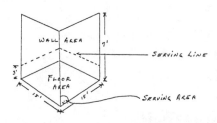

A replay of point is called any time a player hinders an opponent's play or hides the ball with his body.

Variations: *(1) Doubles, Mixed Doubles*—Playing area can be enlarged as wished. Teams alternate hitting the ball, though team members do not have to take turns. *(2)* Plastic scoops and plastic "Fun" ball may be used instead of table tennis ball and paddles, by enlarging the court to about 17 feet square, especially for doubles play. (See Scoop Cornerball rules.) *(3)* Racquetball equipment can be used by enlarging the area to a 20-foot square. (See Scoop Cornerball, Variations, rules.)

189. Volley-Pong

A volleyball variation using table tennis equipment

Age level: 10 and up
Organizational level: Low
Number of players: Singles, doubles or triples
Supervision: None
Playing time: 20–30 minutes

Space needed: Badminton court, or equivalent space 20′ × 44′ with net 5′ high
Equipment: Table tennis paddle for each player, table tennis ball (which can be taped, so it will withstand harder play)

Directions: Basic volleyball rules, except the ball is played on the paddles, and cannot touch the body. Serves are made from the backcourt, alternating right and left halves as in tennis.

Variations: *Mini Volley-Pong*—Same game, except court is only 10′ × 24′ with the net at 7′ height. *Mini Badminton-Pong*—Same 10′ × 24′ court, but badminton rules are used in playing the ball.

190. Paddle Volleyball

Teaches basic volleyball rules, as well as beginner skills for paddle tennis and racquetball and hand-eye coordination for other games

Age level: 12 and up
Organizational level: Medium
Number of players: 2 teams, up to 9 each, depending on size of court laid out
Supervision: Referee and scorekeeper
Playing time: 20–30 minutes per game, average
Space needed: Court with net can vary from

badminton size for younger and novice players to volleyball size for older, better skilled players
Equipment: Tennis ball, paddle tennis paddles (½″ thick wooden paddles about twice the size of table tennis paddles, with additional wood tacked to each side of the handles for comfortable grip)

Directions: Basic volleyball rules, except the tennis ball is passed to teammates and returned over the net with the paddles. Ball may be hit on the fly or after one court bounce by each player "handling" it on the same side (limit 3 players).

Variations: *Pong Badminton*—Badminton rules, except using a table tennis ball with badminton racquets, instead of a shuttlecock.

Game source: Adapted from the Paddle Volleyball game that Grace Arnold, women's director,

Ypsilanti, MI Recreation Department, innovated and used for two years in her school program. It was published in *Recreation* magazine, June 1952.

191. Cesta Cornerball

Variation on jai alai type games

Age level: 10 and up
Organizational level: Medium
Supervision: None, after players have
learned game

Playing time: 15 points, about 30 minutes
Space needed: Corner area 20′ × 20′
Equipment: Whiffleball, plastic cestas (hand
scoops) for each player

Directions: Server has choice of courts. If serving from the right-hand court, he throws the ball from his cesta (scoop) against the right-hand wall, so it caroms off the left wall and into the left-hand court. (Opposite if serving from left court.) Penalty for failure: loss of serve. Only server scores.

Ball may be caught on the fly or one bounce, and must be returned immediately, caroming always first from wall bordering a player's court, to the adjoining wall and into the opponent's court. The ball must always hit both walls. Penalty: loss of point or serve.

Player blocking opponent's view, or otherwise hindering his return, results in a replay, with no points awarded.

Points are awarded, or serve lost, by: (1) illegal serve, (2) ball hit out of bounds, (3) ball not hitting both walls on a return, (4) ball bouncing more than once on floor, (5) holding ball in cesta more than 10 seconds while ball is in play.

192. Jug Ball

Simplified version to teach basics of lacrosse.
Good for hand-eye coordination training.

Age level: 6 up
Organizational level: Medium
Number of players: Two even-numbered
teams, 4–12 players each
Supervision: Referee
Space needed: Minimum 20′ × 50′, unless
played on beach or in shallow pool area,
when area can be made to fit what's available

Equipment: 1 Whiffleball (outside) or soft
foam ball (inside), hand scoop (commercial
ones available, or can make them by cutting bottoms off gallon plastic milk jugs),
two goal standards, which can be anything
from commercial soccer or field hockey
goals to boxes set on their sides, lime or
chalk for marking playing field

Directions: Goals ideally are posts 4′ high set 4′ apart with crossbar on top, or rope stretched across top.

Only goalies may be inside goal circles.

To start play, opposing centers face each other at mid-court, with ball on

ground between them. Each center faces opponent's goal. On referee signal both try to scoop or hit ball to one of their players.

One-point goals are scored by scoop-throwing the ball between the opponent's goalposts on the fly or bounce.

Balls can't be touched with hands. Penalty is loss out of bounds to opposing team at nearest point to infraction. Balls may be blocked away with scoop or body, however. Last team touching ball before it goes out of bounds loses possession at that point.

Defenders may not touch an attacker who has possession of ball.

Disputes over possession (held balls, etc.) will be decided at point of conflict with a "face-off" as done at start of game, between the two players involved.

Play either to predetermined number of goals or time limit, with or without periods for rest, depending upon age, fitness and skill of players.

193. Cesta Wallball (or Baby Jai Alai)

Teaches a mini-version of the Spanish game of jai alai

Age level: 10 and up
Organizational level: Medium
Number of players: Singles or doubles games
Supervision: None
Playing time: 15-point game, about 30 minutes

Space needed: 20′ × 20′ apron with adjoining 9–15′ tall wall
Equipment: Whiffleball and cesta (plastic hand scoop—commercial or made by cutting bottoms or side off plastic gallon milk jugs) for each player

Directions: Ball is played—picked up, thrown and caught—with the cesta, never touched with the hands.

Server stands behind midline, receiver behind "mark," until the ball has rebounded across the midline. Bad first serve gets a second serve.

Ball may be played on the fly or first bounce, and returned on the fly to the wall (before touching the floor).

Points are scored when opponent: (1) makes illegal serve, (2) makes illegal return, (3) hits ball out of bounds, (4) fails to return held ball within 10 seconds,

(5) allows ball to touch floor more than once before a return, (6) touches ball with hands.

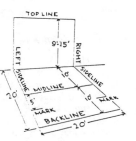

When a player is blocked from the ball, or otherwise hindered by his opponent, or the ball hits him (other than intentionally letting it hit him), it is called a replay. Intentional hinderment is a fault and a point for the opponent.

194. Lob Hockey

Hockey-type play utilizing hand skills

Age level: 12 and up
Organizational level: Medium
Number of players: 2 teams, 7–10 each
Supervision: Referee-scorekeeper
Playing time: 21-point game, about 40 minutes

Space needed: 50′ × 100′ area
Equipment: Whiffle or Fun Ball, hand scoop for each player (commercial scoops and Fun Ball available from Cosom Company)

Directions: Toss coin to decide which team serves first. Player making serve stands behind serve line and hurls ball with scoop into opposing team's playing area. Members of opposing team try to catch or scoop ball to prevent it from going over goal line, and volley it back. Each time a team scores, the ball must be served again. Positions should be rotated so all players get a chance to serve.

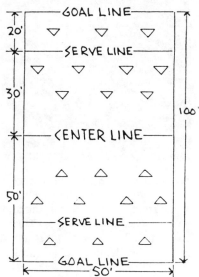

Object of the game is to throw ball over opponents' goal line and prevent them from catching ball. While throwing ball back and forth, each team tries to force the play back to the other's goal line, increasing its chances of scoring.

When player catches ball, he can take *only one step* before returning it. No player is allowed to step over the center line. All caught balls must be thrown directly back into the other team's area and cannot be passed to a teammate.

Scoring: There are 21 points to a game. Three points are scored if team gets ball over opponent's goal that is not caught. Two points are scored if ball is thrown over opponent's goal and is caught. One point is scored if opposing player throws ball out of bounds.

195. Jai Alai–Volleyball

Utilizes skills using hand scoop in a volleyball-type format

Age level: 12 and up
Organizational level: Medium
Number of players: 2 teams, 4–9 each
Supervision: Referee-scorekeeper
Playing time: 21-point game, about 30 minutes
Space needed: Volleyball court, or similar

30′ × 60′ area with 8′ high net. (Can also be played over a fence.)
Equipment: Whiffleball (or Fun Ball), hand scoop for each player (which can be made by cutting sides or bottoms off gallon plastic milk or juice jugs)

Directions: Basic volleyball rules, except ball can't be touched with hands, but must be caught in, and thrown from, hand scoops. Player cannot hold ball in his scoop longer than 5 seconds before playing it while ball is in play.

Players cannot touch net with either bodies or scoops.

196. Jug Tennis

Simpler variation of tennis for small fry play almost anywhere

Age level: 10 and up
Organizational level: Low
Number of players: 2 sides, 1–4 per side
Supervision: None
Playing time: 4-point game, 3 game match, about 20 minutes
Space needed: Badminton court, or equivalent 20′ × 44′ with 5′ high net (or rope)

Equipment: Tennis or Whiffleball (or commercial Fun Ball available from Cosom Co.), jug cesta for each player (made from cutting bottoms or one side off gallon plastic milk jugs or commercial "Scoops" available from Cosom Co.)

Directions: Starting with a gallon plastic milk jug (see picture at left) mark the area to be cut off with a felt-tip pen, cut along the marked lines with heavy scissors or knife, and the end result is a jug cesta.

Utilizing a rope stretched between two

trees as a net, the cesta jugs serve as catching *and* throwing tools. The ball (made from a wad of paper, taped) is never touched with the hands. Throwing the ball from the jug takes a little practice, involving a scoop motion, sort of jerking the scoop back toward you once the ball has momentum.

Use basic tennis rules.

Ball must be caught and returned immediately. Player can take only one and a half steps before throwing it.

Variations: *Jug Racquetball* — Play ball against a wall instead of over a net, using basic racquetball rules. *Anty-Over* — Use jug cestas to catch and throw ball over a small building. If ball is caught, catcher, or catching team, may run around the building and try to tag an opponent with the ball (by throwing it from the cesta). Any tagged player joins the team that tagged him.

197. Pin Hit

Interest rejuvenator, a totally different game

Age level: 8 and up
Organizational level: Medium
Number of players: 2
Supervision: None
Playing time: 21-point game, about 30
  minutes

Space needed: 60′ × 60′ area
Equipment: 1 Bowlite pin (available through Cosom Co. or quart milk cartons can be used), 4–8 Frisbees (marketed by Wham-O Mfg.)

Directions: Players stand 30′ on either side of the pin, as shown in diagram below. On "go" signal, each tries to be first to knock over the pin by throwing, skipping or skidding his Frisbee at it. If there is no hit, each player gathers up the Frisbees his opponent has thrown, goes back to his throwing spot, and resumes throwing as soon as he can (no second "go" signal needed).

Player knocking over pin earns a point. Then, pin is set up again and the game starts again from a "go" signal, with player not scoring the hit throwing first. First to 21 points is winner.

Variations: *Open Field Jai Alai* — Same game as above except each player uses a hand cesta (scoop) (commercial scoops from Cosom Co., or made from plastic milk jugs, as shown on page 144) to throw a Whiffleball (or tennis ball) at the pin. Only one ball is used, so opponents take turns throwing back and forth until a hit is scored.

Spilled Milk — Stack 17–21 or more, pint or quart milk cartons up into a pyramid configuration (depending on a person's stacking skill). One way to do it is to place 9 cartons like figure on previous page.

Then stack 4–8 more on their sides atop each bottom level pair (again, depending upon stacking skill). Then stack 4–8

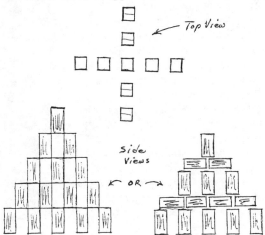

more cartons vertically atop those. (If players have the skill and enough cartons, the stack can go even higher.)

Either Frisbees or cestas and a ball may be used in trying to knock over this pyramid. Player who knocks over the last pin standing is the winner.

198. Rolling Scoop Throw

Teaches use of scoops (hand cestas)
while, at same time, playing a game

Age level: 10 and up
Organizational level: Low
Number of players: 2 teams, 4–6 each
Supervision: Scorekeeper, target rollers (2)
Playing time: 30–60 minutes
Space needed: Area about 20′ × 60′

Equipment: Scoop for each player (plastic scoops marketed by Cosom Co.), 2 Fun Balls (available through Cosom Co., or Whiffleball or sponge balls) per player, 1 auto tire

Directions: Line up groups facing each other about 20′ apart. Assign a player from each group to act as roller. Two rollers stand in the center area, one at each end (see diagram).

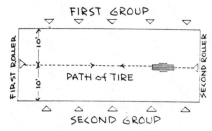

Each player in the first group to throw has a scoop and a Fun Ball. Players in second group do not have to have scoops and balls and can take turns using equipment with the first group. On signal, one roller rolls tire down center of area between the 2 groups. Each player of the first group, using his scoop, attempts to throw ball through tire as it passes. Scoops are tossed over to second group (if every player doesn't have one). Then the second roller sets the tire in motion and the second group tries to throw the balls through it.

The rollers then join their respective groups and 2 other players act as rollers. Continue game until each player has acted as roller. Each ball tossed through the tire counts one point. The player or team with the highest score wins.

Variation: *Human Hoop* — For older players, 13 and up. Same game, except one person sits inside the tire, with legs sticking out on each side to help guide it, and is rolled between the lines. Players try to hit person in the tire as he passes. (Riders get very dizzy, so need new rider each roll.)

199. Scoop Jai Alai

*Active field game while teaches use
of scoops as forerunner to understanding lacrosse*

Age level: 10 and up
Organizational level: High
Number of players: 2 teams, 5–10 each
Supervision: 2 referees and 1 scorekeeper
Playing time: 4 10-minute quarters
Space needed: 60' × 120' area
Equipment: A hand scoop for each player

(plastic scoops available through Cosom Company or may be made by cutting the bottom or one side off a gallon plastic milk or juice jug as shown in illustration on page 144), Whiffleball (or sponge on Fun Ball [Fun Ball available through Cosom Company]), 2 6' × 10' × 5" tall goals of netting

Directions: Toss coin, or otherwise decide which team gets choice of possession of ball or goal. Reverse to start second half. Teams exchange goals for second and fourth quarters.

Starting the Play: Place ball on center spot. Offensive center takes position to one side of the ball with his scoop placed over ball. Both teams line up on their own side of ball. Defensive center may have his scoop on ground to one side of ball, so he is in good position to recover a muffled flip of the ball. The offensive center flips ball to a member of his team. The offensive team, passing the ball with scoops, moves ball down field to throw it into their opponent's goal.

The defensive team tries to intercept passes or steal the ball by flicking it out of opponent's scoops. The defensive team tries to protect its goal by using a man-to-man defense, a zone defense or a combination of both.

Only the goaltender can enter the goal crease. However, he may leave his zone and advance as far as the midfield line when his team is on the offensive. While tending goal, he may deflect a shot with his scoop or a hand. He may catch the ball with a scoop but not in his hand. When he is out of his zone he must play the ball like any other player. He is allowed to protect his goal when a penalty shot is attempted, but must stay within his zone.

When a ball goes out of bounds, it is put into play from that point by a member of the team which did not touch it last. Exception: a ball going out of bounds through the goal crease, is always put into play by the goaltender, no matter what team caused it to go out of bounds. An out-of-bounds ball must be thrown to a team mate and not dropped into his scoop.

When a team wants a time-out called, their captain notifies the referee, who signals timeout when that team has possession of the ball. Each team is allowed 2 time-outs of 3 minutes per quarter.

Substitutions are unlimited, but can be made only when the ball is dead.

When a goal is scored, the team scored upon puts ball in play with a center flip from the center spot.

When a penalty shot is awarded, all players except player attempting the shot and the goaltender must retire to a neutral area.

Fouls which allow the fouled team to take a penalty shot are: (1) Slashing or striking an opponent's scoop or body. (2) Unnecessary body contact such as shouldering, clipping, tripping, body checking, etc. (3) Playing ball in own or opponent's goal crease. (4) Goaltender coming out of own goal crease when penalty shot is being attempted at his goal. (5) Having too many men on the field. (6) Throwing the scoop. (7) Interfering with an opponent's play, such as holding his scoop, holding him, running or falling in front of him to keep him from the ball or prevent his movement.

The ball shall be awarded to opponents and be put in play from out of bounds when a team (1) is offside, (2) causes the ball to go out of bounds, (3) player holds the ball in his scoop over five seconds, (4) player touches the ball with his hand, (5) player takes more than three steps with the ball in his possession, (6) player holds the ball on the ground, (7) player plays ball when not on feet, (8) player kicks the ball, (9) player dribbles the ball on ground, (10) player passes the ball to himself on the ground or in the air, (11) goaltender catches ball with hand, (12) player enters either team's goal crease when on offensive or defense, (13) goaltender goes over midfield line.

200. Badminiature

Active game that can be played in the house. Good for rainy days.

Age level: 8 and up
Organizational level: Low
Number of players: 2 or 4, singles or doubles
Supervision: None
Playing time: Free play, games of 15 points
Space needed: 10′ square minimum, inside or outside; optional, to fit area

Equipment: Chalk or tape to mark court boundaries, net (can be string stretched between two chair backs), newspaper (double sheets folded over string net), paper cup (as shuttlecock), cardboard record album covers or folded magazines (as paddles)

Directions: Indoors, players are seated or kneeling; outdoors they may stand. Area of play is optional, to fit circumstances.

Basic badminton rules are used—singles, doubles or mixed doubles.

Variation: Imagination in use of other playing equipment will add variety to the game, such as using a yarn ball or even a paper ball with rubber bands around it in place of the paper cup. With these materials the open hand may be used in place of the album covers, too.

201. Pingminton

Badminton in a small area, teaches accuracy in stroking

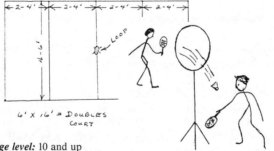

6′ X 16′ = DOUBLES COURT

Age level: 10 and up
Organizational level: Low
Number of players: 1 on 1, 2 on 2
Supervision: None

Playing time: About 30 minutes per game
Space needed: Area 4′ × 8′ inside or outside away from wind
Equipment: Shuttlecock (or yard ball or table tennis ball), badminton racquets for each player (or table tennis paddles, or cardboard L.P. album covers, or round "palm" paddles cut from plywood or stiff cardboard), hoop (commercial or hula hoop or 2′ × 4′ square wooden frame mounted atop a tall pole)

Directions: Basic badminton rules, but hitting the Shuttlecock back and forth through a hoop.

Serve from behind service line, through hoop and over the reception/serve line on opponent's side. Only server scores. Game is 15 points.

202. Winter Badminton

Kookie game to play in the snow

Age level: 12 and up
Organizational level: Low
Number of players: 1 on 1 or 2 on 2
Supervision: None
Playing time: 15-point game, about 15–20 minutes

Space needed: Badminton-sized court, but with net raised to 8′–9′
Equipment: Large wooden racquetball paddles for each player, outdoors shuttlecock, set of snowshoes for each player, food coloring to mark court lines

Directions: Basic badminton rules, played on snowshoes. Higher net gives players more time to move about to return the shuttlecock.

Variations: *(1)* Same as above, except players wear one snowshoe and use the other one as a racquet. (Extra strings may need to be added so the shuttlecock won't slip through.) *(2)* The Russians are playing tennis on ice, wearing ice skates and using an orange ball and conventional racquets. (Report from London Times, 1976.) *(3)* Volleyball in the snow, with players wearing snowshoes, has been played annually in winter at a community sports weekend in Priest Lake, Idaho for years. Ball is painted red and court lines marked with food coloring. *(4)* Trac Ball sets, with curved plastic racquets and plastic balls, have been available from Wham-O Mfg. Co. and may be used for another variation.

203. Bird Dunk

Sample a kookie Russian game invention

Age level: 12 and up
Organizational level: Medium
Number of players: 2 teams, 5–10 each
Supervision: Referee-scorekeeper
Playing time: 4 10-minute quarters, with 3 minutes between each as rest period

Space needed: Basketball court
Equipment: Several shuttlecocks (outdoor plastic type), badminton racquets for each player

Directions: Start game with one team in possession of shuttlecock at mid court. Teams alternate possession to start each quarter.

Object of game is to hit shuttlecock to teammates until one is in position to hit the bird (shuttlecock) into the basketball hoop (from the top only). A player may pass the bird to himself. A shuttlecock may also be juggled or held on the racquet, so long as no steps are taken.

If the shuttle hits the floor, it is put into play at that point immediately by the nearest opposing player to the player last touching it. It must be scooped up on the racquet. Hands cannot be used to touch the bird at any time. (Penalty is loss of possession at point of contact.)

A goal counts 2 points. A "free hit" from the free throw line counts 1 point.

A "free hit on goal" is awarded for these fouls: roughing a player by shoving, tripping, moving, blocking, holding, hitting body or racquet with racquet.

After each score, the team scored on takes shuttlecock under the basket and hits it into play. Must be done within 10 seconds.

Variation: *Flicker Shuttle*—Same game, except a Flicker Ball goal (see Flicker Ball sheet in Football section) is used in place of the basketball goal.

Game source: Adapted from Russian game.

204. Pickle Ball

Variation on the game of tennis

Age level: 10 and up
Organizational level: Medium
Number of players: 1 on 1, 2 on 2
Supervision: None informally, referee and scorekeeper otherwise
Playing time: 11-point game, win by 2 points, about 20 minutes

Space needed: Badminton court, or equivalent 20′ × 44′ (22′ wide for doubles) area
Equipment: Paddles for all players, baseball sized plastic ball, badminton net (or Trac-ball set, available from Wham-O-Mfg.)

Directions: Basic tennis rules, except different equipment (paddle and ball, or Trac-ball plastic racquet and ball) is used.

Serve is made underhand and below the waist, with one foot behind the back line. Ball must clear the penalty zone and land in the diagonally opposite court from the server. Server switches right and left courts each serve, for as long as he continues to make points, but only one serve is allowed each time, instead of two, like in tennis. In doubles, partners take turns serving, not switching courts as in tennis. One partner serves until an error is made, then the other serves.

Both sides must make their *first* return shot off a bounce. After that, the ball may be hit on the volley or one bounce. Exception: a player may not hit the ball except after a bounce when in the penalty zone. Violations are points for opponent.

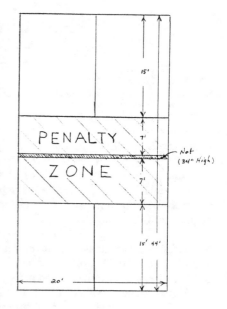

Game source: It is said to have been informally originated by a tennis coach at Washington State University. It is known to have been played in 1976 in the Longview Public Schools system. This is a modified version.

205. Serving Games

A tennis skills exercise for serving,
smashing and driving the ball for accuracy

Age level: 10 and up
Organizational level: Low
Number of players: One at a time, any number in sequence
Supervision: None
Playing time: 60 minutes

Space needed: Tennis court or 27′ × 39′ frontage on a wall or fence backstop
Equipment: 10 pins (Indian clubs, bowling pins, tennis cans, half-gallon milk containers), 12 tennis balls, tennis racquet

Directions: Spot pins on court as shown in Figure 1. Player stands behind net and on (1) first round, throws ball into air and with serving motion tries to knock a pin down, (2) second round, throws ball overhead and lets it drop to court and rebound for a smash to try to knock a pin down, and (3) drop a ball to the court (at service line behind the net) and drive it over the net to hit a pin. Six balls each round. Winner is high total scorer.

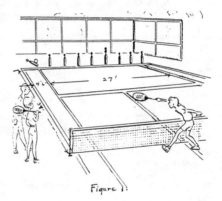

Variations: *Serve Accuracy*—Place pins on court as shown in Figure 2. Player serves from standard serving area and tries to call where shots will hit pins. One point award for hitting any pin, 3 points for directly hitting

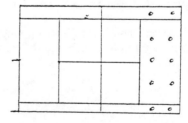

Figure 1:

the pin called. Pins are not reset until all six serves are taken, though ones knocked over are removed. *Drive Accuracy*— Place pins as shown in Figure 3. Player stands at baseline, or in back court, and drops ball, hitting it on the

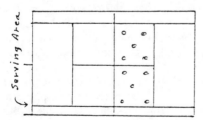

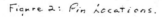

Figure 2: Pin Locations.   Figure 3: Pin Locations.

rebound and driving the ball across court, trying to hit called pins. One point awarded for any pin hit, 3 points for hitting called pin. Six balls. Hit pins removed, but pins not reset until after the six tries.

Game source: Variations on a Russian game idea.

206. Three-Man Tennis

When three tennis players can't find a fourth for doubles

Age level: 16 and up
Organizational level: Low
Number of players: 3
Supervision: None
Playing time: 4-point games, 3 game match, about an hour

Space needed: Tennis court
Equipment: Tennis racquets for all players, several tennis balls

Directions: Basic tennis, except one player plays against two, rotating as single each game.

Single player plays into the doubles court; doubles team must play into the singles court boundaries.

Single player gets two serves, doubles players get one.

Variations: *(1)* Same idea may be used for most racquet or paddle sports. *(2) Triples Tennis* — Back in 1978 a group of octogenarians invented tennis with three players on each side, at the Philippine Columbian Association club in Manila. The advantage is a lot less running and chasing balls.

Game source: Modified from an innovation at the U.S. Navy Special Services Training Facility, 1972.

207. Pole Tennis

It borrows from the games of tennis, tetherball and basketball.
Good family game since all ages can play together.

Age level: 10 and up
Organizational level: Low
Supervision: None
Playing time: 20-point game, about 30–60 minutes
Space needed: Area 15′ × 15′ outside

Equipment: Whiffleball tied to 7′ length of light rope (like clothesline) with the rope attached to the swivel atop a tetherball pole, wooden racquetball paddles for each player, 2 goals (which may be boxes nailed atop 5½′ tall posts)

Directions: Serve as in tennis, overhand from behind serve line, always from right-hand side of court. Doubles partners switch sides each time the serve comes to their side. Each server gets 5 serves in a row, before serve goes to opponent.

Server tries to hit ball into opponent's goal, but opponents may block it and, in turn, try to hit it back into the server's goal. Play is continuous until a goal or foul.

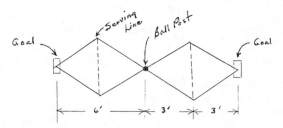

Fouls are called for player: (1) stepping outside court to hit or block ball, (2) blocking ball with body, (3) blocking mouth of goal with stationary paddle. Penalty: free hit by fouled team at goal from own court next to the ball pole.

Variations: *Loop Tennis*—Court is same size. No serve lines. Use rubber ball attached by cord to swivel atop 9′ tall center post (or pipe). Goals set 4′ high.

Players start play next to the ball pole.

Server hits ball toward his own goal. As it rebounds toward opponent, opponent tries to knock it into *either* goal. Opponents may swing at ball anytime it is in their court, trying for either goal. They may strike the rubber string to spoil an opponent's shot (but may not let string wrap around their paddle, which is a foul).

Other fouls and penalties same as Pole Tennis.

Game source: G. E. Macy, an engineer in the Street Traffic Department of Chicago, fashioned the first set by hand—a table model tetherball—in 1928. Howard A. Danforth, director of Physical Education, Florida State University, Tallahassee, FL., wrote about it in *Recreation* magazine, June 1954. And, Zimm-Zamm, a thetherball-type game, with the addition of racquets was later introduced by Fonas Co.

TABLE GAMES

208. Solo Survivor Puzzle

A puzzle to pass time for one person

Age level: 10 and up
Organizational level: Low
Number of players: 1
Supervision: None
Playing time: 20–60 minutes

Space needed: Tabletop
Equipment: Triangular block of wood (6″ per side), 14 golf tees, nails or wooden matchsticks, wood drill (used only by adult)

Craft directions: Bore or drill 15 holes part way into the triangular block in design shown in figure 1, so the holes are aligned anyway you look at them. Holes should be large enough to hold the tees/nails/matchsticks erect.

Play directions: Tees are placed in all holes but the middle one in the third line. To solve the puzzle, pegs are jumped over one another until only one is left on the board. But, each jump is limited to one space, landing in the space immediately past the jumped peg. The jumped pegs are then removed.

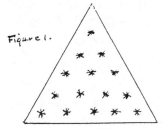

Figure 1.

Anytime the player cannot make a jump within these rules, he's lost the game.

209. Rubberband Writing

Novelty game for parties, camp, etc.

Age level: 10 and up
Organizational level: Low
Number of players: Stunt for one
Supervision: None
Playing time: Open ended

Space needed: Tabletop, chair and scotch tape
Equipment: Pad of unlined paper, pencil and long rubberband

Directions: Tape piece of paper to tabletop. Attach one end of rubberband to the chair, as shown in the adjoining illustration, and the other end to the pencil just above where it is grasped to write.

To use it, hold the pencil as in preparing to write, stretching the rubberband towards you about a foot. Keeping the band stretched tight, start writing. Try to keep the lines even, though the more you write, the harder it will become because the band must be stretched further and further.

When finished, have someone else try to read what you've written.

210. Sea War

War held on paper

Age level: 10 and up
Organizational level: Low
Number of players: 2, or teams of 2
Supervision: None
Playing time: 15–20 minutes
Space needed: Tabletop, 2 facing chairs

Equipment: Graph paper sheets, pencil for each player, some sort of an obstacle that can be placed between the players as they face each other so they can't see each other's papers as they play

Directions: Cut out two four-squares long sized battleships, two three-squares long cruisers and four two-squares long submarines from unlined paper.

Each player, or team, marks off graph paper sheets with two 10–20 square areas, and smaller sections encompassing 4, 3, 2 and 2 spaces. Then each player places his ships somewhere on one of the two crosshatched grids.

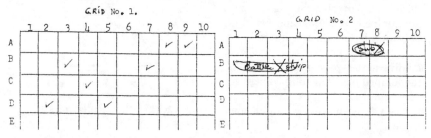

Players then take turns calling their shots (7 shot volleys) at their opponent's fleet, marking each shot called on their second grid as a record, so they know, in

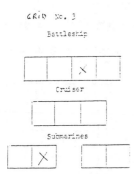

GRID No. 3

Battleship

Cruiser

Submarines

successive volleys, which squares they've already used. Shots are called by listing a number and a letter, which designates the squares they intersect on.

Called volley: A8 + 9, B3 + 7, C4, D2 + 5.

Hits scored on grid 2: (B3, A8) are marked on grid 3, where all squares must be marked to sink the ships indicated.

Each time a ship is sunk, the person, or team, sinking it gets a bonus volley of 7 shots.

Winner is one who sinks all the other's ships first.

Game source: Adapted from an old game from the author's father's childhood.

211. Nisei Go

Adaptation of the Japanese game of Go to a paper and pencil game

Age level: 10 and up
Organizational level: Medium
Number of players: 2
Supervision: Teacher
Playing time: 30–45 minutes

Space needed: Tabletop
Equipment: Pad of graph paper (or lined paper crosshatched to form squares) and 2 pencils

Directions: Should players wish to make their own permanent board game, they may do so by marking any desired number of squares on a piece of plywood, or two pieces of plywood taped together so they fold up like a checkerboard. Then drill indentations at the corner of every square, including the boundary ones (something like the holes in Chinese Checkers board). Then get enough marbles for as many players as will be playing, a different color for each player. The size of the board may dictate this, for the larger the board, the more players it will accommodate.

Basically it is Japanese Go, but with the added feature that any number of people may play at the same time. Scoring has been simplified, too. The marble-using version will be more similar to Go as it uses corners to "square-in" spaces. The paper-and-pencil version uses the lines connecting corners (see diagrams for further explanations). Both versions amount to the same thing in the long run though, as there are four corners and four sides.

Decide who will play first, second, and so on, then take seats in that order clockwise around the table.

Mark a boundary around the number of squares to be used in the game, an even number for the number of players preferably, so the number of moves will end with each person having the same number of turns.

Players then take turns adding a line (or a marble, on the permanent board). A "line-move" includes the mark between any two square-corners (no diagonal lines). The idea is to try to make the last line that "squares-in" a space (or play the last marble that completes a square-in) so your initial may be put in that space. (Players using the marbles and board should make small pieces of paper with their initials on them before starting the game, so they may be dropped on the board as a square is "captured." This makes it a lot easier to count each person's squares at the end of the game, taking them up as you count them — being very careful not to pick up those that count twice, for being used in two different directional strings.)

A somewhat faster and higher-scoring, though more complex, game can also be played by allowing *two* line-fills (or marble-plays) per turn.

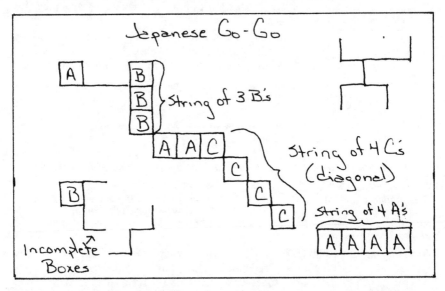

When all spaces have been filled in, start counting up the scores. To avoid arguments, this should be done by one person, with the others checking him, and the results written down immediately, rather than trying to remember them.

Scoring: Score 3 points for a string of three, 4 for a string of four, and so on, counting squares in any direction — across, up and down and diagonal (corner-wise). Nothing under 3 counted. The same space may be counted *twice* if it is used to complete a string in two different directions; three times if used in strings going in three directions. The person with the highest total of points is the winner.

212. Auto Race

Learn a Japanese card game

Age level: 10 and up
Organizational level: Medium
Number of players: 2 or 4
Supervision: Teacher

Playing time: About 20 minutes
Space needed: Tabletop
Equipment: Deck of Bridge cards, paper and pencil

Directions: All black cards given to one player, red cards to the other. Each shuffles the other person's stack.

On command, both start turning over their cards (face up) playing the first two aces — regardless of which person's stack they come from — into the middle of the table. Both players continue turning over their cards as fast as they can, playing them onto the aces in increasing order (ace, 2, 3, etc., up to the King). Both persons play on both stacks, and color of cards does not matter.

When both Kings are reached, the game is continued by playing into the center of the table the other two Kings and playing off both player's stacks backwards down to the aces again.

Cards can not be picked out of the hand stacks in any random order, but must be played onto the middle stacks as they are turned up in order from the hand stacks. Winner is the one to get rid of his cards first.

213. Elimination

Card game simple enough for children to play, yet containing challenge enough for adults, too

Age level: 10 and up
Organizational level: Medium
Number of players: 2–8
Supervision: Teacher

Playing time: About 34 minutes
Space needed: Tabletop
Equipment: Deck of Bridge cards

Directions: Deal 7 cards around, turn the next card face up, as trump suit. Play to the left of the dealer. Players must first play to follow suit, then, if unable to follow suit, to trump, or, if unable to trump, to sluff-off any other card wished. Each player must take one trick to stay in the game. If a player fails, he is out of the game and must wait until the next hand is dealt.

The winner is the person taking the most tricks in each hand. He is dealer for the next hand and, instead of turning up a card to name trump, he can look at his hand first, then name trump himself.

One card less is dealt in each succeeding hand, 6 for the second hand, 5 for the next, etc., down to 1 card each. Overall winner is player taking most total tricks for the 7 hands.

Variation: *Giant Elimination*—Combine 2 decks of cards for more than 8 players.

Game source: An old European game, with variations in rules under different names.

214. "Free Hand" Pinochle

Pinochle game for 3 players

Age level: 12 and up
Number of players: 3
Supervision: Instructions
Playing time: 20–30 minutes

Space needed: Tabletop
Equipment: Pinochle deck, scorepad and pencil

Directions: Regular Pinochle rules, except players bid for the "free hand" and the right to name trump.

Deal 4 regular 12-card hands, face down. The three players pick up their hands and bid. High bidder names trump from his hand, then turns the free hand face up and organizes it into suits. He selects 4 cards from the free hand to make his own playing hand as strong as possible, discarding 4 of his cards into the free hand, but *faced down*. During play, he may refresh his memory by looking at them, but no one else sees them.

Melds are made all around (without the 4 face down cards), and counted. Then play starts, with the bid winner playing first, and also playing the free hand each time as though it was opposite him (second to his left). The bid winner, thus, plays against the other two players in the game who become partners for that hand.

Since partners may change each deal, scoring is done individually.

Meld and trick counting remains the same as regular Pinochle. Each partner, after each deal, gets to claim the points by that partnership on that deal.

The first player to earn 1500 points is the winner.

215. Bermuda Bridge

Innovative format of rubber Bridge for 5-6 players

Age level: 16 and up
Organizational level: High
Number of players: 5-6
Supervision: Teacher

Playing time: 30-60 minutes
Space needed: Tabletop
Equipment: Deck of Bridge cards, score pad and pencil

Directions: At the start of Bermuda rubber, for five players, each of the players draws a card from a spread pack to choose sides.

The two players cutting high are to be the "Pair in the Box," and will oppose the three remaining players, who, as a team, will Chouette for the entire rubber.

Of the three players cutting low — the Chouette Team — the two higher will play the first hand of the rubber while the third sits out. On the second hand, the third man goes in and second man sits out, and for the third hand, second man goes in and first sits out. The three players continue to rotate in this manner until the rubber is completed.

At the start of the second rubber, the two players who kept the same partnership throughout are "out of the box" and now become members of the Chouette. The other three players again cut to determine which two will become the "Pair in the Box" for this rubber. The three remaining will make up the opposing team, who will Chouette in and out after every hand as described above.

At the start of the third rubber, the two players who kept the same partnership throughout are now "out of the box." Of the three players who made up the opposing team, the one who has not yet had a turn "in the box" is now automatically "in"; the other two cut to determine who shall be his partner. The lower man becomes the third member of the Chouetting team.

At the start of the fourth rubber, the cycle is complete, and the five players again draw to choose sides and repeat the cycle.

Scoring is the same as in rubber Bridge, except that the "Pair in the Box" — since they are competing against three opponents — win or lose 50 percent more than the actual amount of the rubber. Suppose they win a 10 rubber. Then each of the three members of the Chouette side pays up 10, which gives each box player 15. Conversely, if the "Pair in the Box" lose a 10, it costs them 15 each to provide 10 for each of the three on the Chouette Team.

To play Bermuda Bridge with six, the players simply cut at the start of each rubber to choose two teams of three. Then the members of each team Chouette in and out of the rubber after every hand until the rubber is completed.

Two in the Box play one rubber versus two pairs who alternate. In this variation, the pair in the box play for double stakes.

Game source: The principle of the game has been taken from the Chouette at Backgammon (where two players are matched against three), but while the origin of Bermuda Bridge is vague, it was really popularized on Bermuda, where it was refined with a set of rules about 1964, which were later printed in the New York Herald Tribune and credited to Florence Osborne.

216. Board Golf

Game of golf relegated to a board

Age level: 8 and up
Organizational level: Medium
Number of players: 2–4
Supervision: Instructions
Playing time: 15–30 minutes

Space needed: Tabletop; larger boards may be placed on floor or ground
Equipment: Playing board, 4 different colored markers (as golf balls), scorecard, pencil and 1 die

Directions: On a large piece of plywood, canvas or heavy paper (size depending on how big the players want to draw their golf course) draw out a 9 or an 18-hole golf course, inserting 3 water, 2 sand traps, trees, brush and other hazards at various spots. The playing track on which the markers will be moved should be marked off in 1″ long sections.

The 9-hole course should include 3 par-5 holes (30 spaces), 4 par-4s (24 spaces) and 2 par-3s (18 spaces). Double that for an 18-hole course or just play twice around.

Players roll the die for high to determine order of teeing off.

Each player will move his marker along the course as many spaces as the number on the die he rolled. The player farthest from the hole rolls each time thereafter, until all players have "holed out." If a player rolls a number that takes his marker past a hole, he then must move his marker backwards, because all players must roll the exact number of spaces needed for them to hole out. Every roll counts as one stroke and the number of strokes each player takes for each hole is written on the scorecard.

After each hole is completed, the player with the lowest stroke score on that hole, then the next in order, and so on, roll in order.

If a player lands in a water hazard, he must move his ball back 2 spaces. If he lands in a sand trap, he loses a turn, but that turn counts a stroke.

217. Blow Ball

Builds lung power

Age level: 6 and up
Organizational level: Low
Number of players: 4 or 8
Supervision: None

Playing time: 4 5-minute periods with 2-minute rests
Space needed: Card table and 4 chairs
Equipment: Table tennis ball and plastic lid

Directions: Players are seated on the 4 sides of the table. The ball is placed in the plastic can lid in the exact center of the table. On "go" signal, all players try to blow the ball off the table on the side directly opposite them. Players may not use hands or body to stop the ball or touch it in any way, may not put their hands or any other body part on the table and may not get out of their chairs. Penalty: one minus point (−1) awarded the person fouling.

Any player that has the ball drop off his side of the table is penalized a minus point (−1).

A player who reaches 15 minus points (−15), is out of the game. Winner is last person in, or player with the least minus points at the end of the 4 periods.

Variations: *Fan Ball*—Same game, except each player uses a fan or square piece of cardboard to fan the ball off an opponent's table edge. *Fan Race*—Mark off a race course with as many lanes as racers, across a floor. On "go" signal, racers start fanning their balls, with a fan or square piece of cardboard, down the race course. If a ball goes outside its lane boundaries, the fanner must go back to the start again.

A race relay may also be run by teams, fanning balls down and back on two lanes.

218. Poker Dice

Combination of the card game poker and dice rolling

Age level: 8 and up
Organizational level: Medium
Number of players: 2–6
Supervision: None

Playing time: 20–30 minutes
Space needed: Table top
Equipment: Five dice

Directions: The object is to roll matching pairs, triplets, four or five of a kind, a sequence of 1-2-3-4-5 (straight). These are ranked, high to low: 5 of a kind, 4 of a kind, straight, 3 of a kind plus high pair (full house), 3 of a kind, two pair, pair.

Each player gets up to three throws, but may stand on first, second or third throws. Or he may change which dice he keeps out from each of the first or second throws. But whichever dice are kept out of the throw, along with the dice thrown, on the third cast is his hand.

219. "Wind" Hockey

Age level: All ages
Number of players: 2 or 4; can be adapted for team use
Space needed: Table top, optional size; the more players, the larger the table, or floor area

Equipment: Table tennis ball (or yarn fluff ball), two halves of any packaged food box about the size of a two-pound sugar package, table covering (to keep ball from being so "lively")

Directions: Players put their goals on a table, open ends toward the table center, then station themselves behind them. The table tennis ball is placed in the middle of the table. Goals placed at opposite ends of the table.

On signal both players, or teams, start blowing the ball, trying to blow it into the opposition goal. If it goes off the table it is replaced where it went off and opponents can't begin blowing again until the signal is given.

If the ball goes out of bounds over one or the other goal lines, it is placed on the table where it went out and the player, or players, at that end get a "penalty" blow, with opponents not allowed to start blowing again until the ball reaches the midpoint of the table.

Winner is person or team to get a pre-determined number of goals first, or the person or team ahead after a pre-determined length of play. Four three-minute quarters make a good time limit for tournaments.

Four players may also play, each individually blowing to protect his goal and to blow the ball into one of the other 3 goals. Scores are "minus" points against goalie scored on.

Players drop from competition as 3 goals are scored in their goal. Winner is one left with least goals against him at a time limit, or the last one remaining when all others have been subtracted out.

CAUTION: Watch playing for too long a period. Players may get lightheaded and feel faint from hyperventilation. Use good judgment here.

220. Clock Golf

Substitutes tiddley-winks for golf balls in an old golf practice game

Age level: 10 and up
Organizational level: Medium
Number of players: 2, or 2 teams of 2
Supervision: Instructions
Playing time: About 30 minutes

Space needed: Tabletop
Equipment: Playing board, a "tiddley" (shooter) and a different colored "wink" (smaller than shooter) for each player, scoresheet and pencil

Directions: Mark diagram of playing field on a paper sheet that can be taped to the table, as shown in figure 1.

Set a paper butter dishlet (type used in fast food restaurants) anywhere in the circle, but off-set from the very center. (It can be changed in location for the second nine holes.)

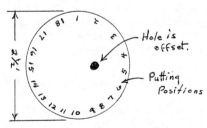

Players start on #1 and tiddley their winks into the hole with the least number of snaps (shots) possible. Snaps are taken as in golf, the person farthest from the hole taking each shot. The number of snaps taken for each hole is recorded on the scoresheet. Lowest overall total for 18 holes is winner.

On #2, the players take turns, in order of least number of snaps taken, in teeing off. The same follows for each succeeding hole.

221. Wink Golf

A game for golf addicts on a rainy day, using tiddley-winks

Age level: 8 and up
Organizational level: Low
Number of players: 2-4
Supervision: Instructions
Playing time: About 30 minutes
Space needed: 15' × 15' floor area
Equipment: A tiddley (shooter) and different colored winks (smaller than shooter) for each player, 9 cups (paper dishlets for butter, catsup, etc., in fast food restaurants), plus various materials to simulate hazards on the course, like a platter of water as a lake to shoot over, or around, a piece of newspaper with sand (or salt) on it as a sand trap, a small shag rug that's "rough" alongside one boundary of the course, plants as trees, a throw pillow as a hillock, etc., string can be used to mark out-of-bounds lines

Directions: Lay out a 9-hole golf course on floor or carpet.

Decide on tee-off order. After that, the player farthest from the hole shoots, even if the same player takes 2 or 3 strokes in a row. Every snap is a stroke and the number of snaps taken to hole-out in each one is recorded for all players on the score card.

After each hole is finished, the player with the least number of strokes for it tees off for the next hole, followed by the other players in least-strokes order.

Winks going out of bounds add a penalty stroke to the player's stroke total for that hole. A wink going into a water hazard can be removed and placed beside it, but costs the shooter 2 penalty strokes. A wink in a sand trap must be played out. A wink into any other hazard that's unplayable can also be removed and set beside it, but also costs 2 penalty strokes.

222. Wink Tennis

New challenge for tiddley-wink players

Age level: 10 and up
Organizational level: Medium
Number of players: 2 or 4
Supervision: None
Playing time: 45-60 minutes
Space needed: Card table or equivalent table area
Equipment: Playing court with net, 1 small white wink (as ball), 2 shooter winks

Craft directions: All you need to make a playing court is a 32" square piece of felt for a card table cover; four 6" lengths of ¼" elastic braid; a needle and thread or sewing machine for sewing the elastic on the corners of the felt; a black felt pen for marking the court lines; two large tiddleys and one small wink from a Tiddley-wink game to use as racquets and ball (or four large tiddleys if four people play). In addition you'll need a cardboard "net" 1½" or 2" high; a score sheet or pad and a pencil for keeping score.

The drawing shows the dimensions for cutting the felt and laying out the court lines.

Directions: The game is played and scored the same as tennis, except that instead of hitting the ball over the net, each player, at his turn, presses on the edge of the wink with the tiddledy and at the same time draws it towards himself to snap the wink over the net. It may take several practice tries before you can do it accurately.

You can play either singles or doubles.

Decide who will serve first. One person serves the entire game of four points (in tennis they're called 15, 30, 40, game; zero is called "love"). Both sides may score points, regardless of who serves. The victor must win by at least two points.

Service is made from behind the end line and must land in the diagonally opposite, smaller, service court. Start from the right side, then alternate with the left side. The server gets two tries to get each serve into the correct court. If he does not, the point goes to the opponent and the server moves to the other court for his next serve.

If the wink hits the net and falls into the correct court on a serve, it is replayed with no penalty on either side. During the course of play, the same situation is ruled "good" and no replay is necessary.

In doubles, partners take turns serving and returning shots.

The wink must land inbounds (on or within the court lines) but it is allowed to slide out-of-bounds after first hitting fair territory. The opponent must then return it from where it lies.

The first player to win six games wins a set, although he must win by two games. Best three of five sets wins the match.

223. Wink Basketball

An alternative for standard tiddley-wink players

Age level: 10 and up
Organizational level: Medium
Number of players: 2 or 2 teams of 2–5
Supervision: Instructions
Playing time: 2 10-minute halves

Space needed: Tabletop
Equipment: Coffee cup, a tiddley (shooter) for each player, 1 wink (smaller than tiddley), chalk for marking playing area, scorepad and pencil

Directions: Determine which team goes first.

Teams alternate snaps, with players on each team taking turns (in same rotation throughout game), all using the same ball/wink. Each player snaps it from where it last landed. The player who snaps it into the cup gets 2 points for his team.

After each goal, the non-scoring team starts the snapping again at the starting line.

If a player shoots out of turn, or snaps the ball/wink off the table or out of the target area, it is a foul and the other team shoots a free shot from anywhere

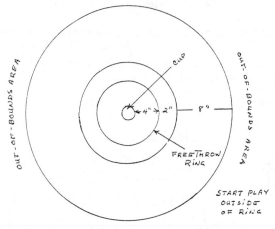

inside the free throw circle. If the FT-snap goes into the cup, it counts 1 point.

If a wink goes into the cup, but bounces out again, it is not a goal.

Variation: *Horse—* Same game, except score is kept by the scoring team getting a letter of H-O-R-S-E on the score-pad for every snap into the cup. First team to spell HORSE, wins.

This can be made more difficult by adding a follow-the-leader role, whereby each player making a goal forces the next opponent to also make it from the same place and in the same manner (left handed, two-handed, standing on one leg or whatever your imagination dreams up). If he misses, the opponent starts over from the starting line. If he makes it, he gets double points—4.

224. Tiddley Baseball

A version of baseball played with tiddley-winks

Age level: 10 and up
Organizational level: Medium
Number of players: 2 teams, 4–8 each
Supervision: Instructions
Playing time: 9-inning game, about 45–60 minutes
Space needed: 9' × 9' area on smooth or hard surface

Equipment: 2 tiddleys (shooters), 1 white wink (smaller than tiddley), 4 different colored winks (as runners), string or tape for field lines and boundaries, scoresheet, pencil and 4 paper catsup cups (type from fast food restaurant)

Directions: Pitcher snaps the tiddley on the wink (ball) towards home plate from the pitcher's rubber. If he snaps it into the cup, it is a strike. Three strikes is an out. If he snaps it beyond the home base line, over or to either side of the home base cup, it is a ball. Four balls gives a walk. If he snaps it so it lands anywhere inside the infield area, the batting team gets to snap a runner-wink toward the first base cup from the home base line. Then, that batter-runner alternates snaps with the defensive player fielding the ball, who snaps the ball towards the first base cup, too. Whichever wink goes in the cup first, determines if it's a hit or an out.

If other runners are on base already, they also get turns to snap their runner-winks toward the next base, in rotation: batter, then fielder, runner on first, runner on second and for a runner on third. If the fielder can snap the ball-wink into more than one cup before the runners reach them, he scores a double or triple out.

When one play is completed, the pitcher pitches again, and play continues until 3 outs are made. Then teams switch places. This continues until 9 innings have been completed.

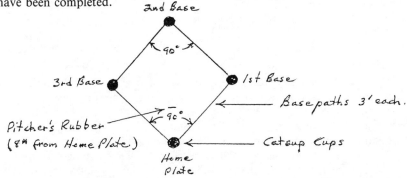

If a wink is snapped on top of an opponent's, or one of its own runners-winks, the player has to play his own wink without his tiddley touching the opposition's wink, or other player's wink. It doesn't matter if the wink moves the other one on this snap, but if the tiddley touches it, it is an out for the shooter. The moved wink is then shot from where it lands.

Pitcher snaps that end in foul territory, without going past the home base line, are called balls.

225. Box Basketball

Game that can be hand crafted from materials anyone can gather.
Good rainy-day game for indoors that is active, yet won't tear up the house.

Age level: 9 and up
Organizational level: Low
Number of players: 2, or 2 teams with players taking turns
Supervision: None
Playing time: Free play. Game may be set at any number of even points.

Space needed: Table game or open space 8' square or larger
Equipment: Box game (two shoeboxes), 4 bottle caps, 4 quart milk containers, (or smaller), glue, 3" piece of string, pencil, ruler

Directions: To make the box game draw 3" (radius) circle in the exact center of the bottom (open end up) of both boxes. Use ruler to find center and string and pencil for circle.

Cut milk containers off about 1" up from bottoms.

Set shoe boxes on end and glue a milk-container bottom inside the end of each shoe box about ⅓ the way down from the open top, centered. When dry, set the boxes on their other ends and glue the other two milk-container bottoms to those ends, as before. Let dry.

Rules: Place two bottle caps inside the ring on the bottom of each box. Place one hand at each end of the box (each player taking a different box). Flip the box so the bottle caps fly into the air, then maneuver the box under them so they will fall onto the milk-container bottoms (which are the "baskets"). Keep trying, because the first person to do it gets 2 points.

If bottle caps fall out of the box, the only penalty is the time lost in picking them up and putting them back into the box (in the circle).

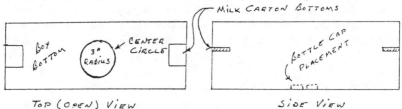

TOP (OPEN) VIEW   SIDE VIEW

When a basket is scored, both players stop and return their bottle caps to the circles on the bottoms of their boxes. Start over again on signal.

Game can be any number of points agreed (15 make a good game), or the winner may be the one scoring the most points in 10 tries, or the game may be played to a time limit of 10 minutes, highest score winning.

Variations: The character of the game can be changed to add a "gambling" element by allowing 8 points to be scored if a player can get bottle caps on both basket-platforms at the same time.

The gambling element comes in by allowing *either* player scoring a single basket to call off the double-play, even if that person did not score the *first* basket. (For example, one player may need 8 points to win, so goes for a double basket. Meanwhile, the other player scores a single basket, so he decides to call off the try so his opponent can't win. Both baskets are cancelled when this happens. Of course, the second player to get the single basket *could* continue play, trying to get the double basket before his opponent. If he didn't, he would lose the game, though.)

226. Muhle (or Nine-Man Morris)

Re-introduce a game older than the United States

Age level: 10 and up
Organizational level: Medium
Number of players: 2
Supervision: Instructions
Playing time: 30 minutes average

Space needed: Tabletop (as shown in diagram below), or floor version
Equipment: Playing board, 18 playing pieces (9 each of 2 contrasting colors)

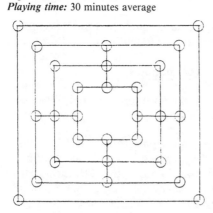

Directions: There are two players, each of whom has nine "men." Each player has a different color. To start the game, each player places a man on the board, in alternation, until all nine men have been placed. The object is to get a muhle, three men in a row. A muhle must run horizontally or vertically on a line. *It cannot lie diagonally.*

When a player has formed a muhle, he may take one of his opponent's men. This is called "pounding."

A player cannot take a man which forms a part of a muhle unless no other piece is available.

When each player has placed his nine men, the play takes the form of moving, it still being the object to make muhles. A man must always be moved on a line. Diagonal moving is not allowed. Moves may be made only from one intersection to the next one. Every time a muhle is made, or remade after "opening" it, the player may "pound."

When a player has been reduced to three men, he may jump, that is, he may put a man from any part of the board to any other part of the board. The player reduced to two men loses the game.

Game source: Unknown, but it has been played in basic form for at least 1,000 years, its name being taken from the 9 "men" (moving pieces) in the game each player has. It's mentioned in Shakespeare's "A Midsummer Night's Dream" and a playing board was found scratched into a rock outcropping in the basement of a house built on which is now 204th street in New York City that was constructed shortly after the American Revolution by William Dyckman, whose grandfather had emigrated from Germany more than a century earlier.

227. Overthrow Checkers

Variation of checkers, requiring more complex planning of moves

Age level: 10 and up
Organizational level: Low
Number of players: 2
Supervision: None, except referee and timekeeper for tournaments
Playing time: Varies with skill of players; average time on playground is 20–30 minutes

Space needed: Table game
Equipment: Checker board and set of checkers, with six extra checkers of each color (or cardboard discs the size of checkers with the words "Emperor" and "Dictator" written on them, six of each, three of each colored red and black)

Directions: Rules of checkers apply, with the following additions:

When a King (a checker that has moved into the opponent's back row, gaining the second checker and the moves of a King) moves back to its own back row, then works its way into the opponent's back row *again*, it gains a third checker on top of the other two (or an Emperor disc) and becomes an Emperor, and thereafter must be jumped *twice* before it is lost to an opponent. An Emperor's moves remain the same as a King's. An Emperor may take an opponent's Emperor by jumping it once.

When an Emperor moves back into his own back row, then makes his way *again* into the opponent's back row, it gains a fourth checker on top of the others (or a Dictator disc) and the title of Dictator. His moves remain the same as a King's, but he cannot be jumped except by another Dictator.

228. Double-Decker Checkers

A more complex, 3-dimensional format for the game of checkers

Age level: 12 and up
Organizational level: Medium
Number of players: 2 or two 2-person teams
Supervision: Instructions
Playing time: 30–45 minutes

Space needed: Tabletop
Equipment: One regular checkerboard and a second one on glass or clear, stiff plastic, sets of checkers and 4 blocks of wood 8″ high

Directions: To make board, cut piece of safety glass or clear, stiff plastic ½″ larger on all sides than the regular checker board. Tape its edges to avoid cuts. Mark the same squares on the glass board as on the standard board, using a grease pencil or thin tape. Place 4 blocks of wood at the 4 corners of the standard board as it sets ready for play on the table, then set the glass board on the blocks directly above the regular board, so the squares may be seen directly over those of the bottom board by looking down through the glass.

Rules: Players line up playing pieces on top board as in starting regular checkers, but play is on two levels.

Each move consists of a 2-space move of one checker—2 spaces on the same level, or one forward on one level and one forward on the bottom board, which transfers that checker to the bottom board. Checkers may be moved onto any level or onto unoccupied space, even though that same space on the other board is occupied. An opponent's piece may be jumped only if the mover's checker is already on, or is moved onto, the same board as the piece to be jumped.

Other rules remain as in regular checkers play, including King's moves, except Kings also can play on any level.

Variation: *Triple Decker Checkers*—Use 3 stacked boards, the top 2 made of glass, and play on all three levels simultaneously. Each play, in turn, gets a 3-space move, however, taken on any level or combination of levels by the same checker. Start play on the middle board. Otherwise, it's the same as Double-Decker.

229. Scramble-Amble Checkers

A more complex game for regular Chinese
Checker players to move up to

Age level: 10 and up
Organizational level: Low
Number of players: 3–4
Supervision: Instructions

Playing time: 10–15 minutes
Space needed: Tabletop
Equipment: Playing board, 4 sets of different colored marbles (12 of each color)

Directions: Mark out a playing board on a 20″ × 20″ sheet of heavy paper, as in figure 1 (shown on next page).

Each player places his colored marbles in his "home base" section of the board. Each player is playing against all other players.

Players take turns moving, clockwise, from whoever moves first. A move is one space forward, sideways or diagonally forward. No backward moves allowed. A move can only be made onto an unoccupied space.

The exception to this one-space move rule is jumping an opposition marble, where the jump is made over the attacked marble into the space beyond, with the jumped marble being removed from the board. A jump may be made forward, diagonally or sideways also, (never backwards), but only if there is an empty space on the other side of the marble to be jumped. (And a player may never jump his own marbles.)

The object of the game is to move as many of one's marbles as possible into the "home base" of the player directly opposite, while, at the same time, trying to keep other players from moving into their opposition home bases. Person who gets the *most* in wins, and that's decided only after all players have completed all moves possible. If a player has marbles so placed he has no possible move,

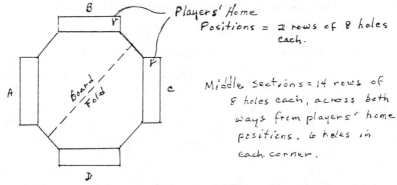

he loses that turn and the next player in the rotation moves. If all remaining players on the board are so stymied, the game is ended and the winner determined as noted above.

230. Bocce Dice

Basic idea of Italian game of bocce, but using dice
in an unusual way to format a board game

Age level: 10 and up
Organizational level: Medium
Number of players: 2, or 2 teams of 2
Playing time: 100-point game, about 20–30 minutes
Space needed: 4' × 9' floor area, or equivalent sized tabletop

Equipment: 2 pair of dice (about the size of a table tennis ball, with rounded corners and each pair a different color), two 6" high, 4' wide backstops (at each end of court), two 4' wide target drawings, with a bullseye and 4 equivalent rings around it which can be taped to the playing area, scorepad and pencil

Directions: Each player, or team, has a different colored pair of dice. They roll for high to determine first roller.

One player rolls one die toward the target at the court end opposite him, trying to stop it, or carom it off the backboard, on the bullseye, or as close

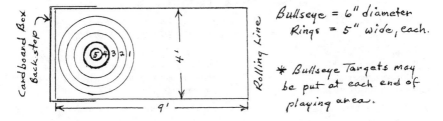

to it as possible. Then, the opponent throws one, and he may knock opponent's die away, if he can. Then each takes a second throw. The scores are figured by multiplying the numbers showing uppermost on all dice in the target area by the number of the ring it rests most in. (A bullseye with a die showing a 6, for example, would be the highest score for one die, 30 points.)

When the scores have been figured, the players then roll at the opposite end target, continuing back and forth until one team reaches 100 points.

231. Golfers Dice

Good game for golf club houses; dice game that involves strategy

Age level: 8 and up
Organizational level: Low
Number of players: 2 to 8
Supervision: None

Playing time: About 20 minutes for 2 players
Space needed: Table or floor area of similar size
Equipment: 5 dice, score sheet and pencil

Directions: Players take turns rolling 5 dice. Each turn consists of three rolls. All three rolls do not have to be taken, and all dice need not be rolled each time, but the third roll is final.

The total of the 5 dice on the third roll may be entered on the scoresheet for any open golf hole, in any order. Once entered, it cannot be changed.

HOLES PLAYERS	1	2	3	PAR-3 4	5	6	7	PAR 3 8	Full Hs 9	TOTAL
A.										
B.										

Par-3 holes must have three matching numbers turn up on the dice before a total can be put in those spaces, but the total of all five dice is entered on the score sheet.

A "full house" must be rolled—three dice showing the same number and the other two dice showing another number alike, as, for example, three 4s and two 6s, to enter the total for hole #9.

If these special holes are not filled as required (within the nine turns that make up a game), they are filled with penalty strokes: a full five-dice count of 30 plus 10 penalty points for a total of 40 points.

A game is comprised of nine turns for each player, in rotation. Low total is winner.

232. Dice Baseball

A "parlor" baseball game, using dice, that is "based upon the similar percentages of rolling dice and baseball scoring"

Age level: 10 and up
Organizational level: Medium
Number of players: 2
Supervision: Instructions

Playing time: 30–40 minutes
Space needed: Tabletop
Equipment: Pair of dice, baseball scorepad and pencil

Directions: Each player tosses the dice until he is retired with 3 outs. Play is 9 innings.

Dice totals:
1–1   Home run
1–2   Double play (Counts as one out with bases empty.)
1–3   Out (If 2 on base and none out, it's a triple play.)
2–2   Stolen base. (If no one on base, it's an out.) Another roll is taken to

determine if a stolen base is successful; for an attempted steal of second base, 2–8 is successful, 9–12 is out; for a steal of third base, 2–7 is successful, 8–12 is out; for a steal of home base, 2–6 is successful, 7–12 is out.)

2–3 Two-base hit
3–3 Base on error
1–4 Two base hit
2–4 Fly out
3–4 Strike out
4–4 Single
1–5 Ground out
2–5 Fly out
3–5 Single
4–5 Ground out
5–5 Base on balls
1–6 Fly out
2–6 Single
3–6 Ground out
4–6 Base on balls
5–6 Sacrifice out. Runners move up one base.
6–6 Three base hit

Game source: Adapted from 2 sources—Kinnon McLamb of Goldsboro, N.C., who innovated his version in 1958, and Robert Ricken of Brooklyn, N.Y., who played a different version as a child.

233. Mini Shuffleboard

Miniature version of shuffleboard that can be used to teach basics of the game

Age level: 8 and up
Organizational level: Medium
Number of players: 2 or 4
Supervision: Instructions
Playing time: 21-point game
Space needed: Tabletop or uncarpeted floor area 6″ × 52″

Equipment: Shuffleboard court drawn on heavy, slick butcher paper, 4 buttons (2 each of different colors) and 2 non-spring type clothes pins (as pushers)

Directions: Regular shuffleboard rules, except the clothes pins are used as stick-pushers and buttons as pucks.

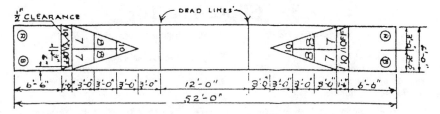

Variation: *21-or-Break*—Player must score exactly 21 points to win. If he doesn't, he loses 10 points.

234. Pencil Pool

Children can learn fundamentals of pool with common items

Age level: 10 and up
Organizational level: Medium
Number of players: 2–4
Supervision: Instructions
Playing time: 30–45 minutes
Space needed: Tabletop with cloth cover, or carpeted floor area 18″ × 39″

Equipment: Rubber-tipped pencil (as pool cue) for each player, 16 marbles (as pool balls) numbered 1–15 with a marking pen, one un-numbered, enough books or thick magazines to form a bumper boundary around the playing area and a triangle (for positioning balls)

Directions: To arrange table, place 12 or more books with their backs forming the 18″ × 39″ rectangular playing area. Leave 1½″–2″ gaps in the six usual spots for "holes." A triangle can be cut from corrugated cardboard by first measuring the inside of it to the size of the 14 marbles.

Use basic pool rules. (Players take turns shooting, but can keep shooting as long as they keep pocketing balls by caroming the cue ball off them.)

Variations: *Rotation*—Balls must be pocketed in numbered order, unless caromed off the numbered ball being shot. *Star and Stripes*—One player shoots only #1–7 (usually plain colored balls) and the other shoots #9–15 (usually striped balls) with the #8 ball (all black) as the last ball shot by either player, and must be shot last.

235. Go-Mo-Ko

Learn a Japanese game

Age level: 10 and up
Organizational level: Low
Number of players: 2 or 4
Supervision: None
Playing time: 20–30 minutes average

Space needed: Tabletop
Equipment: Go-Mo-Ko board, 25 pegs (golf tees or wooden matchsticks) for each player, different colors for teams

Directions: Board may be made from a single square of acoustic tile of even-punch design, or from a 1′ square of peg-board.

Object of the game is for one team to line up 5 of its pegs in a straight line, any direction, without the opponent placing a peg to block the line. Players alternate turns. Winner is the first player, or team, forming a 5-peg line.

236. Clip-a-Tac-Toe

Progression of tic-tac-toe game from paper and pencil to action

Age level: 8 and up
Organizational level: Low
Number of players: 2
Playing time: 5 minutes

Space needed: Tabletop
Equipment: Tic-tac-toe playing board, 12 medium sized paper clips per player

Directions: To make board, cut a 4″ square of styrofoam or corrugated cardboard. Stick 9 pins at 1″ intervals as shown in figure 1 and 2 on next page. (A block of wood and small nails without heads may also be used.)

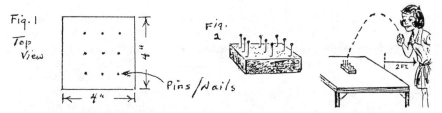

Players take turns tossing the paper clips from about 2′ away, trying to ring a tic-tac-toe, 3 pins in a row in any direction, vertical, horizontal or diagonal.

237. Junk Jackstraws

Return of a game played by our grandparents in their childhood,
using everyday items from around the house to test hand steadiness

Age level: 10 and up
Organizational level: Low
Number of players: 2–4
Supervision: None
Playing time: 20 minutes

Space needed: Tabletop with smooth, hard surface
Equipment: Collection of jackstraws, scoring pad and holding jar

Directions: Collect items to be used as jackstraws: paper clips, pins and needles, thumbtacks, hairpins of various types and sizes, safety pins, buttons and anything else imagination warrants. Put them into a jar, shake them up a bit, then dump them out onto a tabletop in a heap.

Players take turns removing one item at a time from the heap, without moving other pieces. A player continues as long as he is successful. He may use any piece he has already removed to help in removing other items. When all items have been removed that can be, points are totalled to determine winner.

Point values:

Nail – small	3
Nail – large	4
Hairpin	9
Bobbypin	8
Safety Pin – small	8
Safety Pin – large	10
Soda Straw	6
Toothpick	2
Thumbtack	4
Pen Point	3
Pebble	1
Paper Clip – small	10
Paper Clip – large	7

238. Peg Ball

Board game that can be homemade and used at home, picnic, camp or carnival

Age level: 10 and up
Organizational level: Low
Number of players: 1–4

Supervision: 20–30 minutes
Playing time: Quick games, played until players tire of it

Space needed: Table
Equipment: Board 54″ × 70″, 3 small Whiffle- balls, 63 nails without heads, hammer, ruler, pencil and marking pen

Directions: Prepare board with nails spaced 8″ apart in 7 rows of 9 each, as shown in sketch, and mark the board as shown below. Place board flat.

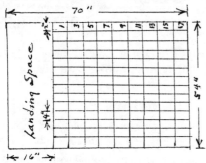

Players each get 3 throws from 2–3 feet in front of the board. Balls must land first on the "Landing Space" then onto the nail area where hopefully, each will hook onto a nail. No points are scored if a ball doesn't impale. If it does, the thrower gains the number of points of the line of nails it ends up in: 1, 3, 5, 7, 9, 11 or 13.

Winner is one with the highest 3-ball total.

Game source: Adaptations on an ideas from a Naval Special Services Training School class, 1972.

239. Flick Football

A football format relegated to a table top

Age level: 10 and up
Organizational level: Low
Number of players: 2
Supervision: None
Playing time: 2 5-minute periods
Space needed: Tabletop on which each player can reach the opposite side, like a card table; sidelines should be no more than 2½′ apart
Equipment: Ball (1½″ triangular cut of corrugated cardboard, or sheet of paper folded into a triangle), tape or chalk (to mark sidelines and 6″ lines at both ends of "field")

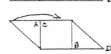

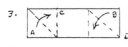

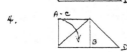

Directions: To make the "football," fold a sheet of paper in the following way: (1) Fold it horizontally in half, (2) fold it in half again, so you have a strip which you fold into thirds, (3) then fold corner A triangularly up and corner B triangularly down, (4) fold left triangular folded end inward upon the middle section, (5) fold C corner down to meet B corner, (6) tuck D corner into open side A–C to form a compact triangular package.

Decide who kicks off. (Other team then automatically kicks off for second period.) Ball is placed at midfield and flicked with a finger as a kickoff.

Then, taking turns, each side is allowed two finger flicks per offensive series. Touchdowns are scored when any part of the ball extends over the edge of the table (inbounds) without falling off. If the ball falls off or is flicked over the table edge, the offense forfeits any remaining flicks in that series and the other team gets the ball at a point 6″ from its edge of the table, plus, a penalty kick, before taking its next offensive series of flicks as well.

If a TD is scored, the extra point attempt is flicked from mid-field. The defensive player forms crossbars by placing the tips of his index fingers together and extending his thumbs downward to the table's surface at the edge. Ball must rest between thumbs, partly off the table's edge, to count.

After a TD extra point attempt, the team scored on gets the ball for kickoff at a point 6″ in from its table edge.

Field goals are kicked anytime the ball is flicked out of bounds, by the team that didn't flick it out. The ball is placed at the sideline point where it went out, and flicked from there, counting 3 points if successful. If not successful, defense gets the ball at the 6″ marker from it's table edge.

Players may not interfere with flicks, or ball, when in opponent's possession.

Variation: *Flick Hockey* — Same game, except a 4″ wide scoring area is taped on the table edge instead of allowing the entire table edge to be a goal line. Balls ending up hanging over the edge, outside these scoring areas, are treated as any other ball. And, of course, there are no TD extra point field on field goal tries. Penalty kicks remain the same for out of bounds play.

TRACK & FIELD, TAG AND RELAY GAMES

240. A Cup of Blow

Relay activity

Age level: 8 and up
Organizational level: Medium
Number of players: Any number of teams of 3 or more
Supervision: None

Playing time: 15 minutes
Space needed: Space to fit number participants, about 3′ × 10′ per team
Equipment: Paper cup and 7′ length of string for each team, punch (nail or pencil)

Directions: Carefully punch holes in center of bottoms of cups (so the bottoms don't come loose). Put one end of each string through the hole in each cup, with the open end of cup at the shoot end.

Line teams up side by side as shown in figure 1 on next page.

Strings, with cups at point A, are held tight by number 2 and 6 players. (An extra 6″ has been added to the end of the strings, so they may be marked with a dark marking pen 6″ in from each end. These marks are the relay race finish lines. Every cup must start from behind one of these marks and isn't a completed run until it passes the line at the other end. It also allows teams to tie a small loop in the string ends so they may be held stretched tight more easily.)

Relay starts on "go" signal, with #1 blower trying to move the cup to the other end of the string by blowing into the open end. When his cup is over the finish line, he takes that end of the string from #6, and #6 pushes the cup, by hand, back to the starting point, then takes his place behind #5. At the same time he's doing this, #2 gives his end of the string to #3 to hold. And, as soon as the cup is in legal starting position, #2 starts blowing the cup. This entire process of exchanges continues until players and cup are back in original starting positions shown in figure 1.

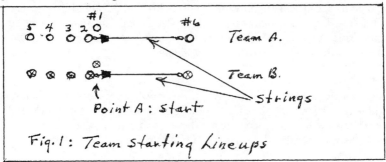

Fig. 1: Team Starting Lineups

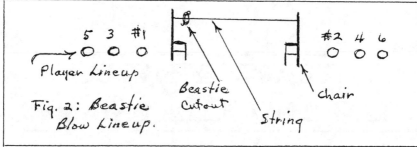

Fig. 2: Beastie Blow Lineup.

Variation: *Beastie Blow*—Instead of cups, cardboard cutouts of horses, greyhounds, pigeons, airplanes, spaceships or hares and tortoises may be put on the strings for relay racing. Since these may be blown from either side, strings may be attached to chair backs and not held. This way, teams can be placed half at each end of their strings and blowers just go one length, then takes their place behind the last person in line, in numbered sequence as shown in figure 2.

241. Frog Hunt

Adds more action to the usual game of tag

Age level: 8 and up
Organizational level: Low
Number of players: 2 teams; 2–10 each
Supervision: Umpire

Playing time: 2 15-minute periods, or to a time limit
Space needed: Area at least 20′ × 20′
Equipment: None

Directions: Choose up teams. One team becomes "frogs," the other, hunters.

During game everyone must hop on one leg, holding the other ankle with one hand. Players may change hopping-and-holding legs, so long as both do not touch down at the same time.

On "play" signal, hunters try to tag frogs, with a hand on the back. A tagged frog is out of play and is escorted to the pond, where he must stay. If the hunter is, in turn, tagged by another frog, before getting his caught frog into the pond, his frog goes free again and the hunger has to wait in the pond. Frogs in pond may be exchanged for hunters in pond, one for one, so both get back into the game. Tagged frogs may also be made into hunters instead of going into the pond, and tagged hunters may likewise be made into frogs instead of going into the pond. If one side captures all opponents, it wins the half. Otherwise, team with most opponents in pond at end of period wins.

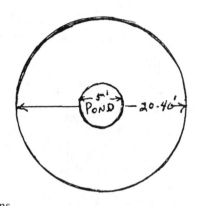

Teams exchange at the half, hunters becoming frogs and vice versa. If each team wins a half, game is a tie, no playoff.

242. Happy Hooligan Race

A handicap race, named after an old cartoon character from 60 years ago named "Happy" Hooligan, who wore a can on top of his head instead of a hat

Age level: 8 and up
Organizational level: Low
Number of players: Any number
Supervision: None
Playing time: 15 minutes

Space needed: 25 yard long course, 3–4' wide lanes for racers
Equipment: Paper cup for each runner, bucket of water to fill them from

Directions: Each runner gets a half-filled cup of water, which he balances on top of his head throughout a race of 25 yards. If the cup falls or is touched by the runner's hands, he must go back to the starting line and begin with a half-filled cup again.

243. Kleenex Sprint

Excellent game for giving stomach muscles a workout

Age level: 6 and up
Organizational level: Low
Number of players: Any number
Supervision: None

Playing time: 10 minutes
Space needed: 25 yard course, 3–4 feet wide racing lanes for each racer
Equipment: Kleenex tissue for each racer

Directions: On "go" signal, racers each "throw" an unfolded Kleenex tissue out ahead of them, go to it, bend, and pick it up, and repeat this process until they cross the finish line.

If a tissue is caught, or touched, after it is thrown, but before it lands on the ground, that racer is penalized 2 giant steps backwards before he can throw again. No runner may move ahead while holding a tissue or letting it blow against his body or clothes. Penalty: two giant steps backwards for every step taken forward while fouling.

244. Lame Dog Race

A handicap race

Age level: 6 and up
Organizational lavel: Low
Number of players: Any number
Supervision: None

Playing time: 15 minutes
Space needed: 25-yard course, 3–4′ lanes for racers
Equipment: None

Directions: Each racer lines up on the starting line on his hands and feet (not knees), face down position. On "go" signal, each one raises one foot off the ground and the entire race must be run that way.

If a player touches the raised foot to the ground, he must immediately resume the raised-leg position and turn completely around twice, before continuing.

Variations: *Crab Race*—Players sit on ground. On "go" signal, they raise their seats from the ground and scuttle down the course on hands and feet (without touching their backsides to the ground until they pass the finish line). Any racer so touching down must scuttle in a complete circle, twice, before continuing. *Lame Ape Race*—Each racer holds his left foot up in front of him with his right hand and hops one-legged to the finish line. Same penalty as above in case his raised foot is released or touched down.

245. Mother Nature's Relay

A handicap relay race

Organizational level: Medium
Number of players: 4-person teams
Supervision: Referee

Playing time: 5–10 minutes
Space needed: 25-yard course
Equipment: None

Directions: Teams decide which members will emulate which animals in the relay: 1st—hop like a frog, 2nd—scuttle like a crab (on hands and feet, backside to ground), 3rd—hop like a kangaroo (hop with both feet at the same time) and 4th—waddle like a duck (squat and hold ankles with both hands).

Numbers 2 and 4 of each team go to the far end of the race course. On "go" signal, all frogs hop the length of the course, tagging the crabs at the end, who, in turn, tag the kangaroos, who tag the ducks. Each must travel the entire course maintaining animal position, unless he comes to a full stop to rest, and each cannot pass the starting line until the previous racer tags him. Penalty: disqualification of team.

246. Handicap Race

A race with a series of handicaps incorporated

Age level: 8 and up
Organizational level: Medium
Number of players: Any number, divided into relay teams
Supervision: Play leader-referee

Playing time: 30 minutes
Space needed: 25-yard course, 3–4′ wide lanes for racers
Equipment: Volleyball, hula hoop and tin pie plate for each team

Directions: Racers line up at starting line, each with a volleyball clamped between his knees. On "go" signal, they waddle to the other end of the course, keeping the ball between their knees. If they drop it, or touch it with their hands, they are penalized 2 giant steps backwards from the point where they dropped, or touched it, and then start again from there. At the end of this lap, they drop the ball and pick up the hula hoop (placed there before the start) and run the course back to their original starting point, while, at the same time, "skinning the cat" (jumping through the hoop) 6 times during the run.

At the starting line, they drop the hoop and pick up the pie tin (placed there before the start of the game), place it on their head and run the course once more, without dropping, or touching, the tin plate. If it falls, or is touched, the runner is penalized 2 giant steps backwards from where the infraction occurred before he can move forward again.

If individuals are racing, the race is over with the three laps. If teams are racing, however, half of each team is placed at each end of the course. As the first racer completes three laps, the second racer would start from the opposite end of the course from the first racer, when he completed his three laps, the next racer would be from the end opposite his start, and so on until every team member has run.

As the last runner crosses the finish line, all of his team's players at that end of the course must somersault down the course and join their other teammates. First team joined together at one end is the winner.

247. Trio Racing

Variation of the three-legged race for picnics, field days,
scout troop meetings, camping groups and playground competitions

Age level: 8 and up
Organizational level: Medium
Number of players: 3 per team, any number of teams in race
Supervision: Referee
Playing time: Organization: 20–30 minutes; race: 2–4 minutes

Space needed: 50 to 100-yard race area, inside or outside
Equipment: 4 3-foot rope lengths per team, towels, small pillows or other padding may be used under the ropes so legs won't be chafed

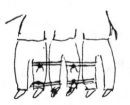

Directions: Each threesome stand side by side to have their legs tied together at ankles and knees, as shown at the left.

Teams line up and on "go" signal, race to the finish line. All three must be across the line, with leg wrappings intact, before any other trio, to win.

Variations: *Amoeba Race*— Threesome stand in a small triangle, backs toward each other. They lock arms at the elbows, line up and run the race in this position. *Witch Race*—Three people straddle a broom, but with the middle person *backwards* to the other two. The race is run that way. (Each team can furnish its own broom, or plain sticks 4–6' long may be used.)

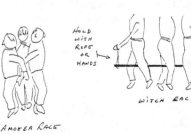

HOLD WITH ROPE OR HANDS

WITCH RACE

AMOEBA RACE

248. Commando Obstacle Course

A physical exercise that uses all body muscles and
tests a variety of skills in a short time in a small space

Age level: 8 and up
Organizational level: Medium
Number of players: Any number
Supervision: Judge and recorder
Playing time: 10 minutes per person

Space needed: 30 yards by 50 yards area, or gym
Equipment: Game Time Co. obstacle course equipment package, or appropriate substitute obstacles as described

Directions: (1) Slalom run—zig-zag running around 5 rocks or stakes. (2) Tunnel crawl—3' high pipe (or two oil barrels with ends cut off) or roof frame, to crawl through or under. (3) Balance beam—2" wide board set on blocks, or section of railroad rail, to walk across and do a full squat and a one-leg balance on. (If racer steps off he must go back and start the beam over.) (4) Limbo bar—chest high bar that racers "limbo" under (bend backwards and shuffle under it). (5) High jump bar—set at 1½–3' depending upon age group. (6) Parallel bars—3–4' high bars that racer must walk along with his hands, as he hold his arms stiffly at his sides with feet hanging down between the bars. (7) Fence climb—8' fence, with rungs to climb up and over on. (8) Monkey bars—racers swing forward, hand over hand, down an overhead ladder. (9) Headstand mat—racers must do a headstand for 3 seconds (or a broad jump, across a 3–4' marked area on mats). (10) Run backwards to the starting line.

249. Blackout

A team capture game with special handicaps built in for night play

Age level: 8 and up
Organizational level: Low
Number of players: 2 teams, any equal number the play area can accommodate
Supervision: Referee
Playing time: 10 minutes

Space needed: Gym or multi-purpose room, where lights can be easily turned off or on
Equipment: Rip-flag belt (or pair of bandannas to tuck into belt at both sides) for each player

Directions: Select 2 teams. All players put on rip-flag belts, or bandanna flags. Each team should have different colored flags. Teams line up against opposite walls.

When referee turns out lights, it is the signal for all players to advance and try to de-flag as many opponents as possible in the dark. The referee will flick the lights on and off again, periodically, to give players a quick glimpse of where everyone is. But, players may not speak, or make vocal noices, or use noise-making implements (whistles, clickers, etc.) to let team members recognize them or to confuse opponents.

When the time period is up, the referee turns the lights on, sends teams back to their walls, and totals up the flags each team has collected, subtracting each teammate's flag collected from the total opponent's flags collected. Team with the most opponent's belts is winner.

Game source: Modified from innovation by Angie Acuna, Sports and Playground director, Pima County Parks and Recreation Department, Tucson, AZ in the mid 1970s.

250. The Hexathlon

*A track and field meet parody, using events that anyone can
have fun doing. Better than a formal track meet at informal places
like camp. Some of the activities can be competed in by handicapped also.*

Age level: 8–10, 11–13, 14–17
Organizational level: High
Number of players: Any number, like a track
and field meet
Supervision: Clerk of the course, field judges
(2–4), starters, recorders
Playing time: Figure an hour per event
average, jumping events taking longer than
the racing events

Space needed: Track and field area, or any
large, open area where the necessary events
and equipment may be set up, inside or
outside
Equipment: Tape measure, high jump
standards (1 set), 6 1-foot high hurdles per
racing lane, tumbling mats (or similar pads)
for high jump pit

Directions: Each participant competes in all six events. Placings are added up
(as a first and a third equal 4) and divided by the number of events where the
contestant placed first through tenth. (Example: This runner placed in two
events, a 1 plus a 3 for a 4, so divide the 4 by the 2 and get 2.00 as that person's
score.) Winner will be the *lowest* score, thus figured.

Events include: *Long Step*—Standing start, though takeoff may be from
one foot. (Replaces the long jump.) Three trials per person. *Standing High
Jump*—No running start. Takeoff may be from one or two feet. (Replaced the
running high jump.) *100-Foot Shuffle*—Each foot must be placed directly in
front of the other, heel tight to toe. (Replaces 100-yard dash.) *100-Hop
Hurdles*—Feet must be kept together, ankle to ankle, so the racer hops down the
course and over the hurdles. (Replaces the 100-yard hurdles.) *Triple Hop*—
Standing start. Hop to same foot, step to opposite foot, and jump to both feet.
Total distance covered is counted. Longest triple hop from three tries is winner.
(Replaces the triple jump.) *Backward Race*—100-foot shuffle, backwards, plac-
ing toe tight to heel. (Replaces long, stamina races.)

251. Jelly Roll Relay

*Good action activity for handling relatively large groups in small
space with little equipment and supervision. Teaches team cooperation.*

Age level: 6 and up
Organizational level: Medium
Number of players: 2 teams: 10 players each
Supervision: 2 referees
Playing time: Varies considerably, depend-
ing upon number of players, but minimum
of half-hour to get organized and run off

Space needed: Level area 50′ × 20′, indoors or
outside
Equipment: 2 Whiffleballs or sponge balls,
4 plastic hand scoops, either commercial
ones (available from Cosom Company) or
homemade (from cutting bottoms or sides
off gallon plastic milk jugs)

Directions: Team members line up as in drawing shown on next page.

To start relay, #5 players on each team pick up balls on ground at their feet
in hand-held scoops and throw them across the jelly-roll area to teammates #6.
Then #5s run across the jelly-roll area to line up behind their #10 teammates,
after giving their scoops to their #7 teammates.

If #6s catch balls thrown to them, they throw them across the field to #4
teammates. If they don't catch the ball, they must retrieve and pick it up in their

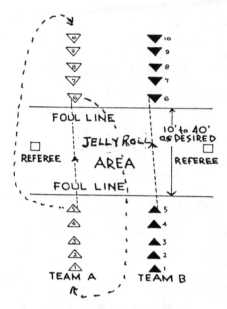

scoops before returning to their throwing spot and throwing.

Each thrower continues in this way, running to stand at the end of his team's line on the opposite end of court, after giving his scoop to the next thrower in line without one. When everyone has had 2 turns, and the #5 player has returned to his original position, the team yells, "Jelly Roll!"

If any player does not throw his ball over the jelly-roll area, he must retrieve it with his scoop, return to his throwing area, and try again.

A foul is called if: (1) thrower or catcher steps over the foul lines, (2) ball is touched with hand by thrower or catcher, (3) any teammate helps recover thrower's or catcher's fumble. Penalty is to drop the ball at point of infraction, then fumbler must retrieve it with his scoop and return to position.

First team to finish and yell "Jelly Roll!" is winner. Losers then have to drop to floor/ground and execute a "jelly roll," a complete rollover.

252. Tunnel Race

A team handicap relay race

Age level: 6 and up
Organizational level: Medium
Number of players: Any number that may be divided into evenly numbered teams, from 6 up

Playing time: 30–40 minutes
Space needed: 70′ race course, 10′ wide raceway (lane) for each team
Equipment: Stake or rock to mark end of each racing lane

Directions: Line teams up behind starting line, all facing the starting line. On "go" signal, all players straddle their legs and the last person in each line crawls on his hands and knees between all the legs.

At the starting line, he gets to his feet and races to the end of the course, around the marker there and back to his team. Upon crossing the starting line after this run, he yells "go" to the new last man in his line, while he takes his place at the front of the line. This is repeated until the last person in line crosses the starting line on his return run. Upon crossing the line he yells "Drop," and all his teammates drop to the ground. First team "down" wins.

Fouls that can disqualify a team: (1) Player not crawling between the legs of all his teammates, (2) player pushing, pulling, carrying, or otherwise aiding a teammate, (3) runner calling "go" or "down" before he crosses the line at the end of his run, and (4) player interfering physically with a member of another team.

Variation: *Mole race* — Blindfold all players, except each team "caller," who calls out directions to his teammates in the same relay as above. Caller cannot touch his players. (This game should not be played where safety hazards exist, like near water, trees in the race course, steps or drop offs, etc.) Caller can stand anywhere in his team's racing lane, even running beside players as he gives instructions.

Game source: Tunnel Race is adapted and modified from a game innovated by Angie Acuna, Sports and Playground director, Pima County Park and Recreation Department, Tuscon, AZ, in the mid-1970s.

253. Ball Dogging

Agility training. Good exercise for running backs in football.

Age level: 8 and up
Organizational level: Low
Number of players: 2 teams: 6–12 each
Supervision: Dice roller-caller
Playing time: 30–60 minutes. Play to preset score or to time limit.

Space needed: Area 15′ × 50′
Equipment: Ball (any type), though any other object can be used (rock, stick, etc.), kerchiefs for all players, pair of dice

Directions: Divide players into two teams. Line teams up about 50′ apart.

Each player tucks corner of kerchief into belt in back, with rest of it hanging free. Ball is placed midway between two teams, in the middle of the area. Players number off: 1 to 6 or 1 to 12 on each side.

If six players being used, use one of dice (die); if 12 players, use both dice. Caller rolls dice and calls number that comes up. Those numbered players from both sides race toward the ball and attempt to grab it and take it back to their side. The one who grabs it must then try to keep the opponent from grabbing his neckerchief out of his belt. If he gets the ball safely to his side, his team gets a point; if he is de-flagged first, the other team gets the point.

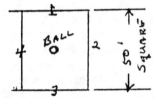

Variation: *4-Way Ball Dogging* — Same game, except use four teams arranged in a square all facing the ball in the center.

Game source: Adapted from an old Indian punishment ritual, where person to be punished had to run between two rows of people flogging him with belts and rawhide strips and, sometimes, clubs.

254. Land Grab

Capture game

Age level: 8 and up
Organizational level: Low
Number of players: 2 teams, any even number the play area can accommodate
Supervision: Referee

Playing time: 30–60 minutes
Space needed: 50 yards × 40 yards
Equipment: Rip-flag belt for each player, 3–4 backless benches, ball (soccer, playground, volley, etc.)

Directions: Select teams. Put on rip-flag belts. Team captains number off players in order he wants them to compete.

Object of the game: to capture the ball (at midfield) without being de-flagged.

On "go" signal by referee, the first competitor from each team rushes to midfield and tries to grab the ball (which has been placed atop a bottle cap or plastic can lid to keep it from rolling out of position), and take it back to his team's safety zone. The player who doesn't get the ball, tries to de-flag the one with the ball before he gets back to safety. If the ball carrier returns safely, he earns a point for his team. If he is deflagged (either flag on his belt), he is out of the game.

The ball is returned to the midfield spot and the #2 players on each team compete. (Some groups prefer to use a bucket in place of the ball.)

If a ball is dropped while the carrier is in the field of play, it may be re-covered by either player. Ball cannot be knocked out of player's hands, how-ever.

One special rule is that the ball may only be grabbed from its position when a player has at least one foot in the oppo-nent's No Man's Land. That means he must straddle, or jump, the midfield benches to do it. Penalty: player banished from the game; point to opposing team.

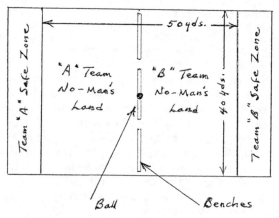

Variation: *Land Grab II*—Same game except 2, or even 3, players play at the same time, trying to get the ball. One added rule: players may bounce-pass the ball among teammates in the playing area.

Game source: Modified from game by Angie Acuna, Sports and Playground director, Pima County Parks and Recreations Department, Tucson, AZ, in the mid–1970s.

255. Gauntlet

Teaches running and dodging skills (perhaps as training element for football and rugby running backs). Good group game that gets everyone actively involved in a small area.

Age level: 10 and over
Organizational level: Low
Number of players: 2 teams, 8–14 each
Supervision: Referee
Playing time: 30 minutes
Space needed: 6′ × 80–100′ runway area
Equipment: 2 buckets or small boxes, as many tennis balls (or rocks) as there are

members on each team, 2 flag football-type belts with 2 "flags" attached by grippers or velcro at the sides (or 2 bandannas may be tucked into the belt by one corner each, at the sides), something to mark the gauntlet's runway lines (depending on whether game is played on ground, grass or floor)

Directions: Place balls in one bucket at one end of runway and empty bucket at other end.

Defensive team lines up along both sides of runway, between the 2 safety zones. Offensive team lines up at the end of the runway where the empty bucket is. The first 2 players in line put on the flag belts (or bandannas).

On "go" signal, the first runner runs the gauntlet, takes a ball out of the full bucket, then runs the gauntlet back to put the ball in the empty bucket. If he makes it all the way, without the defensive players plucking *both* flags from his belt during his run, the ball goes into the bucket. If he doesn't succeed, the ball is given to the defensive team captain. The team with the most balls, when all offensive team members have completed their runs, is winner of that half of the game.

Then the teams switch places and repeat the game. If the same team wins both halves, it is the game winner. If the teams split wins, it's a tie.

Offensive players may not run out of the runway. Penalty: his run is over at that point and his ball goes to the opponents. Defensive players may not step into the runway, or into the safety zones, to grab flags from runners. Penalty: that runner automatically gets his ball in the bucket. No blocking or holding runners.

As soon as one runner puts his ball into the bucket, or gives it to the opponents, and as soon as the next runner has a flag belt on, he may run, whether the defense if ready or not. (Quick changes with the 2 belts, therefore, becomes important. Other players may help fast changes.)

Variations: *Sockball Gauntlet*—Same game, except buckets and flag belts are not needed and Whiffleballs or sponge balls—enough so every defensive player has one or two—are thrown at the runners. Every hit is a point. Team with most points after the two halves is the winner. Ball may be recovered and thrown from anywhere outside the runway and safety zone, but the runner cannot be hit while in either safety zone. *Dropsy Gauntlet*—Same basic game idea as above, except the runner holds a volleyball behind him with both hands. The defensive team throws balls (volley, tennis or small playground balls) at the volleyball, trying to knock it out of the runner's hands. If they succeed, he gets no points. But, if he makes it safely down the runway one way, the runner gets one point, and if he makes it both ways still holding the ball, he gets 2 points for his team.

As before, defense team members can throw balls from anywhere outside the runway and safety zones, but, cannot throw when a runner is in a safety zone.

The defensive team is penalized 2 points if a runner is hit in the head with a thrown ball (so long as he doesn't dodge into it.)

Game source: Adapted from an old Indian game.

256. Fox and Geese

Winter snow game, transformed into a year-round game

Age level: 6 and up
Organizational level: Low
Number of players: Up to 12
Supervision: None
Playing time: Open ended

Space needed: 60′ × 60′ area at playground, beach, park or gym/multi-purpose room
Equipment: Chalk or string to mark off playing area

Directions: Select one player as the "Fox." He is the chaser, trying to tag (two hand touch) the "geese" (the other players).

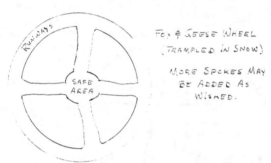

FOX & GEESE WHEEL
(TRAMPLED IN SNOW)

MORE SPOKES MAY
BE ADDED AS
WISHED.

Geese are safe when in the "pond," but only 2 may be in the pond at any one time. Both fox and geese must remain on the circular and cross paths. A player taking a shortcut, or going outside the boundaries, is out of the game and must go into the fox's den, until another goose rescues him. A rescue is accomplished by taking the hand of the goose in the den and both getting back to the pond without being tagged by the fox.

If the fox succeeds in tagging a goose while in the playing paths, the tagged goose becomes the fox and the fox becomes a goose and play continues. The new fox cannot tag the new goose, however, until he has first attempted to tag another goose.

Variation: *Tag Team Fox and Geese*—With large groups playing on large playing areas, more cross paths may be used, and two foxes may work as a team.

257. Hare and Hounds

A classic chase game rejuvenated from Grandpa's boyhood

Age level: 10 and up
Organizational level: Low
Number of players: 1–2 hares, as many hounds as wish
Supervision: Referee
Playing time: Open-ended, until hare gets back to its home or the hounds catch him

Space needed: A regional park, wooded area, or an urban neighborhood
Equipment: Bag of rice or birdseed, or box of colored Kleenex tissues

Directions: One or two players are selected as hares. They get the bag of rice or birdseed or box of Kleenex to carry with them. They use it to leave clues to their trail, leaving a handful at places that are in the open, yet not easy to find for the hounds — around a corner they have turned, on the top step of a long flight of stairs, in the low crotch of a tree, or wherever ingenuity may dictate. The hares must indicate direction taken at intersections, etc., but may double back on the trail, circle behind the hounds, borrow a bicycle (so as not to leave footprints, or to just gain time), etc.

The hares get 10 minutes head start before the hounds start tracking them. If the kleenex tissues are being left by the hares, the hounds pick them up as they find them (no litter), so they may be recycled for use in another game.

If the hares get back to the starting point without being tagged by the hounds, he/they win. If the hounds tag first, they win.

Game source: An old English game, first played in the U.S. Christmas Day 1877 in Westchester, N.Y., by Walter S. Vosburgh.

258. Criss-Cross Tag

A team tag game, with an innovation

Age level: 8 and up
Organizational level: Medium
Number of players: 4 teams, any equal
  number to 10
Supervision: Referee

Playing time: 60 minutes
Space needed: 50 yards × 50 yards area
Equipment: Chalk to mark boundaries (or
  stakes at all four corners, string connecting
  them optional)

Directions: Line up one team on each of the four sides of the playing area. The front 4 go into the "box" (playing area) to become the first "taggers."

On "go" signal by referee, all players on all four sides run across to the opposite side from where they're starting, while trying to keep from getting tagged (two-hand touch anywhere except on the head) while inside the box. Each person tagged must hold a hand in the air as he gets to his opposite side, so the referee can tabulate scores. Taggers may not tag their own teammates, but may tag any player on any of the 3 other teams. Referee counts one point for each hand raised (tagged player) from each team.

If a player has been tagged, but does not raise his hand, the referee may give a point *and* a penalty point to that team.

Then the taggers take their places with their own teams, and another player from each team becomes tag-

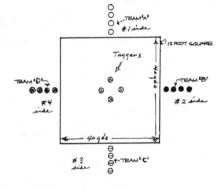

ger. This rotation continues until all players have had a turn as tagger. Then the referee totals the points for each team, for all runs, and the *lowest* point team (one with least tagged players) wins.

259. Bronco Roundup

A team captive game

Age level: 8 and up
Organizational level: Medium
Number of players: 2 teams, any even
  number to 8
Supervision: Foreman (referee)
Playing time: 20 minutes

Space needed: 45 yards × 45 yards area
Equipment: Chalk, or other marking
  substance, to mark boundary lines, rip-flag
  belt (or 2 bandannas to tuck into each
  "bronco" belt)

Directions: Objective: Cowboys catch and "tame" broncos, by deflagging them.
Choose up teams.

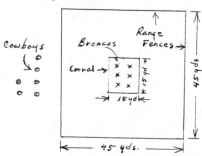

Game starts on "go" signal from
"foreman" with "cowboys" outside
the "range fences" and the "broncos"
inside anywhere. All broncos wear 2
bandannas, one tucked into the belt
on either side. The cowboys move
into the ranch and try to grab the flags
from the broncos. A bronco has to
lose both flags before he is captured.
When that happens, he is out of the
game and must move outside the
ranch fences. To avoid being deflagged, broncos may dodge, twist and turn, leap
and use their folded arms to ward off cowboys. They may also dodge back into
the corral to get away or to take a rest, since that is a safe haven. But only 2
broncos may be in there at the same time. (If more are in, any one of them may
be deflagged.)

If all broncos are deflagged by the end of the time period, the cowboys win.
If not, the broncos win.

Teams change sides and play again.

260. Invasion

A team capture game simulating basic military maneuvers

Age level: 14 and over
Organizational level: Medium
Number of players: 2 teams, any equal
  number to 12
Supervision: Referee
Playing time: Open-ended until one team
  captures the other's flag, or one team has all
  been captured

Space needed: Football or soccer field, or
  equivalent area, but better played in a
  wooded area or over an entire one-block
  urban area
Equipment: Rip-flag belts for all players, 2
  pennants (or bandannas tied to stakes at
  least 5' high)

Directions: Select armies (teams); armies select sergeants to lead them. All
players put on rip-flag belts (or 2 bandannas tucked into the belt, one on each
side). Each team should have different colored rip-flags. Each army sets up a jail
area near the rear of its playing area and a headquarters area, where the army's
pennant post is situated.

One player may be ordered to remain near each area (jail and headquarters)
to protect them. They may call for assistance when threatened.

To start the game, the two armies line up along the No Man's Line. After the referee gives the "go" signal, any members of either army may dash into the opponent's territory and attempt to grab the army pennant-stake and take it back to their home headquarters. If successful, the game is won. If these players are deflagged (one flag) before they can get back, the flag is rescued and replaced and the belts of the deflagged players are put into the capturer's jail. The deflagged players are out of the game (until they can be rescued) and must go outside their captors' area.

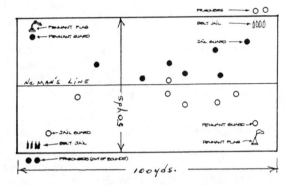

Any player may rescue a teammate by grabbing a rip-flag belt out of the opponent's jail and returning with it back over the No Man's Line, without being deflagged himself.

He may choose the prisoner he wants returned.

A temporary truce may be called at any time by the opposing sergeants, to exchange prisoners. A team may also win, however, by capturing (deflagging) all its opponents, even though their pennant hasn't been captured.

Variation: *Invasion II*—Same game, except each team may have one, or two, designated "convoy" players. They do not wear rip-flag belts, so cannot be captured, but they also cannot rescue teammates or capture the opponent's flag. Their only duty is to "convoy" another teammate into enemy territory and protect him from opposing players (via body blocking with arms crossed on the chest, and no pushing, tripping or kicking) while the teammate tries to rescue players, or capture the flag. A convoy may also help guard his own team's jail and headquarters when called upon.

Game source: May have spun off from Kick the Can, but was popularized in the 1940s as a game for Boy Scout groups. It's also long been played in much more complex manner by military organizations' war gaming.

261. Moving Maze Race

A chase game with moving hazards

Age level: 12 and up
Organizational level: Medium
Number of players: 18 or more
Supervision: Referee
Playing time: Open ended, 5 minute maximum session for "runners" and "chasers"

Space needed: 20′ × 20′ area minimum; the more players, the more space required
Equipment: A rip-flag football belt, or a belt with 2 bandannas tucked in at the sides

Directions: Select "runner" and "chaser." Line up other players in ranks, 4–6 per line, all facing the same way.

Select a leader who can be part of the lines or not. He gives the ranks letters and has the players in the ranks "number down," as shown in the sketch, so he can call instructions to them.

Runner puts on rip-flag belt. He gets a 5-second head start over the chaser (or the runner and chaser can be started at diagonally opposite corners of the

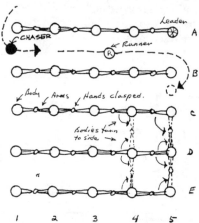

formation). Then, the leader helps the runner elude the chaser by calling out commands for various pairs of players in the ranks to wheel and block the chaser's passage.

At the start, the leader commands, "clasp hands," and all the players in each rank (line) clasp hands. The runner and chaser run up and down the alleys, thus formed between the ranks. But, if it looks like the chaser is going to catch the runner, the leader commands, "C and D #5, sweep together," for example, and those 2 players, turn left and right, respectively, and clasp each other's hands, thus blocking the chaser after the runner has passed them.

If the chaser grabs a flag off the runner, he wins. If he doesn't within 3–5 minutes, new runner, chaser and leader are selected.

Variation: *Advanced Maze Race*—When players become good enough at the basic game, two chasers may be introduced into the game to chase one runner.

WORD-PLAY AND STORY-TELLING GAMES

262. Your Name's the Game (or Name-Bingo)

Originated as a fill-in time-passer for spectators waiting for softball games to begin. (Can also be used in school classes, at scout meetings, company picnics, dance intermissions, basketball or football halftimes, etc.)

Age level: Open
Organizational level: High
Number of players: Open
Supervision: Master-of-ceremonies and recorder
Playing time: 15–30 minutes
Space needed: Tabletop (for MC and recorder)

Equipment: Cardboard spinner card with all letters of the alphabet and one "Free Letter" space on it, pad of paper and pencil (for all players), public address system (if necessary). Name-bingo sheets are all alike, each having a complete alphabet, but each in random order, in its squares

Directions: Someone from crowd is called in as "spinner." MC announces the letters that come up as he spins them, and the recorder lists them in order. Players try to bingo! by crossing out all the letters of their first and last names (as given on their driver's license or credit card or, in the case of children, their school activity card). Duplicate letters may be crossed or checked more than once. The "free letter" may be used as any one letter once, unless spun more than once.

When a name-bingo is called, the person calling out brings his sheet to the recorder for verification, and, if correct, ends the game. Prizes can be announced, like tickets to some event, snack food, drinks or merchandise.

263. Deft-nitions

A word-play game to increase vocabulary

Age level: 12 and up
Organizational level: Medium
Number of players: Open
Supervision: Play leader or teacher

Playing time: Open-ended
Space needed: Tabletop
Equipment: Several dictionaries, paper pads and pencils for all players

Directions: Divide group into 2–3 person teams to make up 10 deft-nitions (or as many as possible) in a 20-minute period. Each deft-nition includes a rhyming couplet, each word about the same number of syllables, and a short deft-nition (definition) of the couplet.

When time is up, each group takes its turn as quiz-show hosts, presenting the overall group with its deft-nitions and the number of syllables in the couplet words as clues (which can be humorous), so they can try to guess the correct rhyming couplet that goes with it.

Here are examples. The first two are answered correctly. See if you can get the answers for the others. They are in a mixed-up order.

Deft-nition:	Number of Syllables:	Rhyming Couplet Answers:
A pale Romeo might be described as a :	One	Wan Don
A tonsorial expert operating on the waterfront could be called a:	Two	Harbor Barber
A spotted feline potted full of holes might be a:	Two	Quaint Saint
Any car owner knows that a damp carwash cloth is a:	Two	Brash Pash
An unwashed "knight of the open road" might, with delicacy, be labeled as:	Two	School Jewel
Bug bliss could also be called:	One	Dreamy Mimi
A Germanic cheerleader has just been selected at school. A good nickname for him might be the:	Two	Gluesome Twosome

A new robot, put on the market in the year 1990, was advertised to have a Mona Lisa smile. The indelicate press headlined it as "The robot with the:	One	Hen Pen
An egotistical lover, in the vernacular of the teen-age, would be a:	One	Flea Glee
A Big Man on Campus would immediately know it was his keen queen being referred to if someone asked after his:	One	Beach Peach
A bikinied Riviera rave would become, in Americanese, a:	One	Peppered Leopard
A lackadaisical Model-T was once the ultimate in campus cars, but today it would be called a:	One	Rootin' Teuton
What would the shepherd call the meanest ram in his flock?	Two	Bored Ford
Any woman's dorm on any campus might well be labeled:	One	Fragrant Vagrant
A bit of French fluff comes to school on the foreign exchange program. All the boys are likely to start calling her a:	Two	Clammy Chamois
As a reporter for the local paper you have just finished a story on a new midget guided missile, and you need a catch term for the headline. You might use:	Two	Fizzle Missile
An old-fashioned priest might be called by those who know him a:	One	Power Flour
A couple who have gone steady for the past two years might be known among their friends as a:	Two	Tin Grin Wooly Bully High Guy Gringo Lingo Pocket Rocket

Now, in un-muddled order, are the answers: Wan Don, Harbor Barber, Peppered Leopard, Clammy Chamois, Fragrant Vagrant, Flea Glee, Rootin' Teuton, Tin Grin, Brash Pash, School Jewel, Beach Peach, Bored Ford, Wooly Bully, Hen Pen, Dreamy Mimi, Pocket Rocket, Quaint Saint, Gluesome Twosome.

264. Dictionary Doodling

Test of ingenuity in doodling words so they become self-defining

Age level: 14 and up
Number of players: Open
Supervision: Teacher
Playing time: Open-ended

Space needed: Tabletop
Equipment: Several dictionaries, paper pads and pencils for all players

Directions: Teacher should show examples in explanation:

The teams may be chosen to work on 8 suggested words by the teacher, 5 minutes per word. At the end of that time, the groups may put their doodled words on the chalkboard.

The class may vote on the best ones and they may be reproduced on poster paper and placed on the bulletin board.

265. Math Matching

Game to create interest in learning simple mathematics

Age level: 8 and up
Organizational level: Medium
Number of players: 4–15
Supervision: Instructor

Playing time: Open-ended
Space needed: 20′ × 20′ area
Equipment: Tablet, marking pen, safety pins for all players

Directions: Players form circle, facing inward. Each draws a number out of a hat (from #1 to however many are playing). That number is put onto a sheet of paper and pinned to his chest.

The player drawing #1 becomes the game leader (with the instructor's aid), and calls out directions. For example, he may call out any number (from 2 to however many players there are), like "#4." Number 4 then listens for the next directions, which might be, "Double it." Number 4 would have to come up with the answer "#8." If missed, the leader calls on someone else for the answer.

The leader may also use subtraction, multiplication and division directions. For older, better schooled players, he may involve 2 players in a single computation, or even several, like "#9," subtract #3 and add #2, then divide #2. All 4 players would have to come up with the answer.

When everyone in the circle has been involved, the number tags may be redistributed for another game with a different leader.

266. Trademark Recall

*Make a game of a poll of sorts—find out
how well we remember company trademarks*

Age level: 14 and up
Organizational level: Medium

Number of players: Open
Supervision: Game leader

Playing time: 20–30 minutes
Space needed: Wall space for taping up pictures
Equipment: Selection of 25 or so advertisements of well known companies, with the trademark names cut out, but with hints in the pictures to help viewers guess them, like packaging, colors, slogans, etc. (Keep the trademarks and company names on an answer sheet for later reference.) Paper and pencils for each player.

Directions: Post the ads and number them. Players try guessing the company names/trademarks the ads represent (being sure to match numbers on ads with their answers).

At the end of the time period, the game leader reads the answers so everyone can check their papers. Winner is one with most correct answers.

267. Ad Tic-Tac-Toe

Variation of old tic-tac-toe game

Age level: 8 and up
Organizational level: Medium
Number of players: 2
Supervision: None

Playing time: 10–20 minutes
Space needed: Tabletop
Equipment: Stack of old magazines, paper pad and two pencils

Directions: Make tic-tac-toe forms on paper pad. Several games may be played at once, if wished, each being played with a different T-T-T diagram.

Players go through magazines looking for pictures of personalities, ads for various products, company trademarks, etc. Each time one is found they think they can duplicate, they make a note on magazine and page where it was found. They then put an X and O, or their initials, whichever they are using, in one of the T-T-T squares. If he can find another one quickly, he can mark a second square of his choice, since players don't have to take turns (as in regular tic-tac-toe). First player with 3 marks in a row, any direction, is winner. It's a better contest if 3–5 games are played at the same time. Then the winner is the player winning the most games.

Variations: *Ad T3*—Same game, but played while watching TV. *License Tic-Tac-Toe*—Played while traveling. Player to first see an out-of-state license plate, gets to mark a form. Whatever out-of-state license his opponent sees first also goes on that sheet. As either player sees other out-of-state licenses, they are put on other T3 forms, so a number of games will be going on simultaneously. (Games may continue for days.) *Giant Tic-Tac-Toe*—Playing time per game may be extended by using larger T3 designs; any of the variations can use these. Or they can be used for teams to play on.

268. Baby Says

Making a game of captioning baby pictures

Age level: 14 and up
Organizational level: Low
Number of players: Open
Supervision: 2–3 judges
Playing time: 30 minutes

Space needed: Wall area where pictures may be taped up for viewing.
Equipment: Collection of 25 or so baby pictures cut from newspapers and magazines (unusual facial expressions preferred), paper and pencil for each player

Directions: Pictures numbered and posted. Each player numbers his sheet to correspond to the pictures. Then they all look at the pictures and write humorous captions or quotations of what the babies in the pictures might be saying (judging from their expressions, poses and clothes), being sure to match pictures, numbers and captions.

When everyone has written all the captions they can think up, they go down the picture list and everyone reads his captions.

Variation: *Ad-Glibs*—Same game can be played using pictures in ads.

269. Imagineering (or Tell and Spell)

Word game for group play. Good for family or party.

Age level: 10 and up
Organizational level: Low
Number of players: Open
Supervision: Referee-recorder
Playing time: 30–60 minutes

Space needed: Room with seating for all players
Equipment: Dictionary, paper and pencil for players

Directions: First player says a word (which may be a real or a made-up word). The next person in order, either accepts or challenges the word. If he is correct, the word-giver must pay a penalty; if wrong, he pays the penalty. A penalty may be any funny thing the winner thinks up, like reciting a poem, singing a lullaby in rap style, making the ugliest face he can, demonstrating a yoga pose or hopping like a toad around the group.

When the penalty has been paid, the second player must give a word, starting with the last letter of the first player's word. (The referee-recorder keeps track of all words used.) Then the same sequence is repeated until everyone has played.

The game may then be continued by everyone using the list of words they've used in the game in a story. This may be done in several ways: (1) By each person taking a turn telling the story orally, until he has used one of the words, then the next person taking over, and so on. (2) By each person writing a story using all the words, then reading them to the group. (3) By each person telling a segment of the story orally, ending with one of the words (even if it comes in mid-sentence). (4) Same as above, but in writing, with the entire story read to the group when completed.

270. Who Am I?

Age level: Any age
Number of players: Any number
Space needed: Any area, indoors or outdoors

Equipment: Paper pad, pins, pencil or felt pen, list of names in various categories to be used in the game, as cartoon characters, politicians, actors and actresses, etc.

Directions: Decide on category to use in the game. Mark names on sheets of paper.

Pin a name on the back of each player, so he cannot see it.

On signal each player starts circulating among other players. Each is allowed to ask one question and answer one question from each other player, all of which must be answered "yes" or "no." By asking questions in this manner each person tries to determine the name on his back. First one to guess is the winner.

271. Ego Trip

A psychological game played to make people in a group friends and to build up everyone's ego. Good family game.

Age level: 10 and up
Organizational level: Low
Number of players: 10–12 easy to handle. Needs playleader to get game started.
Playing time: 30–60 minutes
Space needed: Area where group can be seated in a circle, all facing each other

Equipment: Chairs or stools can be used, if wished, for participants, but the more informal crossed-legged sitting on the floor or ground seems to break down inhibitions better. A tape recorder may be used to record everything so children can play it again whenever they wish.

Directions: Seat participants in circle facing each other. The leader asks for volunteers first, each one to say something he likes about one of the others in the circle. Once something has been said about someone, that person cannot be complimented by anyone again until everyone in the circle has been complimented. As the game goes on, and players get into it, the rule can be made that the person complimented must then be the one to compliment someone else, and so on until everyone has been covered. Then another round may be started.

    Variations: *Ego Trip II*—Same basic idea, except one person at a time takes his place in the center of the ring of players. Then each person in the ring tells him one thing he likes about him. This continues until everyone has been in the center. *Ego Strip*—Same idea as either game above, except people are made humorous fun of or told things others *don't* like about them. This needs careful handling, preferably humorously, like a "roast."

272. Stage Coach

Good social mixer at party, camp or playground

Age level: 8 and up
Organizational level: Low
Number of players: 3 teams: cowboys, Indians, coach drivers (equal number of each) and story teller

Space needed: Circular area large enough to hold all participants
Equipment: Chairs or stools for all participants, except the story teller

Directions: Seat players in a circle all facing toward the story teller in the center. Choose up teams of cowboys, Indians and stagecoach drivers, then have them take seats in rotation around the circle—a cowboy, then an Indian, then a coach driver, then repeat the sequence all around the circle. (This is so the story teller can tell quickly if any member of a team makes a mistake.)

    Story teller starts telling a story about cowboys, Indians and stagecoach drivers. Everytime he says any of those names in the story, all its team members must jump to their feet and act out their parts—cowboys galloping like a horse or shooting a gun or whatever and making appropriate noises at the same time,

Indians war whooping and war dancing, scalping or whatever, coach drivers likewise doing their thing. Periodically, the story teller will throw the word "stagecoach" into this story, then everyone has to immediately stand and go into their acts and, at the same time, move one seat clockwise. While this is happening, the story teller tries to sneak into a seat before one of the circle players does. If he succeeds, the player without a seat exchanges places with the story teller and must continue telling the story until he can sneak into a seat and exchange places with someone else.

Variations: *Pony Express*—This game can be made more tricky for older players by adding the words "Pony Express" into the story. When it is said, everyone stands, goes into their acts and moves *2* spaces over, clockwise.

273. Story Board
Practice the sequencing of storytelling

Age level: 10 and up
Organizational level: Medium
Number of players: 1–12
Supervision: Reader
Playing time: 30–60 minutes
Space needed: Tables, covered with protective newspapers

Equipment: Stack of magazines (for cutting up), snub-nosed scissors for each player or team, large sheets of wrapping paper, pencil for each player or team, and glue

Directions: Reader reads a short story to the group. Then, each player, or team of two, rewrites it in his/their own words, changing it as wished as they go along. At the same time, they are looking through the magazines for pictures that might be used to illustrate their story. This accounts for the changing of the story as they write it, to make it easier to illustrate. Each player, or team, must have at least 6 pictures in the appropriate spots in the story text.

Variation: *Story Board II*—Players may cut out a group of related pictures, put them into a story sequence, then write a short story to fit.

SPECIAL EQUIPMENT GAMES

274. Belli-Ball
Social game, for picnic, camp, etc.,
that is as much fun to watch as participate in

Age level: 6 and up
Organizational level: Low
Number of players: 1
Supervision: None

Playing time: 21 points, 15–20 minutes
Space needed: Standing space
Equipment: Belli-ball set (or homemade one)

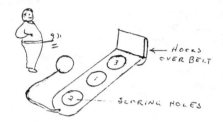

Directions: Belli-ball form is fitted over the belt as shown in the sketch, then is jiggled up and down to bounce the ball into and out of the holes until a total of 21 points is reached. Holes count 1, 2, or 3 points as shown, each time the ball lands in one of them.

Game source: Belli-ball unit marketed by Miles Kimball of Oshkosh, WI., 1978.

275. Balance Beam

Teaches body balancing skills

Age level: 8 and up
Organizational level: Medium
Number of players: 1 or 2 at a time
Supervision: Instructor
Playing time: Open
Space needed: 6′ × 25′ area, heavily sanded, or with tumbling mats

Equipment: Balance beam (commercial cable unit, called Tite-Roper, marketed by Wise Engineering Company or can be made from a section of old railroad or trolley track, or a metal cable, ¾″ or larger, stretched tightly between two anchored platforms or cement blocks)

Directions: Various balancing stunts may be learned, like one leg jumps, spins, squats, somersaults, or a lead-in to gymnastics and circus stunts.

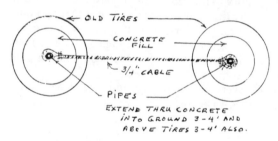

When enough people have learned some skills, a competition may be held with each contestant allowed a few minutes to show his skills on the beam in a "routine." Judging would be on: (1) body and beam control, (2) difficulty of stunts, (3) originality of routine, and (4) how well the stunts are done.

276. Button Capture

A sitdown game with simple materials

Age level: 10 and up
Organizational level: Low
Number of players: 4
Supervision: None

Playing time: 15–20 minutes
Space needed: 10′ × 10′ area
Equipment: 1 large button with 4 holes in it, 4 10′ lengths of string, 4 chairs

Directions: Tie 4 strings to the holes in the button as in figure 1 (shown on next page). Place chairs 8′ from the button. Players each hold a string end, using the extra 2′ of length for maneuvering.

On "go" signal, players try to maneuver their strings by pulling, snapping, loosing suddenly to throw another player off balance, or jerking quickly when another player tries to loose or take up slack — until one player captures the button.

If a player's string breaks, he's out of the match, while the others continue.

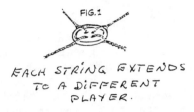

FIG. 1

Variation: *String Chew*—Same game, except chairs eliminated. Players get on knees, place the ends of the strings in their mouths, holding them with their teeth.

EACH STRING EXTENDS TO A DIFFERENT PLAYER.

On "go" signal, each tries to chew the string into his mouth faster than the others. Winner is the one to get the button in his teeth. Hands cannot be used to touch the string. If anyone drops the string from his mouth, he can try to get it back using only his mouth and teeth. If he fails, he's out of the match.

277. Jackstones

*Revives a popular game in Grandma's day,
requiring hand-eye coordination*

Age level: 6 and up
Organizational level: Low
Number of players: 1–4
Playing time: 20–30 minutes
Space needed: 5' × 5' area with smooth, hard surface

Equipment: Semi-hard rubber ball (about golf ball size) and 12 jackstones (or pebbles of a like size)

Directions: May be determined by lagging. This is done by tossing six jackstones up and catching them on the back of one hand, then tossing the jacks caught up and catching on the palm of the hand. The one catching the most jacks plays first and so on in order.

Fouls or Misses: Using wrong hand to catch ball. (Left handers reverse rules.)

Failure to pick up the proper number of jacks.

Allowing the ball to bounce more than once before catching.

Catching the ball against clothing, body or with both hands.

Touching any other jack while attempting to pick up a jack or group of jacks.

Drop jack and/or ball.

Failure to hold the ball or jacks until movement has been completed.

Failure to begin a turn with the proper stunt.

Changing sitting or standing position after jacks have been scattered.

Order of Events: *Babies*—Scatter all jacks upon the playing surface by a single movement. Toss the ball up, pick up one jack and, after ball has bounced once, catch the ball in the same (right) hand. Transfer the jack to the left hand and proceed as before until all six jacks are in the left hand.

For Twos—Jacks are picked up by twos; otherwise proceed as in ones. Same for threes, fours (four and two, or two and four) fives and sixes.

In the Basket—Scatter jacks, toss ball up, pick up one jack in right hand and, while the ball bounces once, transfer jack to the left hand, then catch ball with the right hand. When all jacks have been picked up and transferred to the left hand, proceed through twos, threes, fours, fives and sixes.

Ups — Scatter jacks, toss ball up with right hand, pick up one jack with right hand and catch the ball in the right hand after it has bounced once, same as in Babies. Toss ball upward and transfer the jack to the left hand, while ball bounces once, then catch the ball with the right hand. Continue through sixes.

Downs — Scatter jacks. Toss the ball up with right hand, pick up one jack with the right hand and catch the ball in the right hand after it has bounced once, same as in Babies. Bounce the ball downward and transfer the jack to the left hand, while ball bounces once, then catch the ball with the right hand.

Double Ups — Scatter jacks, toss the ball upward with right hand, pick up one jack with right hand and catch the ball in the right hand after it has bounced once. Toss ball upward and transfer the jack to the left hand while the ball is bouncing only once. When last jack has been transferred to left hand, tap surface with right hand for last pick up. Continue through sixes.

Double-Downs — Scatter jacks, toss the ball up with right hand, pick up one jack with right hand, catch the ball in the right hand after it has bounced once. Bounce the ball downward and transfer the jack to the left hand while the ball is bouncing only once. When last jack has been transferred to left hand, tap surface with right hand for last pick up. Continue through sixes.

Strike the Match — Scatter jacks, toss ball up, pick up one jack and scratch it across the playing surface with a striking movement. Keep the jack in right hand and after ball has bounced once, catch the ball in the same hand. Transfer jack to left hand and proceed until all six jacks have been struck. Re-scatter jacks and continue through sixes.

Orbit the Moon — Scatter jacks. Throw ball up. In one continuous movement, pick up all jacks at once and make a complete circle around the ball (still holding jacks in hand). Then catch ball in the same hand, after it has bounced only once.

Game source: Rules revision written by the Jacksonville, FL, Recreation Department.

278. Snake Stomp (or Dragon Dodge)

Variation of rope jumping, requiring more agility. Interests boys also.

Age level: 6 and up
Organizational level: Low
Number of players: 2–4 at a time, one rope holder and from 1 to 3 jumpers, depending upon the length of the rope used
Supervision: None
Playing time: Free play
Space needed: Sidewalk or playground area of similar size
Equipment: Jump rope 10'–20' long

Directions: Rope holder takes one end and whips it back and forth, causing it to wiggle and dace. Jumpers can start from a straddle position over the rope

Directions: Rope holder takes one end and whips it back and forth, causing it to wiggle and dance. Jumpers can start from a straddle position over the rope or can "jump in" when the holder gives the "go" signal. Jumpers must avoid being touched by the rope. Any player touched is out and must go to the sidelines. Last one to remain is the winner. Winner has choice of becoming the rope holder or selecting which loser will become the holder.

Variations: *Snake Stompers*—For larger groups, where everyone gets to play. Jumpers, either one or two at a time, jump into play, make three successful jumps, then get back out of play all without being touched by the rope. As soon as one is touched out or jumps out of play, the next player in line jumps in for three jumps, and so on until only one jumper remains in the game. Touched jumpers are eliminated.

Game source: Unknown origin. Played at Bell, CA, city playground, 1962, with variations added by author.

279. Woggle Sticks

Teach body balance and control

Age level: 8 and up
Organizational level: None
Number of players: Any number materials available for and a craft instructor can handle
Supervision: Craft instructor
Playing time: 30 minutes for crafting; play is unstructured

Space needed: Any flat area (in woodshop, if sticks have to be cut)
Equipment: 2 barrel staves (if they can still be found), or 2 boards 1″ × 4″ and 3–4′ long, 2 rope pieces 2′ long each, ski wax or beeswax

Directions: Cut wood pieces to size, if necessary. Sandpaper and wax bottoms, so they'll slide easier in snow (not necessary, if using them on land). Tie them to feet, across instep, with a loop around the ankles, keeping knot on top of stick. (Groove can be cut into bottom of stick to fit rope into, if wished, to cut down "drag" and wear on rope and make binding to foot more secure.)

Walking requires a balancing of the body back and forth sideways as one steps forward, since the sticks extend well beyond the toes of the foot (thus the name "woggle sticks"). Or walking may be done in herringbone ski fashion, placing sticks forward at about 30-degree angles, pointing out to the sides on each step forward. This is the easiest way to climb any hillock especially.

Races over flat areas or over obstacle courses may be run one-on-one or by teams against each other, with each pairs' winner earning a team point.

280. Tilt Tennis

An active board game that can be handcrafted. Teaches finesse and
soft, precise reactions, good hand and eye coordination.

Age level: 10 and up
Organizational level: Low
Number of players: 1 or 2
Supervision: None

Playing time: Free play; game of 21 points
Space needed: Any open space 8′ × 8′
Equipment: Tilt Tennis board (available from many mail-order companies), table tennis ball

Directions: Opponents may sit, kneel or stand facing each other, holding the board between them, inside the boundary lines.

Server starts play by tossing ball into air so it bounces on his half of the board, then goes toward opponent's side. Players then take turns hitting the ball

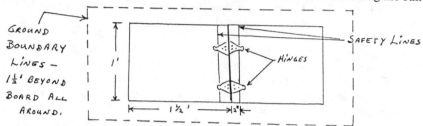

with their board halves until the opponent misses the ball or hits it out of bounds, or allows it to hit more than once on his board half. Any of these "faults" give a point to the other player. Game is usually 21 points, but can be varied by agreement of players before starting.

Each player must allow the other freedom to maneuver the board to play the ball within the boundaries when it is his turn to play. If he doesn't, it is a fault and a point for the opponent.

Variations: *Super Tilt Tennis*—The boundary area may be enlarged if 3-foot lengths of rope are attached between the board halves. This allows players more maneuverability.

281. Jungle Climb

Make and set up a piece of playground equipment by recycling old auto tires

Age level: (crafting) teenagers; (play) 8 and up
Organizational level: Medium craft, low play
Supervision: Project manager to oversee construction
Playing time: Weekend (to collect materials and set up climber) play on climber afterward is free, unstructured
Space needed: Flat ground area where frames for climber can be set into cement in ground, about 20′ × 20′ area
Equipment: Five saplings of 2 × 2″ boards or metal pipe lengths 15′ long, 10 old, but

sturdy auto tires (all as near alike as possible), 75′ of clothesline rope or plastic line, 2 3-way end & 8 t-connectors, 2 3′ and 2 5′ long braces (wood or metal pipe to match longer lengths being used), 8 2½″ bolts, washers and nuts, bag quick-dry cement and container to mix it in (with sand and water), shovel, pipe cutter, pipe wrenches, wood drill (if using wood frame), knife (to cut rope lengths), garden hoe (to help mix cement), tape measure, marking pencil

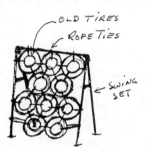

Directions: *Mountain Climb*—Free, unstructured play, with children pretending mountain climbing, boarding a pirate ship, or whatever.

Ape Race—Two people race each other up one side and down the other. They must touch a tire in each of the four tiers with a foot, both going up and down. They can't jump to the second tier to start, for example, or drop from the top on the slanted backside of the climber.

Snake Race—Two people race each other up and down, but they must "slither" their bodies through a tire in each of the four tiers both up and down.

282. Snow Snake Slinging

Sample traditional Indian winter sport

Age level: 8–11, 12–16, 17–18, over 18
Organizational level: High
Number of players: Any number, in rotation
Supervision: Course makers, judge-recorder
Playing time: Constructing and maintaining course takes considerable time. Actual competition takes only a few minutes per person per throw, but then the throws must be measured, too. Tournament can take all day or entire weekend, depending on number participants
Space needed: Straight area a mile long (less for children), 6–8' wide. Course can be made by dragging a log through the snow

to form a trough. This can be watered, then dragged again to smooth all obstructions.
Equipment: Each contestant handcrafts his own 7' long "snake" (throwing stick). They are weighted with lead at head end and grooved at the tail end for the finger to fit, and painted in snake designs. Hickory makes good snakes, because they are flexible so as to follow the minor irregularities in the trough. Snakes can also be waxed, like skis. Course should have stakes at its side marking every 100 yards, after the first 500. Then a tape measure can be used to measure between them.

Directions: Each contestant slings his snake up the trough in turn. Farthest throw wins. Some have been recorded over a mile, at speeds up to 120 mph.

Thus, safety measures call for everyone to stand clear of the trough during a throw.

If snake goes out of trough, distance is recorded at point it left.

Game source: Hun Ya from Iriquois at Six Nations Reservation Brantford, Ont., Canada.

283. Bike Drag Races

Bicycle field day at school or playground, all ages can test their skills in speed and control of their bicycles

Age level: 7–8, 9–10, 11–12, 13–14, 15–16, 17–19, boys and girls divisions, and divisions for gear-shift bikes and standards

Organizational level: High
Supervision: Bike safety inspectors, race registrars, race referee, starter, 2 course

judges, finish recorder, 2 runners (message carriers), timer

Playing time: 2–3 days

Space needed: One short block of city street (blocked off, preferably adjoining a park or playground where all participants can await their turns)

Equipment: P.A. system, starter's gun, 2 clipboards, tablets and pencils (for registrar and finish recorder), 2 stopwatches, 24 wooden blocks, bulletin board (for posting competition brackets and keeping track of winners), ribbon awards and winner's trophies. All riders furnish their own bicycles.

Competition Procedure: All bikes are safety inspected by the Police Department.

Registrants are numbered, in each division, their numbers put on slips of paper and put into large cans for drawings for race pairings.

Mark starting and ending lines on roadway. Use center line to divide racing lanes. (Any racer going across the center line is disqualified.)

Run-offs are single elimination. Times are taken on both racers each race, so fastest losers may be added in place of later "no-shows" when race pairings are called to race. Each division should be run off before starting another division, so racers will know about when they will be racing. (It's proven best to run older age groups first, since they get more impatient and harder to control than younger ones.)

Racers may trade or borrow bikes to compete with. Only the competitors themselves are numbered.

Starter checks false starts. (Two false starts by the same person in the same race disqualifies him.) Course judges make sure bikes do not cross the center line or go outside the course boundaries and that riders do not get off their bikes or interfere with opponents, or receive any help from spectators. Equipment breakdown, such as a loose chain, flat tire, etc., allows for a later re-run. A wreck, caused by the rider's carelessness, though, does not get a re-run. The finish recorder takes the name of finishers, their times, and order of finish. The race referee arbitrates all questions, problems and disputes.

Competition Events: Diaper Derby — A tricycle race may be added as an interesting sidelight event — 50 yards, with balloons given to all finishers.

Bike Drags — A straightaway race, from a standing start, for speed.

Straight Line Riding — Wood blocks are placed on both sides of the center line, about 4″ apart, every 5′ for a 60-foot distance. Riders must pass both bike tires between all the blocks without hitting them. Course judges note all hits or other errors. Winner is rider with least errors *and* fastest time.

Slow Race — Riders run the course as slow as they can, without touching a foot down or holding onto anyone or anything as an aid. A touchdown or illegal aid is an automatic disqualification. Riders cannot cross middle line or course boundaries. Winners are slowest times.

Slalom — 12 wooden blocks are placed down the middle of each lane, starting at 40–50 feet from the starting point and at 10-feet distances thereafter, leaving a "dash" section at the end of the race to the finish line. Riders start from dead stop, then on "go" signal, they must weave to left and right alternately of all 12 blocks, then sprint to finish line.

Pony Express Race — Teams of 4 riders, 2 stationed at each end of the block-long course. Each rider must cross the start-or-finish line, get off the bike and turn it over to the next relay rider. Each rider has to be mounted, with no foot on the ground, *before* he crosses the start-or-finish line at his end of the course, or the course judge will make him go back and re-start his lap from behind the line.

Disqualification fouls include: (1) interfering with an opposing team, (2) crossing the middle line or course boundaries, (3) receiving aid from spectators, (4) two false starts in the same race and (5) running with the bicycle between the start/finish lines.

Mile Marathon — If a city block around the park, school or playground can be blocked off, it makes a good mile marathon course. Measure the course, since blocks register different distances. Course judges keep track of racer's laps. Starter will blow a whistle when the leader starts the last lap.

Disqualification fouls include: (1) intentional interference with an opponent, (2) receiving aid from another rider or a spectator, (3) running with the bicycle and (4) taking any shortcut off the designated course.

284. Bike Polo

A game format challenge for bicycle riders, teaching cooperation and new skills

Age level: 12 and over
Organizational level: Medium
Number of players: 2 teams, 6 each
Supervision: 2 referees
Playing time: 4 5-minute periods
Space needed: Soccer or football field. (Park area may also be used, even with trees, as hazards, on the course to add variety.)
Equipment: 7″ foam ball (or soft rubber playground ball), riders furnish own bicycles, 2 whistles (for referees)

Directions: Teams line up in front of their goal area (soccer or football standards, or 2 stakes, 15′ apart). Referee places ball at mid-field. On whistle, teams race to play the ball.

Ball is kicked, fisted (if bouncing high enough) or headed, by players in trying to advance it into the opponent's goal. Player may not carry the ball or hold it on his person or bike. Penalty: free kick, by opponent nearest him, at point of infraction. Players cannot run into or push over opponents. Penalty: free kick-on-goal, from a point 20 yards in front of opponent's goal. A goal is one point. Referee throws out-of-bounds balls into court.

285. Tot Train

Variation on the playground merry-go-round

Age level: 6 and up
Number of players: 3 (2 riders and a pusher)
Playing time: Open play, once the train has been constructed
Space needed: 10′ × 10′ area on concrete or other solid flooring
Equipment: 2 wooden boxes, each big enough for a child to sit in, plywood platform to hold them end-to-end, 8 free-wheeling casters, floor flange and sections of pipe and connections as indicated in picture on the next page

Directions: Children sit in boxes and another pushes them. The "train" rotates around the floor flange. (One added use found was that a child just learning to walk could learn faster by holding onto the back of this type "train.")

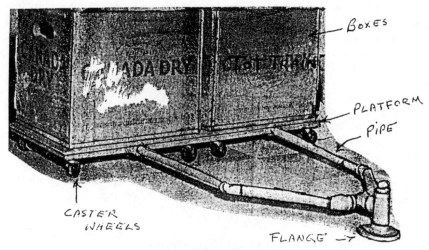

Tot Train

286. Four-Season Sliding

Innovates novel items so sledding becomes a year-round sport

Age level: 12 and up
Organizational level: Medium
Number of players: Open

Supervision: Play leader
Space needed: Smooth sloping hillside

*Directions: Snow Sliding—*Put an old foam sofa cushion inside a strong plastic garbage bag for a different sled ride.

An old plastic or metal garbage can lid, with the handle removed, is another innovative snow vehicle.

*Rainy-day Sliding—*In Hawaii, bunches of the native Ti leaves are used to ride down rain-slick hillsides. But cardboard boxes work, too—one-person ones, as well as bigger pairs-sleds.

Simulated rainy days can also be accomplished by laying commercially-produced slip-n-slide, or similar strip of plastic, on a slope. An old plastic bucket or garbage can may be punctured with several holes on one side, then placed at the high side of the slide to drip water onto it, being replenished with buckets of river, lake or ocean water.

*Grassy Sliding—*Cakes of ice make great sleds for grassy hillside terrain.

American Toys Industry, in 1977, introduced a two-piece mold called a no-sno sled that could be filled with water and placed in a freezer. Removed later, the bottom half becomes an ice sled and the top half a dry seat. This idea could just as well be adapted using a plastic garbage can lid.

*Sand Sliding—*Lay an old VW auto hood upside down on the sand. Tie it with a cable or plastic rope to a 4-wheel-drive vehicle and it can be towed like a surfboard.

287. Push-Bug Derby

*A step up from the Soap Box Derby, where team work counts
in both handcrafting and "running" the finished velocipede*

Age level: 15 and up

Organizational level: High

Number of players: 3 person teams (2 "motormen" pushers and a "jockey," or driver)

Supervision: Starter, course referee and finish judge

Playing time: Construction on own, race time depends on length of course and how many teams competing

Space needed: Connected sidewalk complex wide enough to accommodate two push-bugs side by side, or closed-off street area

Equipment: Starter's whistle, push-bugs (examples in picture) and flags to mark the course

Directions: Each team is composed of two male "motormen" who push (or pull) the push-bug and a female "jockey" who drives it. On the "go" signal, the first two bugs are raced to the end of the pre-selected course, and return. (If the course has turns in it, there should be an even number each way so one bug won't have to travel a longer distance than the other.)

Any foul eliminates a bug: (1) a bug receiving any help from other than its registered team, (2) any bug or team intentionally blocking, holding or running another bug off the course, (3) a jockey getting off a bug for any part of a race (except getting back aboard immediately after a turnover, (4) a bug taking a shortcut from the laid-out race course, and (5) any bug or team using illegal gear or aids of any kind to enhance their chances over other competitors.

Game source: A Pushcart Derby was an annual event at the University of California—Santa Barbara in the 1960s.

288. Bronco Buster

Simulated bronco busting

Age level: 12 and up
Organizational level: Medium
Number of players: Rider, plus 4 rope handlers
Space needed: 15′ × 15′ area filled with sawdust for safety

Equipment: Empty barrel (preferably with lids on both ends), 4 heavy ropes 10′ long, metal drill (to drill holes in barrel for attaching ropes), four 6′ posts (to anchor the drum) and a saddle

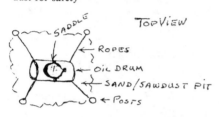

Directions: Oil drum "bronco" is hooked up as shown in diagram. Four rope handlers shake, push and pull them to make the bronco buck.

Riders can be timed and all those staying on for the rodeo-type 10-second ride qualify for the finals of a ride off.

289. Jousting

Historical sport going back to the days of the knights
of the roundtable. Young boys played at jousting and squires
or knights-in-training used the sport in learning skills necessary
to become a knight. The practice of grabbing the brass ring
on a merry-go-round grew out of this sport.

Age level: By age groups 6–8, 9–11, 12–14, 15–17, 18 and over

Organizational level: Low, unless tournament is planned

Number of players: Any number, in rotation

Supervision: None in free play. Tournament: judge, recorder, ring hangers

Playing time: About 15 seconds per run, three runs per person. Ties run off by using smaller rings.

Space needed: Course 80 yards by 40 yards minimum. May be set up in circle form also, or on a racetrack.

Equipment: Several sharpened broomsticks (without the brooms) as lances, wire rings or rope quoits 2″ and 3″ across (about 12 each), 3 7-foot high posts or stands with crossbars, 3 iron or wire ring hangers (for suspending rings from crossbars), stopwatch (for competition)

Directions: Rings are put on ring hangers and suspended from each of three posts' cross-bars. Posts are 30 yards apart; course is 80 yards long.

On go signal, runner trots or runs the length of the course trying to spear the three rings on his lance. Fifteen seconds maximum should be allowed each run. Any run taking longer is cancelled out.

Rings should be hung about shoulder height (the average for the age group participating). Lances are held braced under the armpit or balanced in the hand over the shoulder so the point is at eye level, for better aiming at the rings.

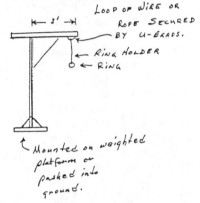

Person who lances most rings in three runs is winner. Ties are run off using smaller rings. If ties still result, more runs may be taken until a winner exists, or less time may be allowed for the runs (11 seconds).

Variations: *Bike Jousting*— Bicycles may be used instead of players running through the course. *Running at the Rings*—This is one of four forms of jousting on horseback, and is the state sport of Maryland, with state-wide organizations in several eastern states, and national championships each autumn in Washington, D.C.

Game source: History shows the sport coming down to us directly from knight jousting in the "middle ages" in Europe. For complete history and rules see *Knight Life: Jousting in the United States* by Robert L. Loeffelbein, from Golden Owl Publishing Company, 117 So. Essex Drive, Lexington Park, MD 20653 ($5).

290. Playground Zoo

Age level: 10 and up
Organizational level: High
Number of players: Any number
Supervision: Play leader

Playing time: 2 or 3 weeks' programming
Space needed: Large room, airy and sun-lit
Equipment: Boxes, chicken wire, tools—
  hammer, nails, saw

Directions: Children gather live "animals"—moths, grasshoppers, bees, crayfish, lizards, mice, etc. Add an ant farm, bird feeders, a hummingbird feeder.

Build display cage—homes for them, like in a zoo. Fix them up with materials as near like their regular habitat as possible under circumstances. (Some knowledge of the "animals" is required in order to do this; this promotes high interest in a reading program, itself a good lead-into a nature program.)

Set up jobs at this "zoo" among the children, making them earn the jobs by their work and interest: *Curator*—who should know the most about animals and their habits and habitat. He "oversees" the "zoo," especially the day-to-day jobs. *Head Animal Handler*—oversees the feeding and cage cleaning among a rotating staff (so all children get a chance to feed and play with the "animals"). *Head Animal Trainer*—to teach the "animals" tricks and exercise them. *Historian*— keep the records of where the animals came from, their histories, and see that a sign describing each "animal" is on its cage-home.

The "zoo" may also be used as a background for a "Wild Animal Pet Parade." Children use their own ingenuity to make up their pets like wild animals, make up wagons, bicycle trailers, etc., as circus wagons or cages for the animals on parade. It should be publicized as open to the public, with awards given in classifications.

RECREATION FOR RAINY DAYS, PLAY DAYS, CARNIVALS AND PARTIES

291. Penny Crawl

Age level: All ages
Number of players: Trick for one

Space needed: Anywhere
Equipment: Four pennies, or washers

Directions: Place penny or washer on the tip of each finger, palm of hand up.

Without using the thumb or the other hand or removing any of them from the hand, work them all into a single pile on the tip of the first finger.

When you master it, then try it on the other hand.

292. American Hopscotch

Teaches U.S. geography in a game format

Age level: 6 and up
Organizational level: Medium
Number of players: Any number, in sequence
Supervision: None informally, referee otherwise

Playing time: 60 minutes minimum
Space needed: About 30′ × 30′ area
Equipment: U.S. map showing all states, chalk or stick to outline map on floor or ground, marker for each player (identifiable by owner's initials on each)

Directions: Hopscotch course is a map of the United States, with a hopping sequence marked out by numbering the states in order of jumping, so all states are covered. This may be done various ways, the easiest being a start from Alaska to Washington, then back and forth in rows across the U.S., taking about 6 sweeps and ending with California to Hawaii. Another way is to circle the perimeter states and corkscrew into the middle ones, being sure to leave entrance—exit areas for hoppers to get on and off the map.

After deciding sequence of hoppers, first one tosses his personal marker (stone, bottlecap, design cut from inner-tube, coin, etc.), onto the state numbered "1." Then he hops on one foot over state #1 and on around the course in the numbered sequence, states #2, 3, 4 and so on, hopping off the map after #50. Then he must return, still hopping on one foot, to state #2, where he must bend over without letting his other foot or any part of his body, except the one hand picking up his marker, touch the ground—and pick up his marker, then hop onto state #1 and so on off the map.

If, at anytime, he misses hopping onto a state in the correct numbered order, or touches the ground with any part of his body except the hopping foot, except for "double states," or fails to toss his marker into the correct state for his next circuit hop, he is through, at that point, for that turn. On his next turn, he must throw into the state missed and hop that circuit before advancing.

If a hopper successfully completes a hop circuit, he throws his marker into the next state in order and continues as before. If not, the next hopper takes over. First one to complete 50 states is the winner.

If markers are on 3 or 4 states in a row, and none of the players have jumped them successfully, the middle marker, or markers, may be advanced to the next state. No hopper may step in any state with anyone's marker in it.

Adjacent states, with the same names (Virginia and West Virginia, North and South Dakota, North and South Carolina) should be marked as "double squares," where one foot is placed in each at the same time (unless one or both have markers on them, in which case they are treated as a single state in hopping sequence).

Game source: Originally reported by Robert Stewart, Principal in Roy, Utah.

293. British Hopscotch

Can take the place of calisthenics type exercising

Age level: 6 and up
Organizational level: Low
Number of players: Any number, in sequence

Supervision: None
Playing time: Open ended
Space needed: 6′ × 6′ area, (as shown in figure)

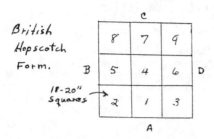

British Hopscotch Form.

18-20" Squares

Equipment: Chalk, etc., to mark court diagram (or court may be painted on a cardboard mat for use anywhere)

Directions: No taws needed. Player starts at side A, jumps into square #1 with both feet, straddles it by jumping into 2 and 3, then back into 1, and jumps out *backwards*. Next, he jumps into square #4 with both feet, straddle jumps into 5 and 6, back into 4, and out again backwards, over #1. Then he jumps into #7, straddle jumps into 8 and 9, back into 7, and out backwards over 4 and 1.

He then goes to side B and repeats. Then to side C and D. He loses his turn when he makes a mistake, and resumes where he left off. First to finish all four sides wins.

Variation: *Standard Hopscotch*—The standard game of hopscotch uses the design in figure 2, or some variation of it. This design may also be painted on a cardboard mat or on the back of an old carpet remnant or on canvas (so it can be rolled up and stored). A vinyl, non-skid one is also manufactured commercially by Hopscotch, Inc., of New York City.

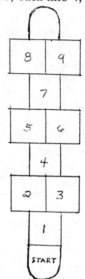

Standard Hopscotch

294. Hop-Scotch Rope Jumping

Age level: 8 and up
Number of players: Two rope turners, any number jumpers, one at a time. No more than 6 for maximum participation

Space needed: Outdoors or indoors in a gym or multi-purpose room
Equipment: Long jump ropes, chalk or tape to mark hopscotchs, and markers (taws)

Directions: Use the British hop-scotch form (see British Hopscoth rules) and play it the same way, while jumping rope at the same time.

The rope must be centered over the hop-scotch and turned slow enough so the jumper can jump into the required spaces. Jumpers must go through each side (A, B, C, and D) without a miss or a stop, and get out of the rope swing without a miss also. All jumpers keep jumping at the same side until they do it without a miss, then move on to the next successive side. First one to complete all sides is the winner.

A variation of this game can be played by using a taw in the middle spaces, which must be picked up after the straddle step each time, while continuing to jump rope.

295. Hopscotch Obstacle Course

Adds zest to the standard game of hopscotch
as well as adds a new challenge for the better players

Age level: 8 and up
Organizational level: Low
Number of players: Any number, in sequence
Supervision: Play leader

Playing time: Open ended
Space needed: 8' × 12' area
Equipment: Markers (taws) for each player, various items to add to play area as obstacles

Directions: Basic hopscotch rules, except differences caused by the handicaps on the course, such as an open cardboard box covering one square which has to be hopped into and out of, a wooden box faced down which has to be hopped up onto, a space requiring a hopper to land on it backwards, a space requiring the hopper to land on it with both feet crossed, a space that requires 10 up and down hops while turning around, and a space requiring the hopper to pick up his marker by reaching backwards.

296. Dutch Rope Jumping

Age level: 6 and up
Number of players: Two rope holders, one to four jumpers

Space needed: Outdoors, or indoors in a gym or multi-purpose room
Equipment: Strands of elastic about 20' long

Directions: Two holders stretch a strand of elastic until it lies limp on the ground at the center spot. Jumper stands on it at that spot.

Holders pull the elastic taut. Jumper jumps into air when ready, then tries to land back on the elastic strand.

To make the game harder, there are various tricks that can be done in the air while jumping. The jumper always has to re-land on the elastic, however. Some of the stunts include a half turn left or right, a full turn right or left, a leg tuck-up, a toe-touch, etc., only limited by imagination.

This game can be played by several jumpers at once, too, with the others either starting to jump on the elastic, or running into the game during a jump. Anyone missing the elastic on the landing, however, is out.

297. Hurricane

Age level: 8 and up
Organizational level: Low
Number of players: 4 or 8
Supervision: None
Playing time: 3–5 minutes

Space needed: Square table and 4 chairs
Equipment: A fan or square piece of cardboard for each player and a number of articles, like a feather, a straw, a cotton ball, a paper wad and a bottlecap, etc.

Directions: Players sit on 4 sides of table. All items are placed in the exact middle of the table inside a large plastic can top. On signal, all players try to fan the items off the table. Each item may be worth a different number of points, depending on how hard it is to be fanned. Any item going off the table gives the number of points it is worth to the player playing that side. When all items have been blown off, scores are totalled. Winner is one with *least* points.

298. Mummy Wrapper Race

Social ice-breaker

Age level: 8 and up
Organizational level: Low
Number of players: Couples, any number
Supervision: Judge
Playing time: 10 minutes

Space needed: No special area required; any relatively open space for as many competing couples as are present
Equipment: Roll of toilet tissue for each couple, wastebasket for cleanup

Directions: Divide group in half (older players may be divided by men and women). Put names of one of the groups in a hat and let the members of the other group draw for partners. Each pair gets a roll of tissue.

On "go" signal one member of each twosome starts wrapping the other from head to toe (like an Egyptian mummy), leaving mouth and nose holes for breathing, with the tissue. Persons being wrapped cannot move to help in any way, even raising the arms or holding the loose end. Winners are the ones done first, correctly and with no gaps in the wrapping.

299. Ego Game (or The Magic Quiet Game)

Control game for quieting a group of children

Age level: 6–13
Organizational level: Low
Number of players: Open
Supervision: Judge-play leader
Playing time: 10 minutes, average

Space needed: Almost anywhere, but especially good in classroom, at camp meeting, etc.
Equipment: None

Directions: When a group of children are all talking at once or causing similar commotion, the leader announces the Ego Game. Everyone may continue talking, arguing, yelling, or whatever, until a person uses the words "I," "Me," "My," or "Mine." As soon as the judge, or any participant, catches someone using these words, they are out of the "conversation" and they become assistant-judges to catch others. The game doesn't take long at all.

300. Flag Pin

*Social group game. Considered better than pinning the tail
on the donkey because it teaches where the U.S. capital is located.
Can also be a good lead-in to teaching something about
the American flag — where and how it was born, et al.*

Age level: 6 and up
Organizational level: Low
Number of players: 12 or less, taking turns
Supervision: Judge and guide (for blind-folded players)
Playing time: About 5 minutes per person

Space needed: Any open space fronting on a wall
Equipment: Map of the United States, a small American flag glued onto a pin for each contestant, blindfold, large piece of corrugated cardboard (to mount the map on and serve as a pincushion for the pins)

Directions: This is a variation of pin-the-tail-on-the-donkey. Each person in turn is blindfolded, turned around a couple of times, pushed toward the map and tries to stick a flag pin on Washington, D.C. Winner is person closest.

Variations: *(1)* Pin the bikini bathing suit on the girl (for girls). *(2)* Pin Snoopy on top of his doghouse, sleeping. *(3)* Pin a worm in the hole in an apple on a tree. *(4)* Pin a bullet hole on the bandit, aiming for the heart.

301. Name Bingo

Age level: 8 and up, including adult
Number of players: Any size group
Space needed: Party, new class, meetings, etc.
Equipment: "Bingo" sheets may be made, (but to cut down errors, it is best to have them mimeographed or xeroxed off beforehand), pencil for each contestant, sign-in sheet, scissors, small box

Directions: Each contestant signs in on sheet prepared in such a way that signatures will be far enough apart to be cut out and placed in box for drawings. As person signs in, he/she gets a Name Bingo playing sheet.

The middle square is for the owner's name and is the traditional "free" space.

All contestants are given 15 minutes to circulate and meet and get the autographs of other contestants in the squares of their Bingo sheets. Each name can only be used once on each sheet, and only one name to a space.

Names on the register are cut out, folded up, and put into a box. The leader moves around the group having different people draw out names and read them off.

Each square 2" x 2"
Your Name Here (Center Space)
Uneven number of Squares: 5, 7, 9 each way.

As a name is read off, any person having that name on his Bingo sheet marks an X through it. This continues until someone has a complete line, in any direction, X'd out. This may include that middle free space, which should be X'd out before play starts.

Note: This idea may be printed on a dance favor, for an intermission game, or as an ice-breaker, on a party napkin, or in a program.

302. Tree Bingo

Age level: 6 and up
Number of players: Up to 25
Space needed: Tables or other flat surfaces
Equipment: Tree Bingo sheets, 15 markers per person (pebbles, corn, etc.)

Directions: Make Tree Bingo sheets: divide a sheet of 8½ × 11 paper into 16 equal rectangles. Draw a different leaf—showing the veins and its fruit—in each rectangle, using common tree leaves seen around the playground.

After this master sheet is made, trace it onto ditto master or xerox copies so the playing sheets can be made.

Cut one of the copies into rectangles, folding each. Put these into container for drawing out in Bingo-type play.

When a player gets four markers in a row, he yells "Tree-O" and becomes the winner.

If more permanent sheets are desired, the drawings can be colored, glued

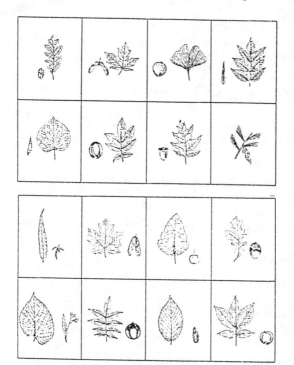

or dry-mounted on cardboard, then sprayed with Krylon or covered with Saran Wrap.

Variations: *(1)* The leader makes believe the tree is describing itself, and gives features of the leaf that will distinguish it. The players guess at the leaf he is describing, marking their guess on their playing card. If a player has a wrong leaf marked when calling Tree-O, he has to drop out of that game, and the play goes on until a true winner is found.

As players get better, the clues may become descriptive terminology, habitat, uses, fruit type, etc., of the tree leaves represented. Later the children may even give the clues, with the leader refereeing. *(2)* Sheets with bird pictures may be used in place of trees — Bird-O, Animal tracks, flowers, or anything children might want to use.

Suggested References: Palmer, E. L. *Fieldbook of Natural History.* New York: McGraw-Hill, 1949.

Watts, May T. *Master Tree Finder.* Nature Study Guild, Box 972, Berkeley, California 94701.

Zim, H. S. and Martin Zim. *Trees.* New York: Simon and Schuster, 1952.

Game source: May T. Watts, Naturalist Emeritus, Morton Arboretum, Lisle, IL.

303. Olympic Seed Spit

Age level: 10 and up
Number of players: Any number. The more the merrier.
Supervision: (a) Starter, to give the go to each contestant and see he doesn't foul.
(b) Field judge, to mark the official landing spots of the seed and oversee the measurements. (c) Course judges, to help mark the landing spots of the seeds with name flags and make the distance measurements.
(d) Clerk of the course, to record names and distances
Equipment: Watermelons, powdered chalk for marking contest field, tape measure, clipboard, paper and pencil, nails or pegs with name tags for all players

Directions: Have a watermelon feed, telling the children to save their seeds for a contest.

Draw two contest areas. (See figure on next page.) Allow practicing on one.

Rules: (a) Contestants can't step over the foul line when seed spitting, but they can take a step or run behind the line to add momentum. The try doesn't count if a foul is made.

(b) Each contestant gets three tries, one after the other, with the best distance counting officially. (Or average of the three can be taken.)

Foul Line
← 5 1-foot markers
← 7 5-foot marks
← World Record= 35'6"

304. Statues

Age level: 6-12
Number of players: 10 is limit for most participation and fun
Supervision: None

Playing time: Open ended
Space needed: Lawn area
Equipment: None

Directions: One person is designated "it." He stands in middle of an open area, takes another participant by the wrist, whirls him three times around, then lets him go. The person swung around is supposed to hold the pose and expression he ends up in on the command "freeze" until all others have been similarly swung into a statue pose.

The "swinger" then chooses the person holding the pose he thinks best exemplifies the conditions he had set up prior to swinging—funniest, most like an animal, most graceful, most like a robot, etc.

Person so selected then becomes the swinger, sets up his classification, and starts swinging the participants.

305. Beastie Dancing

Age level: 6-10
Organizational level: High
Number of players: Any number
Supervision: Play leader or teacher

Playing time: 2 weeks of programming
Space needed: Indoors or outdoors, any relatively clear area
Equipment: Books and movies of animals

Directions: Take a week to prepare. Have a reading program on animals, a children's story session on their pets, movies on various animals, and a trip to the zoo. Children should be reminded throughout this week that they will be making up their own "Beastie Dances" for a review at the end of the week, thus they should be studying the movements of the animals so they will be able to mimic them.

A crafts program can follow this week, where the children may make costumes for their dance—simple things, like a mane for a horse, a neck ruff for a lion, a red comb for a rooster, etc.

Variations: *(a)* The best "beastie dance steps" can be chosen and taught to the rest of the group by the innovators. Then these can be worked into games, like jump rope, tag, ducks and geese. *(b)* The dancers can also be worked by the group into a square dance format, which could then be presented to parents, a real square dance group, other playgrounds. (This often leads into an interest in actual square dancing. All square dance groups are willing to help teach this activity, too. All volunteer experts come free. There are also beginning records on the market to teach square dancing, complete with calls.)

306. Seat Scramble (or Toil & Trouble)

*Especially good game to keep younger
children involved inside on a rainy day*

Age level: 6 and up
Organizational level: Low
Number of players: 6-10 are easy to handle
Supervision: None
Playing time: Open ended

Space needed: Area where group may be
seated in a circle
Equipment: Chairs for all participants, a
broom or mop stick

Directions: Seat all players in a circle facing person who is "it" in the middle. "It" holds a broomstick, which he starts the game with. He makes stirring motions and the incantation, "Bubble, bubble, toil and trouble," at which signal the players rise and march around in a circle outside the ring of chairs. (All chairs must have easy access on both sides.) They recite along with him.

When "it" drops his stick, everyone, including "it," scrambles for a seat. Whoever is left without a seat is "it" for the next round. Game may be played until players tire of it.

"It" may make the game more interesting by having all the players skip, bunny hop or jump on one leg, etc., as they circle.

307. Belly-Laugh

Age level: 6 and up
Number of players: Group participation
Space needed: Indoors or outdoors, 20′ × 20′
area

Equipment: Laughing record or tape recording of people laughing, record or tape
player, if available

Directions: All participants, including director, lay on back on floor in a circle, each with his head resting on the stomach of another person.

One person starts by saying HA. The person whose head was on the first person's belly says HA! HA!, continuing until everyone is giggling. Soon, everyone is laughing and all order disappears.

308. Sardines

New wrinkle on the old game of hide and seek

Age level: 6 and up
Organizational level: Low
Number of players: 4-10
Supervision: None

Playing time: Varies—15-30 minutes
Space needed: Room or small building where
places to hide are available
Equipment: None

Directions: One person is selected as the "hider." He hides somewhere within the prescribed playing area. The other players close their eyes and count to 50 while he's hiding. Then they scatter, searching for him. Each hunter that finds him snuggles quietly in the hiding place with him until all but one are sardined together. That last hunter is given the title of "Booby" for the day.

Game source: Adapted from an English game from about a century ago.

309. Balloons-to-the-Moon*

Age level: Any ages
Number of players: Any number
Space needed: Any open field, free from trees, telephone lines and overhead obstructions

Equipment: Balloons, post cards and 2′ lengths of string for each contestant, a helium balloon filler, pencils, paper punch

Directions: Pre-print message on back of each postcard telling about contest and asking the finder to mail the card back. Leave room for the finder's name and address, for verification and award, if you give finder awards. Also, leave a space for the contestant's name. The return address on each card should be the playground so return records may be kept and verified.

Give each contestant a helium-filled balloon, string and postcard. Have each write his name on his card and tie it to the balloon. (Punch a hole in the card to tie string to.)

On command, all contestants loose their balloons with cards attached and the contest starts. Should run for a week to allow answers to come back, even from several hundred miles away. Post a map showing the mileage distance and the landing spots.

The one whose balloon went the farthest by closing time is the winner.

Alert the local newspaper to take pictures of the send-off, then keep them up-to-date on the returning cards. Other balloon games and events should be held between the start and end, to keep interest high.

Note: In 1981, a balloon sent aloft in Santa Barbara, CA, floated 1700 miles and was picked up in Rankin, TX., just 2 days later. In 1975, one was sent up from the Boy's Club in Camarillo, CA, and found nearly 3,500 miles away in Fajardo, Puerto Rico three weeks later by 14-year-old Orlando Estrada.

310. Balloon Bounce

Agility training in doing two things at the same time

Age level: 10 and up
Organizational level: Low
Number of players: 1–3 at a time, but group participation
Supervision: None
Playing time: Open ended

Space needed: 20′ × 20′ space, or larger, depending on number of participants. Mark a circle.
Equipment: Balloon for every participant, paper cups for every contestant (to drink from), box of toothpicks, large coat

Directions: Players form a ring around the circle. Each one blows up a round balloon and ties it to his ankle with 1½ feet of string. On a "go" signal, each person tries to stamp or sit on others' balloons and break them, while at the same time trying to keep their own from being broken. Balloons can't be pinched or bitten, and no rings or other foreign objects may be used.

Variations: Players can't leave the circle, or they are out of the game. Winner is last one with a whole balloon.

Players take turns keeping their balloons bouncing while tied to one wrist by punching them with their fist on shoulder or head—while, at the same time, putting on the oversize coat, and picking up 20 toothpicks. No winners, just a fun thing to do and watch. The group can think up other things to try to do while keeping one's balloon bouncing.

311. Chopstick Balloon Relay

Age level: Elementary and junior high ages
Number of players: Any number that can be evenly divided into teams

Space needed: Indoors or outdoors
Equipment: Balloon and two sets of chopsticks (or any similar sticks) per team

Directions: Teams line up, one person behind another, facing a goal line. First two people on each team are given sets of chopsticks. First relay runner holds the balloon between the chopsticks.

On a "go" signal, first runners race to turning point and return to the starting point, exchanging the balloon, using only the two sets of chopsticks, with the #2 racer and so on until everyone has run. The first runner gives his sticks to #3, #2 gives his to #4, etc. If a balloon is dropped during the run, it must be recovered only by use of the sticks.

Winning team is the one with all its runners back over the goal line first.

312. Balloon Steeplechase

Party or playground special event

Age level: 8 and up
Organizational level: Medium
Number of players: Any number, in sequence
Supervision: Referee, starter and timekeeper
Playing time: 10 minutes per participant

Space needed: Yard, park, playground, etc.
Equipment: A round balloon for each participant, hand pump for blowing them up, supply of twistems to hold balloons closed and stopwatch

Directions: Set up an obstacle course around the area—over a fence, down a slide, under clotheslines, over a tree limb, up and down steps, etc.—and be sure it is well marked and understood by participants.

Each steeplechaser is given a balloon at the starting point and, at the "go" signal, runs the course while bouncing the balloon up and down, never letting it rest on his hand or other parts of his body. The starter is also the timekeeper. Fastest legal run is winner.

Variation: *Bounce Steeplechase*—Same, except, if no stopwatch is available, the referee counts the balloon bounces each player makes during his run. The player with the least number is the winner. *Chopstick Steeplechase*—Same event, except each participant must carry his balloon over the obstacle course with chopsticks. Players cannot advance if not *holding* the balloon with the chopsticks. Each run is timed, with winner being the fastest time with no penalities.

313. The Candy Tree

*Great surprise for family members, a class of
school children, a club or scout group or children
at camp or playground. Also, a good carnival fund raiser.*

Age level: 6 and up
Organizational level: Medium

Number of players: 6–12 to prepare
Space needed: A tree (live, outside, or

crafted, inside), with lots of low branches

Equipment: Colored paper sheets to make cornucopias from, glue (to secure their ends), and a large selection of nuts and candies, popcorn, caramel corn, and other snack foods (to fill the cornucopias), string and scissors to make hangers for them

Directions: Hang the cornucopias from all the tree limbs.

If the tree is a surprise for a group, the members of the group are allowed to select the cornucopia they want when the surprise is sprung. Outside, they can climb the tree and pick their selected one (make sure all possible safety practices are carried out). For inside, crafted trees, a ladder and a "can-reacher" can be provided. A "can reacher" is a stick ending in a gripper that can be closed on a can on a high shelf in a grocery story. Or the cornucopias may be enclosed, so they can be dislodged with a garden rake or broom and caught as they drop from the tree.

This could also be done making and using Mexican-type pinatas filled with snack foods and small favors. Then, others could be broken open in the traditional way with a blindfolded child swinging a stick at one hanging overhead that can be danced around, via an attached rope, to make contact more difficult (and fun for the onlookers). When one is broken, everyone scrambles for the favors that spill out.

Game source: Adapted from an old German custom.

314. Grab Bag

Can be played almost anywhere, anytime, by anyone

Age level: 8 and up
Organizational level: Medium
Number of players: One at a time in rotation
Supervision: Referee and several recorders
Playing time: 10 minutes per person

Space needed: Almost anywhere
Equipment: Several large paper sacks, 20–30 small objects that can be identified by touch (but which players have not been shown), paper and pencils

Directions: Fill each bag with 10 of the objects. Number each bag. Each is given to contestant who is allowed to put one hand inside. By touch, he identifies as many as he can, while a recorder writes down what he calls off. After the 10-minute time limit contestants switch bags.

Bags are passed around until all players have had a chance to try all of them. Then have each person correct his paper as the referee shows and identifies the objects in each bag.

315. Swap Carnival

Age level: All ages up through 12
Organizational level: High
Number of players: Any number
Supervision: Fair director

Space needed: Outdoors or indoors with a relatively large area
Equipment: Signs and decorations as at a fair, pencils and register sheets for all

Directions: Direct each child to bring a "white elephant" from home (being careful to explain that a "white elephant" is an unwanted item).

Have a playground area decorated like a fair, in which they can help, of course.

On signal, tell them they have one hour (or whatever is required, depending upon the number of persons involved) in which to swap their white elephant with the others. Each swap must be signed into the register sheet each person will carry. The person with the most registered swaps at the end of the given period of time is the winner.

Children can make own sandwich board signs like "Honest John's White Elephants," etc. and can rig mobile shops, like a wagon with the three gold balls of the pawnbroker on it, or a bicycle trailer, etc. Encourage ingenuity.

This event might well be the first phase of a fair, to get the King or Queen of the fair. It could continue with a decorated bicycle and wagon parade, carnival booth, games and contests, a ball game, etc.

316. Cukoo

Carnival type game

Age level: 10 and up
Organizational level: Medium
Number of players: 2-6, or 2 teams, 2-4 each
Space needed: 10' booth frontage, 20' depth

Equipment: 6-12 sponges, 4' high screen 8-9' long, 3 chairs, 3 cycle helmets, 3 pairs safety glasses

Directions: Three "cukoos" sit on chairs behind the screen in the booth, wearing cycle helmets and safety glasses. Supply of sponges and pan (or bucket) of water are set at a throw line 12-14' in front of the screen.

When the throwers dip their sponges in the water, the cukoos start bobbing and weaving behind the screen, poking their heads above it at unexpected angles and places to fool the throwers into missing them with the sponges. Since this bobbing around is tiring, the cukoos should be substituted every 5 minutes.

Teams compete by one throwing and other serving as cukoos. Then they switch roles. Team with most "hits" wins.

Variations: *Face Up to It*—Same idea, except instead of the cukoos behind the screen, a 5-6' high plywood screen is painted with 3 figures (like Arabs, hillbillies, clowns, gangsters or whatever). The faces are cut out so the target team members can put their faces in the cutouts for the throwing team to target with the wet sponges. *The Rainmaker*—Same idea, except balloons are filled with water and hung on nails in a board hung over the heads of the target team. The throwing team uses darts and tries to break the balloons to spill the water down onto the target team sitting on chairs under the balloons. A fine-mesh net should be spread over the heads of those seated so any darts that misfire, or fall, will be caught by the net.

317. Picnic Scramble

Picnic or camp activities

Age level: 12 and up
Organizational level: Low
Number of players: Male-female pairs
Supervision: Referee

Playing time: Open-ended
Space needed: Area to fit number of participants

Directions: Fish Strike: Raw egg is tied atop each male's head securely with a cloth under the chin. Each male's female partner is given a fresh fish. On "go" signal, each female tries to hit and break the eggs on every male's head, except her partner's, with her fish, while, at the same time, helping her partner protect his egg from the other females. No one can go outside the pre-designated game area. Last couple with their egg intact, are winners.

Bombs Away: The male of each couple lays on his back with a teacup sitting in his open mouth. His female partner stands on a chair situated beside his head and tries to drop an egg, from waist high, so it stays — broken or not — in the cup. All cups must be the same and must be completely clean.

Dinosaur Egg Hunt: Several watermelons are hidden. On "go" signal, couples hold a treasure hunt for them.

318. Mud Scrabble

Shows how even a mud puddle can give an idea for a game

Age level: 10 and up
Organizational level: Low
Number of players: 6-15
Supervision: Play leader
Space needed: Dirt area that can be wet down and turned into a boggy mud puddle, big enough to handle the number of participants on hand
Equipment: A good supply of pennies and nickels and maybe some bottlecaps (for free soda pop)

Directions: Scatter the coins and bottlecaps in the mudhole (before participants arrive). On "go" signal, all searchers — dressed in the grubbiest clothes, jump in and start scrabbling for them.

Game source: University of Miami coeds from a few years ago.

319. Mud Sliding

Innovative social and sport outing for teens and adults

Age level: Teens and up
Organizational level: Medium
Number of players: 10-12
Playing time: Open ended
Space needed: A sloping hillside that can be wet down or be used after a rainstorm
Equipment: Enough cardboard boxes, large enough for people to sit inside of, for the party members

Directions: Slider climbs into box, or pairs in larger boxes, and points it downhill, sliding in the mud. Several boxes can be made into a "train" by each person hooking his legs over the back of the box in front of him.

Game source: Adaptation of Hawaiian sport of Ti Leaf Sliding.

320. Mud Disco

A teen dance with a whole new look

Age level: Teens
Organizational level: Medium
Supervision: Dance committee, D.J.
Playing time: Two hours
Space needed: Field that can be watered down until it is boggy mud, size depending on group

Equipment: Tape player and music tapes, like movies score of "Singing in the Rain," for disc jockey, strings of Christmas lights for lighting and decorations

Directions: Dancers wear their grubbiest clothes and go barefoot. (Dressing rooms and showers might be made available afterwards for those who want to change to dry clothes before leaving.)

Variation: Install a movie screen at one side of the dance area and project music videos as dance music.

CRAFTS PLAY AND GAME CONSTRUCTIONS

321. Home-Made Play Dough, Paints, and Bubble Blowing Compound

Play Dough: An easy home-made recipe for making play dough for children:

Mix 5 cups of flour with 2 cups salt. Slowly add 4 tablespoons water. Add several drops of oil of wintergreen or clove. Add 4 tablespoons salad oil (to keep mixture from hardening). Add food coloring to the water if you want the dough colored. Store dough in a tightly covered plastic container.

When children are through playing with it, let them "sculpt" their own creations or use cookie cutters so the play dough creations can be baked and eaten if the dough isn't in too bad shape after playing with it. (If it is dirty or tattered, make up a new batch for sculpting and baking.)

Painting Supplies: If regular painting supplies aren't available, try these make-do ones:

Trim a foam-type egg carton to have four or six of the cups left to hold paints. Put water in each cup and different colored food coloring in all but one cup, leaving the plain water for cleaning the "brush" between colors. Any stick can be tipped with a twisted-on cotton swab for use as a paintbrush. Cut open paper sacks for poster paper. (Any paint on body or clothes washes right out.)

Bubble Blowing Compound: The best soap-based bubble blowing compounds can be made by shaving into a powder a good grade of ordinary Castile soap (not the "super fatted" kind). Here's the recipe: powdered Castile soap—1 part, water (soft or distilled)—20 parts, and glycerine—15 parts. Add a minute amount of fluorescein dye, available at drugstores, to give bubbles opalescent coloring.

322. Bubbling-Up

Keeping children occupied with a minimum of fuss, bother and supervision

Age level: 4–12
Number of players: Any number
Supervision: None
Playing time: Freetime activity, no time schedule
Space needed: Almost anywhere (keep away from fabrics, furniture, etc., which might stain from soap bubbles)

Equipment: Containers of soapy water (with a few drops of food coloring added for colored bubbles), various circular items (tab from an opened can, ring, ring of any size made from pieces of wire). It's even possible to form ring of thumb and index finger, dunk, and blow bubbles through them. Hair curlers make myriad bubbles at same time.

Directions: Just dunk items in soapy water, then either blow through the rings, or wave the items back and forth in the air, to form bubbles.

Variation: *Blow-Up Contest:* See who can make the largest bubbles by using, for examples, wire clothes hangers stretched into circle (or maybe a square), or loops of rope. Need bucket or dishpan of soapy water for these.

Might also have contest for oddest shaped bubbles by trying various kitchen utensils, like colander, strainer, sauce spoons with holes in them, and whatever else imagination seizes on.

323. Box Play

Stretches imagination by playing with boxes

Age level: 4–8
Organizational level: Low
Number of players: 2–4 per set of boxes
Supervision: Any tool used in cutting or changing boxes, ropes, etc., limited to supervisor, or other adult
Playing time: Free play activity, no structured time limitations
Space needed: Almost anywhere: house, porch, back yard, picnic area, playground, beach

Equipment: Collection of cardboard boxes (from large furniture ones to small ones a small child can sit in), plus empty milk cartons, plastic bottles and cardboard packages of all kinds, ball of string, several short lengths of rope (4–6 feet). Tools (heavy scissors, knife, ice pick, scout knife) to be used only by supervisor when needed

Conductor, Engineer: Children put string of boxes together, connecting them with ropes, into a "train" or "engine." String might be pulled by adult supervisor.

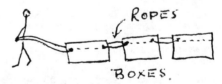

One box might be pulled as a "caboose" by a child on a tricycle.

Chinese Dragon: Open flaps of several (3–6) boxes of similar size may be stapled or attached by rope through holes cut through cardboard together, as shown in sketch. This is the "dragon." It may be painted and decorated with a

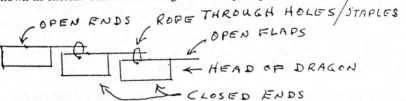

face, big teeth, red tongue hanging down, ears sticking up, and scales along the sides. Then children get under the dragon, each child holding one of the box sections over his head (which is inside the open box), and they make it slither and dance around the room, just like the Chinese do with their ceremonial dragons on special days.

Treat Box: Box large enough to hold child, with cutdown sides, is used as a place where child sits and eats treats (to keep messes in one easily cleaned or discarded place). Child can work with play dough here, eat drippy popsickles, etc., and all can be mopped up with a sponge before box is soaked through. Child can pretend the box is a train dining room, a restaurant, or whatever.

Store: Boxes can become store counter and shelves, stocked with empty containers of all sorts. Money can be made by cutting up paper into bill-sized strips, marking amounts on them, and cutting round bits of cardboard to represent coins. One child becomes a storekeeper and others can be shoppers.

Star Maker: A large box may be used as a television set, by cutting a square piece out of the side big enough for two heads to be seen from inside the box. Children may pretend they are TV performers, with other children out front as TV watchers.

Variation: Smaller box. Put a story-strip on a long sheet of butcher or wrapping paper. Glue one end to one round wooden or cardboard tube (like giftwrap paper comes around) and the other end to the other tube. Set the tubes into holes sized to hold them in both the top and bottom sides of the box, so they can be used as TV knobs, turning the picture-strip as the strip painter narrates.

324. Electricity Play

Teaches basics of static electricity, that electric "charge"
that accompanies a shuffle across a rug and a touch on a
metal doorknob, or the petting of a cat where
its hairs seem to rise up to meet your hand, or
the combing of your hair so it stands up to meet the comb.

Age level: 6 and up
Organizational level: Low
Number of players: Any number for which materials are available
Supervision: Adult craft leader to demonstrate

Playing time: One hour craft period for group
Space needed: Table area, indoors or outdoors

Electric Dancers: Needs: large aluminum pie plate or caserole pan or shallow box, piece of glass or heavy plastic big enough to cover the plate, pan or box, tissue paper sheets or roll toilet tissue, blunt scissors, pieces of fur, wool or soft leather (roughened side).

Cut little paper figurines dancing, skating, or playing soccer, being careful not to make them taller than the plate, pan or box. Place several of them in the bottom of the container, put the glass/plastic lid on the container, and rub the piece of fur-wool-leather back and forth fast on the glass/plastic sheet. The figurines will jump around as the static electricity, caused by the rubbing, reaches them.

Sadie Hawkins Balloon: Blow up a round balloon. Mark a hillbilly face on it with a marking pen, girls making a boy's face, boys making a girl's face.

Put boys in a circle around one girl, or all the girls, if wished. Girl, or girls, rub their balloons vigorously with a piece of fur, wool or rough soft leather. On "Let go" signal, girls let go of balloons to see which boys they will be attracted to.

Then girls form circle around boy, or boys, and repeat procedure.

Angry Balloons: Blow up two balloons, and make angry faces on each. Tie short strings on each. Rub both vigorously with piece of fur, wool or soft rough leather, or against a wool sweater. Try to hold string so the two balloons will "kiss and make up."

325. Snake Swirl

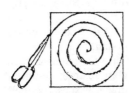

Age level: 5–8
Number of players: Best grouping 15–20
Space needed: Indoors or outdoors
Equipment: Scissors, bond paper, saucer or box top (circular), pencil, piece of thread, cellophane tape

Directions: Cut a circle from bond paper (about 4″ in diameter). A saucer or box top may be used as a guide. Cut out the circle. Place a dot in the center of the circle. Now, cut your circle in a spiral as shown by the dotted line in Figure 1, following round and round, stopping near the dot. With a bit of cellophane tape, secure one end of a piece of thread to the dot as in Figure 2.

The paper spiral will twirl in the breeze, near a source of heat or hanging near an airy spot.

326. Feet Painting

Messy-type painting activity children love, but which can still be structured

Age level: 4 and up
Organizational level: Low
Number of players: 1–10 can be reasonably handled
Supervision: Craft instructor or adult supervisor
Playing time: Keeps painter occupied for 30–60 minutes
Space needed: Hard surfaced floor (wood or cement), either indoors or outdoors out of wind
Equipment: Fingerpaints (or any paint that will wash off bodies, clothes and outdoor floor area easily), newspapers (for spreading on floor if inside), rolls of shelf, wrapping, butcher or other paper to paint on, paper towels for cleanup and a water tap or bucket

Directions: Spread out large sheets of paper for each painter. Wet it slightly.

Painters remove shoes and stockings.

Put globs of various-colored paints around the sheets. Painters are then allowed to slip-and-slide around and feet-paint their own masterpieces.

After cleanup, when the paintings have dried, the paintings may be hung up on a wall as a display. Or each child may select the best portion of his painting to cut out for framing. Then, next craft session can be spent making paper frames, naming paintings, inscribing the artists' names on them, and arranging an outdoor art exhibit.

327. Worm Painting

Makes painting fun

Age level: 4 and up
Organizational level: Low
Number of players: Any number that can be handled in a craft group
Supervision: Craft supervisor, someone to dig and bring in angleworms
Playing time: Painters will be occupied for 30–60 minutes

Space needed: Hard surfaced floor area or tabletop, indoors or outdoors out of wind
Equipment: Fingerpaints, large sheets of wrapping or butcher or poster paper, a number of earthworms (alive, which can be kept in a box of fresh earth if you want to use them over again later), water bucket

Directions: Prepare earth bed for worms. Earth should be very loose, so worms can be easily dug up with hands. Cover area to be used with newspapers to save mess.

Lay down sheets of paper for each painter, and put globs of paint, several colors, in the middle of each paper, wetting paper slightly first.

Clean angleworms in waterbucket, then drop several into the paint on each paper. Children can watch them wriggle around, painting an abstract design as they go. Worms can be moved around to suit the children's wishes for their designs.

When done, clean worms and put them into the dirt. Clean children and area. Let paintings dry.

Then, paper or cardboard frames may be made for pictures and an outdoor art show set up. Children cut out what they think are the best parts of their pictures to frame and inscribe with their signatures.

The worms may also be put on display inside a large glass container of earth.

328. Leaf Ink Prints

Age level: All
Number of players: Any number
Space needed: Craft tables, indoors or outdoors
Equipment: Oil-base printer's ink (or oil or water-based linoleum block printing ink), pane of glass with taped edges (for safety purposes), roller (brayer) for distributing the ink on the glass, paper smooth enough to show leaf veins, turpentine or other solvent for oil-base inks (or water for water-based inks), paper towels or cloths, a good supply of newspapers

Directions: Place a dab of ink on the glass pane and roll it out with the brayer until it is evenly distributed. Place the leaf with vein side down on the ink. Cover the leaf with a piece of newspaper.

Locate the petiole of the leaf under the paper, hold the leaf in place with one hand, and rub over the newspaper evenly (over the leaf) with the other hand. Rub more near the midvein and margin of the leaf.

Remove the newspaper and carefully place the leaf on the print paper. Cover the leaf with clean newspaper and repeat the rubbing to make the print.

Before making the next print, roll out the ink on the glass again. Add ink only when necessary.

Clean the pane of glass and the brayer with the proper solvent, using paper towels on clothes when finished.

329. Leaf Spatter Prints

Age level: All ages
Number of players: Any number
Space needed: Craft or picnic tables, indoors or outdoors
Equipment: Flit gun (or toothbrush and piece of wire screen), straight pins, corrugated cardboard, newspapers and tape (to protect working spaces, walls and surfaces), water-based poster paint, and small jar or can (to hold paint if using screen method)

Directions: Flit gun method: Place a cardboard box on a table. Cover table and adjacent walls with newspapers. Mix poster paint to cream-like consistency and fill flit gun.

Pin or tape a piece of absorbent print paper to the cardboard box. Pin the leaf to the print paper.

Spray paint from flit gun around the margin of the leaf so it is heaviest near the margin of the leaf and fades out toward the edge of the paper. Contrasting colors may be sprayed from separate flit guns.

Clean the flit gun carefully with water, spraying water through it.

Toothbrush Method: Set up box and paper as above. Pin the absorbent print paper to the box, and the leaf to the print paper. Mix paint to consistency of cream in the jar or can.

Dip toothbrush in paint, tapping off surplus paint.

Hold a piece of wire screen in one hand and rub the toothbrush over the top of it. Keep moving the screen and rubbing with the toothbrush around the margin of the leaf until the paint droplets are adequate.

Let dry. Remove leaf and paper and clean equipment.

330. Ink Blot Flowering Plant

Age level: 8 and up
Number of players: Any number; best grouping is 1–4 children to a plant
Space needed: Tables
Equipment: Colored paper scraps, scissors, milk cartons, black ink, glue, small fallen branches and twigs, paper-covered wires (for holding cleaner's hangers together)

Directions: Cut milk carton off at desired depth, usually about 8 inches from bottom. Fill it two-thirds full of dirt or sand.

Stick a branch or twig into the earth/sand, or, if it is too sparse, add the green-paper covered wires, twisted onto the twig, as extra branches.

Make the flowers: (a) Fold a piece of colored paper. Drop an ink blot in the crease, and press it closed with the fingers at the fold. The finger pressure spreads the ink into designs. (b) Open the paper. Cut out around the design. (c) Glue the blot-flower to the end of a twig branch. Make others.

With such varicolored "flowers" at the ends of all branches, you have a flower bush.

331. Creature Crafting

Age level: Any age, but primarily for elementary and junior high ages
Number of players: Any number your area and leaders can handle

Space needed: Indoors or outdoors, wherever you have picnic or crafts tables
Equipment: Scrap materials, toothpicks, glue, paint and brushes, construction paper

Directions: Director tells all children to spend 15 minutes looking around the playground and collecting small objects, like twigs, leaves, pretty or unusually shaped pebbles, feathers, bark, seeds, string, sucker or ice cream sticks, weeds and long grass strands. Tell them it is for a surprise use.

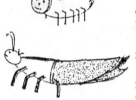

LIMA BEAN SPIDER WITH BENT TOOTHPICK LEGS

PEAPOD GRASSHOPPER

When everyone has reassembled, give out sheets of construction paper and set out glue and paints and brushes.

Tell them to use the materials they have gathered to make paste-up designs, pictures, and animals.

(a) Paint pebbles to look like the animals (or science-fiction creatures) their shapes suggest. Can use colored paper to add to the illusions.

(b) Press leaves, then paste them on paper. Using the leaf as the body of a creature, paint or paste on heads, hands, legs and feet and other appendages from outer space or inner imagination. Or use magazine cut-out additions.

(c) Use substitute materials (which must be supplied beforehand by the craft leader, in case of lack of materials later), such as vegetables—peas, string beans, beans, carrot slices, etc. Use toothpicks or twigs to help make animals or creatures.

LEAF PASTE-ON AND PAINT-UP

332. Bottle Cap Bugs

Age level: 9 and up
Number of players: Any number
Space needed: Crafts table, indoors or outdoors
Equipment: Scraps, like pebbles, bottle caps

of all sorts, old matchsticks, wire, toothpicks, pipe cleaners, leaves, glue, paints and brushes, small hammer and a few nails for making holes

Directions: Gather the scrap craft materials, which can be scavenged on a playground cleanup or pre-arranged to be brought from home.

Show group how to make one type bug, then turn them loose on their own. The "show" bug: Take a bottle cap, punch a hole off center with hammer and nail. Take out cap liner, in one piece. Put wire up through hole as antennae, and six legs extruding from body of the cap. Replace the cap liner to hold antennae and legs in place. Paint eyes on your "bug." Add other ideas as you think of them, as mandibles (jaws), tail, wings, etc. Or you might make a turtle in a similar fashion.

Variations: *(1)* Glue the "bugs" into a three-dimensional insect scene, on twigs, eating leaves, crawling in the grass, etc. Makes interesting display for the playground. *(2)* Miniature Japanese Bonsai plantings may also be simulated growing from the bottle caps, using twigs, grass and bits of leaves, carefully gluing them to look like small plants. *(3)* Bottle caps may be painted light colors — as white or yellow — then mod sayings hand printed on them. Remove the cap liners

BOTTLE CAP BUG

carefully, and by placing the top of the cap on the outside of a shirt or blouse, the liner on the inside, then pushing the liner into the cap so the cloth of the blouse or shirt is held between, the caps may be worn as "pins."

Game source: Oakland, California, Recreation Department.

333. Martian Art

Imagination stretcher

Age level: 9–11, 12–15, 16 and up
Organizational level: Low
Number of players: Any number for which materials are available, space will allow, and instructor can handle
Supervision: Craft instructor
Playing time: Hour session is usually enough time

Space needed: Tables and chairs. (If rough tables, like outdoor picnic tables are used, smoother drawing boards [like plywood] may be needed under drawing-paper sheets.)
Equipment: Supply of poster paper, poster paints and paint brushes, a few science-fiction comic books for inspiration for young artists

Directions: Project is for each artist to draw or paint his own imaginative space alien or monster.

Winner will be the drawing getting the most votes from the artists themselves.

Follow-up: Present an art exhibit of the paintings. Lead the artists into a reading program of science-fiction books, with book reports being given and those who wish going on to illustrate their reports with paintings of the characters or monsters in their book reports.

334. Snip Shopping

Babysitting activity for tykes

Age level: 4–8
Organizational level: Low
Number of players: 1–6
Supervision: Babysitter
Playing time: However long it keeps tykes engrossed
Space needed: Table top, or quiet, free floor area

Equipment: Old general merchandise mail order catalogs (one for every two children), blunt scissors for each participant, self-applying glue containers for each two participants, sheets of wrapping or butcher paper for each participant, rulers

Directions: Draw rooms of a house on wrapping paper, each participant drawing the rooms of his own home. These do not have to be to scale, though they should be roughly sized in relation to actual rooms (bathroom smaller than living room, for example).

Cut pictures out of catalogue to completely furnish house. Those who finish this early may go on to cut out wardrobes for all the members of the family living in the house. After that, they may cut out yard and garden tools and equipment.

Paste pictures in appropriate places in appropriate rooms

Variation: *3-D Paste-Up* — Older children may use a cardboard box as house, pasting pieces of cardboard (cut off other boxes) as room walls inside the box. Then, they can paste their cutout pictures in the appropriate places in the appropriate rooms. They may cut out windows and doors as well, before beginning their pasting.

335. Peephole Binoculars
Make a play item with scrap craft material

Age level: 8 and up
Organizational level: Low
Number of players: As many as materials are available for and craft leader can handle
Supervision: Craft leader (to use or supervise use of tools, like knife and scissors)
Playing time: 30-60 minutes, depending on age group and number participants

Space needed: Work tables and chairs
Equipment: 2 paper or styrofoam cups per participant, pieces of styrofoam that can be cut to shape, blunt scissors, knife (though rough sandpaper might be used to shape wedges instead of cutting them), glue, paint, penny nails

Directions: See sketch: (1) Cut and shape styrofoam wedge to fit between cups, being sure it is wide enough so, when finished, the eye holes in the cups will fit

the width of the eyes on the person who will use the binoculars. (2) Punch holes in middle of cups with penny nail. (3) Glue wedge between cups. (4) Paint finished binoculars (black inside, any other color wished outside).

336. Bottle Cap Boat Racing
Practical craft project

Age level: 8 and up
Organizational level: Low
Number of players: Any number in heat eliminations, 2-10 at a time
Supervision: Commodore (referee), stopwatch
Playing time: Crafting — 30 minutes;

racing — 10-20 minutes, depending upon length of course used
Space needed: Tabletop, or smooth floor, concrete shuffleboard court
Equipment: One per contestant: bottlecap with cork still inside, sheet 5" × 7" paper, thin hairpin, soda straw, piece of beeswax, chalk

Directions: Each contestant makes own bottlecap sailboat. (See sketches on next page.) Contestants may be numbered, and they may put their numbers on their boat sails. Use beeswax to wax bottoms of bottlecap boats (to slide more easily).

Mark off a race course, including hazards like sandbars, underwater wrecks, buoys, etc., with chalk.

Line finished boats up at starting point. On "go" signal, each boat owner "skipper" starts blowing gently through his straw at sail of his boat, guiding it safely over the course. Hazards are marked with penalties, such as "Aground. Move back 6 inches," "Hole in hull, stop 10 seconds for repairs," etc.

STICK PIN THRU CORK FROM CAP AND BEND OVER.

PAPER →

HAIRPIN →

CORK

CAP

If boat tips over, it must be righted again before the skipper may blow on sails again.

Winner is first over the finish line.

Variation: *Windy Racing* — Boat owners take turns "sailing" their boats. Each "skipper's" turn lasts as long as he can blow out in a single breath. If he hits a hazard before his breath is exhausted, his turn is automatically over. Winner is skipper over finish line with least turns. Ties can be run off with a race between/among winners. *River Run* — Jar lids (like instant coffee jars) may

PUT CORK BACK INTO CAP

be used to make larger, more stable boats for actual sailing on water. Races can be held on small creeks, across a swimming pool or a tub of water, or down a street gutter after a rain runoff.

337. Hop Ring

Toy that can be home crafted. New challenge for rope jumpers.

Age level: 8 and up
Number of players: One at a time
Supervision: None
Playing time: Open ended
Space needed: 4′ × 4′ area

Equipment: Hop-ring ("Swing-It" jumping rope from Miles Kimball Co., of Osh Kosh, WI. or can be made from a Whiz-Ring attached to a small weight, like a fisherman's lead sinker, with a 2′ length of string)

Directions: Jumper swings leg to activate ring and get weight swinging in a circle. He must jump the string with his free foot each time it comes around.

Jumpers who become accomplished, can walk while jumping the string, run or even dance. Walking or running races may, thus, be set up.

Variations: *Jumping Jacks and Jills* — Jumping "doubles" may be accomplished by extanding the length of the string. Then a second jumper stands beside the ring wearer, arms

around each other's waists. Both must jump together to keep the ring circling. Contests may be set up with girl pairs versus boy pairs for added interest (and to raise interest of boys in rope jumping programs). *Hoop Ring Dueling* — Two jumpers wearing hoop-rings must stay in a 25′ circle, while each tries to hop his ring near enough to snare the opponent's leg, yet keep the opponent from snaring his leg.

338. Stompers

Remembrance of activity grandpa used to play

Age level: 8 and up
Organizational level: Low
Number of players: 1–10
Supervision: Craft instructor to use or supervise use of tools
Playing time: 30–60 minutes, depending on age and number participants
Space needed: Craft area inside, or any outside area free of traffic

Equipment: 2 coffee cans or other large (#10) cans, 2 lengths of clothesline rope (or plastic rope) long enough to reach from waist down under foot (extended leg) and back up to waist for each participant. Tools: hammer, large nail. Wood blocks 1″ × 3″ × 6–8″ may also be used, if wished.

Directions: Hammer two holes in each can, about an inch up from the can's bottom and opposite each other. (Open end is the bottom here. Open ends can be covered with plastic snap-on covers, which will save lawns, for example, from getting cup up with the stompers.)

Stick rope end through both holes. Tie two ends in square or other knot that won't come loose.

If wooden blocks are to be used as platforms between can and shoe, they are placed across the closed ends of the cans. The ropes are then stuck through the can holes, brought over the wooden block, threaded through the two holes again, and brought up waist high where the two ends are tied together. (The holes in the can may have to be enlarged to take the double rope through them.)

Paint the finished stompers, if wished.

To walk with them, put feet on the cans (closed ends), or on the wooden blocks, pull the ropes up tight with your hands (to hold the cans against your feet) and walk.

Variation: *Bucket Stompers*—Instead of cans, use old buckets with handles removed. Holes can be put through the sides an inch or so down from the closed bottoms for the ropes to go through.

339. Chigger

Variation of Hangman game, rejuvenated from World War I days

Age level: 8 and up
Organizational level: Medium
Number of players: 2–4
Supervision: None
Playing time: 15–20 minutes

Space needed: Tabletop or any smooth hard floor surface
Equipment: Chigger spinning top, pad of paper and pencil. (A square block may be used in place of a top.)

Craft directions for top: Construct the top from a piece of wood 2″ × 2″ × 2½″ long. The corners are planed off until there are eight even sides. Those sides are tapered at the bottom to form a point. A piece of ½″ dowel stick is glued in a hole bored in the top. The sides are labelled E, L, T, F, B, L and H, standing for Eye, Leg, Tail, Feeler, Body, Leg and Head, respectively. The eighth side has a chigger drawn on it which entitles the player to two free spins. A larger top of 4″ × 4″ is also appropriate.

Rules: Each player has paper. A pencil can be passed around for use by all. Players take turns spinning the top. When it falls to its side, the player must draw part of the chigger indicated by the letter uppermost on the top (as explained on previous page). As a player finishes drawing the whole chigger — body, head, 2 eyes, 2 antennae, 6 legs and a tail, he is out of the game. Last one remaining is the winner.

Variations: *Scratch the Chigger* — A stack of papers can be prepared with chiggers already drawn on them, in pencil. Then, players *erase* (or scratch) the body parts as they come up on the top. Winner is one scratching out his chigger first. *Couple Chigger* — Either of the games may be played with partners, each partner taking a turn. This results in faster games.

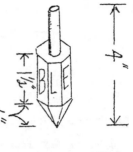

Spinning Top

Game source: During World War I, a game called "Cootie" helped soldiers while away idle hours. This game was named after the source of much discomfiture to the men in the trenches. It was played with a die. The use of a top to play the game is credited to Jacksonville's Superintendent of Recreation, Nathan L. Mallison.

340. Japanese Wish Tree

Learn a bit of Japanese culture

Age level: 6 and up
Organizational level: Low
Number of players: Any number craft instructor can handle
Supervision: Craft instructor or adult leader
Playing time: An hour to an hour and a half, if tree has to be constructed. Less if using prefabbed or real tree.

Space needed: Small tree, with low-hanging branches, or a large bush. Can be constructed from wire attached to a wooden base. Or a metal, plastic or other prefabricated Christmas tree can be used.
Equipment: The tree, 2″ × 6″ slips of colored paper, pencils for all participants, supply of twist-ems

Directions: Set up tree, pick out live one to be used, or construct one. Constructed ones can be made from wire, paper (cutout poster), or wherever imagination leads.

Place box of paper slips and pencils on a stand under, or beside, the tree, along with a sign explaining (perhaps in rhyme) that it is a "wish tree" and anyone may write out a wish and attach it to the tree with a twist-em.

When a wish has been written down, the paper is folded over, twisted into the semblance of a flower shape, and a twist-em is twisted around it and a tree branch.

During the preparation of this event it should be stressed to all concerned that, to come true, wishes should state positive and happy thoughts for self and others, and not be selfish thoughts.

The tree, with all the varicolored paper slips decorating it, makes an eye-catching display, as well as great picture material for publicity purposes, especially with children in the pictures, and for scrapbook and photo album pictures.

A good follow-up program is to invite parents, with their cameras, to see the tree and participate in a program where each child who participated picks one of the wishes off the tree and reads it aloud. (This part can be audio or video taped for further publicity use or for file records.)

341. A Bird Feeder

Learn more about our feathered friends,
by crafting a useful item for one's yard

Age level: 10 and up
Organizational level: Medium
Number of players: 1–10 if materials are
  available
Supervise: Craft instructor or adult to
  supervise use of tools
Playing time: Hour craft period
Space needed: Craft or outdoor picnic tables
Equipment: Per person: 2 same size alumi-

num pie pans (throwaways, not reusable
ones), large juice can (top and bottom removed), wood piece (round or square) 4"
diameter and 1" thick, metal clothes hanger.
Tool needs: Can opener, wire cutter, wood
drill and bit slightly larger than clothes
hanger wire, hammer and metal punch (or
nail about the same size around as the
hanger wire), pliers, tin snips

Directions: Drill a hole through center of the piece of wood. Punch a hole in the center of each pie pan (for the wire clotheshanger to go through).

Snip six triangular holes around the bottom edge of the juice can, for seed outlets.

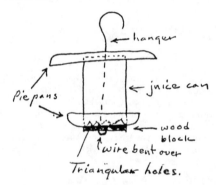

Unwind and straighten the clothes hanger wire, leaving the curved part as is.

Invert one pie pan over the top of the can, the other under it (where the triangular holes are) and the wooden block under that. Run the straight end of the hanger through all of these. Cut it off with about 2 inches to spare. Bend those 2 inches over to hold everything together. If holes are so big the wire fits loosely, add washers made from corrugated cardboard on both sides of the wood block. (A larger pan may be used at the top, if wished, to make rain shelter.)

Feeder can be filled merely by lifting up the top pan and pouring birdseed into the can. It will sift out into the bottom pan as needed, automatically.

342. Dirty Harry

Handcraft materials for target shooting game

Age level: 12 and up
Organizational level: Medium
Number of players: 10–15
Supervision: Craft instructor
Playing time: Average—two craft periods
  (2 hours)
Space needed: Area 8' × 12' or larger
Equipment: Individual: a spring-type clothes

pin, 2 tacks, supply of thick rubber bands
(for shooting) and block of wood 4" × 6", 1–
2" thick (for rubber band shooting gun).
Group: 12–15 targets (pop tops from various
sized cans, like chocolate drink canisters
and some coffee cans), 2 poles (broomsticks, old pieces of pipe), 4–6 10' lengths of
string or twine, marker pen

Directions: Tack clothes pin on the shorter end of wood blocks so the gripping end is slightly higher than the longer length of wood. (See figure 1 on next page.)

Set poles into ground about 10′ apart in area free of traffic (against a building saves steps in rounding up rubber bands after shooting). String the pop top targets on the lengths of twine as you tie the twine to the poles. (See figures 2 and 3).

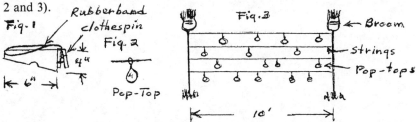

Assign numbers of points various targets are worth. (Smaller ones worth more.) Mark points on targets so shooters can see them from 8′ away, where they shoot from.

Each shooter gets three shots in each of two rounds. Targets are re-arranged for the second round. Winner is shooter with most points in two rounds.